No Place for Plastic Saints

*Earthquakes, Chicken Feet, and Candid
Confessions of a Missionary Wife*

by
Margaret A. Register

Xulon PRESS

Harold ~

Thank you for all
your years "in
Missionaries !

Your "old" friends,

Margaret & Joe Resith

Dedication

To the best granddaughters in the world:
Jennifer, Kyndal,
Tessa, Kaybree,
and Emily.
These stories tell of your heritage.
You are writing our future.

And to aspiring and veteran missionaries –
what a life we lead!

Preface

—❦—

"*G*randma, tell me the story again about the old goat lady. She was *so stinky*...."

"Tell us about when the earthquake shook the whole house."

"Tell me about the dead man on the picnic table, with the yucky stuff dripping in a can...."

The grandchildren beg me to tell them my stories. And the children said, "Mom, write down the stories so they won't be forgotten."

So, I have. But as I wrote the fun stuff, I also remembered times of pain. As I recalled the miracles, I also re-lived the times when God was silent.

You'll soon notice that this is not a typical "religious" book. Neither is it a cutesy-sweet story of picture-perfect missionaries. It is just an abbreviated account of the first thirty-four years of my life.

Some of the people my husband, Joe, and I encountered were cruel and deliberately caused emotional pain. On the other side of the spectrum, we became friends with many dear, dear people who continue to live in our hearts. All of these are part of my story.

I have attempted to be transparent with both the pain and the victories. Every anecdote is true, every person real.

Why do I use the term "Plastic Saint"? Because sometimes I feel like one.

May these words inform, inspire, and challenge you to greater faith, hope, and love as you live out your own story.

Margaret A. Register

Plastic Saints: my definition

The plastic saint stands in front of others and looks good.
She (or he) says the right things. She smiles at the right time and
sheds a tear as needed for effect.
But she is brittle one-on-one.
She finds it difficult to stoop over to kiss the wounded.
Her very hollowness (which could contain the joys and sorrows of
others) remains vacant and unattached.
She is not evil. She is neutral.
She fears being transparent, and thus, vulnerable.
She does not realize that God stands poised, hand outstretched, to
touch, to humanize, to soften the plastic saint—just as soon as she
breaks, melts, *wants* to begin the long journey toward
becoming Christ-like.

Foreword

——◦✛◦——

*I*n my six decades of working in media, I have never met a more creative director than Margaret Register. (No, she's not that old, I am!) She is just brilliant. Besides that, she's bilingual! How does one person get so much talent??

But first and foremost, Margaret is a missionary. She and her husband, Joe, have impacted Latin America with the Gospel in so many dynamic ways. They are the creators of the innovative STAR television ministries, which include the *Secret Place* series and the *Meet God!* series (in several languages). These shows have changed the lives of hundreds of thousands of kids around the world.

But why in the world would a person such as Margaret (who could make a fortune in the entertainment business) dedicate her life to spreading the Gospel in far-away places? There has to be a story behind that! There is one, and it's contained in this marvelous book you now hold in your hands.

I have never known Margaret to do anything that was not highly enjoyable, informative, and inspirational! You're about to get blessed—so, get ready!

Dan Betzer
Pastor / Author / Revivaltime Radio Speaker /
Byline Television Host / Assemblies of God Executive Presbyter /
Dan & Louie Puppet Duo

Acknowledgments

---

*M*ost of these memories spring from the yellowed pages of letters to my mother, Frieda Arnold. She kept the letters; my sister, Jan Hammac, preserved them.

I am also indebted to every major character in these stories. When I contacted them, these added their memories to mine: Bob Bowden, Margaret Bowden, Jeanne Bowden Errichiello, Roland Blount, Chris and Erica Grace, Doris Gaona, Don Jenkins, Victor Hedman, Jan Hammac.

Louisa Jeter Walker's book, "Siembra y Cosecha, Tomo 2," provided historical background, as did the Library of Congress, Country Studies.

I am grateful to the Assemblies of God World Missions Board for allowing Joe and me to serve as foreign missionaries over a span of nearly thirty-eight years.

My deep thanks extend to my *First Readers*, a group of faithful friends who plowed new ground with me week after week for two years: Dr. Steven Fettke, whose words of encouragement sustained and motivated me; Juanita Blackburn, who would not let me stop; and my sister Jan, who kept saying, "Wow, I didn't know you went through all that!" Also *First Readers* and always with words of encouragement: Ingrid Black, Peggy and Dave Norris, Jeanne LaMay, Melody Garber, Betty Wireman, Phyllis Benigas, Gayle Porter, Maritza Segura, Sara Segura, my cousin Carol Punch, and my cousin Agnes Davis.

I can never repay my good friend Juanita Cunningham Blackburn, who not only encouraged me, and gave wonderful formatting ideas, but also searched for dangling participles and other equally dastardly errors.

Two missionary colleagues have empathized with almost every written word and have given me invaluable assistance: Melody Garber, who scanned the photos, and Jeanne LaMay, who drew the maps. Thanks, girls!

My special gratitude goes to my daughter Crysti (she changed the spelling from Christy), who laughed, cried, and kept remembering additional anecdotes.

My son, Tim, caused me to begin to write down these stories once-for-all. He also admonished me to freely include more "fears and feelings." Thanks, Tim.

I could never have persevered without my husband, Joe, who proof-read, added details, and brought me fresh coffee. Thanks, Babe, for your encouragement and patience.

Most of all I thank my Lord Jesus, who inspired and enabled me to remember the joys and the pain and to look back to see personal growth.

CORREO AEREO

Sunday afternoon
Jan. 18, 1970

Dear Mom & Dad,

Just a note to tell you everyone has arrived & everything is in a state of confusion!!!

We spent last week (Jan. 6-11) in Santiago. It was just as bad as before — dust, noise, traffic.

Orlando, a boy from Ivan's church, went with us to see the Bible Institute. He is so sweet. He plans to start B. School in March. Joe wants us to pay his tuition $10 a month. He could use some "deoderant money" if you know anyone who'd like to send him a dollar or two a week, or month. Ivan doesn't know it yet & will hit the ceiling. Orlando, unconciously, told us alot (we've told him nothing) He is the C.A. president & said he wants to train someone else to take his place — He said,

"The pastor just can't work with the young people. I always stand between him & them."

We'd wondered & wondered why he had run off all the adults but had a nice group of young people!!

Jan. 7th
(a week ago)

The Roland Blount arrived in Santiago last Wednesday. They have two children, a boy 11, a girl 4½.

The Bowdens arrived on Friday. Their two girls are 11 + 13.

(Did I write that the Velez are letting us use their big house while they're in the States? (The Bowdens

"This happened so that the work of God might be displayed in [her] life."
Jesus in John 9:3 NIV

Contents

Recipes

Carl and Frieda Arnold with Margaret Ann
1944

Jan, Daddy, Margaret, Mom, David
1947

1

My Illinois Heritage

Margaret Ann Arnold Register
1939–1952

I was conceived at a funeral. Not *conceived* conceived. But that was the first time Daddy saw Momma. And the first time Momma saw Daddy. Momma was sitting up front, behind the casket, with her accordion on her lap, ready to sing a song for the deceased. Daddy came in the door of the one-room schoolhouse–cum–church in his overalls and red plaid flannel shirt. Momma leaned over to the man sitting next to her: "Who is that nice-looking young man?" she asked. "My son, Carl," he replied.

Turns out, there was a revival at the little community school in Patoka, Illinois, and Momma (Frieda Wayman) was the special music. Daddy (Carl Arnold) attended every night. He got saved. And got Momma. They were married just three months later, on April 9, 1939.

Frieda convinced Carl that he would be a great Methodist preacher. So he went to seminary. He was assigned a circuit of three little congregations near Beaucoup, Illinois where we moved so he could travel from there to the seminary during the week and go out from there every Sunday to his "circuit." I was their first child. After my sister and brother, Jan and David, were born, Daddy took a "big" church in Nashville, Illinois. We had nearly a hundred people in that little red brick building.

I was five and ready to start school on the day after Labor Day, 1948. Except I didn't have any shoes because my summer sandals were worn out. So, at breakfast, Momma said, "Carl, Margaret Ann has got to have a pair of shoes. School starts Tuesday." Daddy sighed, "All we can do is pray, we don't have a penny left over for shoes." We knelt at our chairs around the white kitchen table and prayed. Daddy got up and left for the church. Momma got up and started putting the dirty dishes in the sink. I stayed on my knees. I was serious about this shoe business. Finally, I raised up and started looking around.

"Where are they? Where are my shoes?"

Momma looked at me with a mixture of terror and amazement. "Run on out to play. Your shoes are on their way." As soon as the screen door slammed behind me, she knelt again. "Oh, God, you see the faith of this little one. Please answer our prayers!"

Ed Bernreuter was plowing, riding a big Case tractor; he had acres to get plowed that day. "Go take a ten-dollar bill to the preacher," a voice said inside him. Ed plowed another row. "Go take that ten-dollar bill to the preacher," he sensed again. Ed plowed another row. "Now!" Ed stopped the tractor, climbed into his pick-up truck, and headed to town. He knocked on our front screen door and handed Momma "my shoes."

One Sunday night, when I was five years old, Daddy gave the invitation to go forward for salvation. I wanted to go really, really bad. But I was too shy. After we went home and had gone to bed, I couldn't stop thinking about it. I went into Momma and Daddy's bedroom and tapped Momma on the shoulder. She knelt with me and helped me to ask Jesus into my heart.

Though Daddy enjoyed the Methodist seminary, many professors were modernistic in their views, with one even teaching that the blood of Jesus was "nothing more than the blood of a pig." After much prayer and discussion, Daddy and Momma decided to join the Nazarene movement and we moved south to Carbondale, Illinois, where Daddy became a Nazarene pastor.

They came on Halloween, a year after we moved to Carbondale. Three "ghouls" to rob us of our house and to take away Daddy's job. It was during my little sister Jan's fifth birthday party. We were playing pin the tail on the donkey, and since I was 7 going on 8, I was telling Jan and all her little kindergarten friends how to do it. We were laughing when the loud knock sounded on the front door. There stood three men in dark suits, starched white shirts, and striped ties. Their faces were grim as the tall one said to Daddy, "Rev. Arnold, we need to see you. Alone."

Later, we learned that Daddy and the "committee from head-quarters" had differing ideas about how the Holy Spirit worked. We were told to vacate the parsonage within two weeks.

On the following Sunday morning, Daddy resigned from the little Nazarene church in Carbondale, Illinois. He stood behind the polished oak pulpit and told how Momma had heard, two years earlier, about an "infilling" of the Holy Spirit. A neighbor lady up in Nashville, Illinois told her about it. So Momma began to pray, asking God if this were "real."

Then, one morning, Momma was working down in the basement washing clothes in a wringer-style washing machine while she prayed. On a nearby table, her Bible lay open to Psalm 84, where she had just read, "No good thing will He withhold from them that walk uprightly." Momma began to pray out loud. "God, I don't know if this Holy Spirit baptism is a 'good thing' or not. But if it is, I want it!"

Momma started to reach down to take the lid off the washing machine, but instead her hands went up and she began to praise God. She had never seen anyone do this before. Her hands above her head, arms raised toward heaven, she began to speak in a language she had never learned.

She was crying and talking so loudly that the neighbor lady heard her and came running over, thinking Momma had caught her hair in the wringer. Momma was radiant and could hardly wait to tell Daddy what she had experienced.

He was furious! He told her *never* to tell anyone about this weird experience. It would ruin his ministry!

But he, too, was curious. What if it were true? He began to pray privately, asking God to fill him, too, if indeed this Holy Spirit baptism was "a good thing."

"And just a few days ago," Daddy told the congregation, "as I sat praying, alone in my study, I felt a warmth pour over me. I began to speak quietly in a language I had never heard before. I thought my heart would burst with the pure joy of it!" Daddy's face glowed.

"Later, I mentioned this experience to a few friends and somehow the church hierarchy found out about it. They've asked me to resign."

Daddy announced his resignation, effective immediately. After the service, he did not go to the door to shake hands with everyone as he usually did. Instead, he fled to his office. When everyone had left the church, Daddy came out of his office, locked the church door, and headed reluctantly to the parsonage.

When he arrived, he saw people in the yard. They were crowding onto the porch, inside the front door, in the living room. A deacon hollered out, "Preacher, if you really believe this experience is from God, we all want it, too."

So they kept the same deacons, the same Sunday school teachers, the same ushers, and they formed a new church. They rented a room over a local bar and began to pray. Every person received this "baptism in the Holy Spirit" (except one elderly lady who chose not to change denominations). Today, that "relocated" church is First Assembly of God in Carbondale, Illinois.

The only house Daddy could quickly find for us to move into was on the outskirts of town. Actually, the little rental house sat on a dirt road, and though the interior was framed in, it did not have all the drywall. Momma cried a lot. But Jan and I loved the rope swing in the front yard and we liked the dirt road because it had a big hump that Daddy would "fly over" to drop down on the other side. But Momma kept crying and at one point she and Daddy had the only really big shouting fight that I ever remember.

Soon after that, Daddy found a large lot (to build the new church on) with a lovely brick house on the side of the property. Momma loved that house--hardwood floors, stairs to the attic, and a full basement--full, that is, with dog poop! Daddy shoveled, gagged, shoveled, and gagged. He gagged so loudly that it made us kids gag upstairs, just listening to him gag in the basement.

A couple of years later, Roy Sherrill, an evangelist, came to town with a big tent. He asked Daddy to come and be his full-time traveling assistant, to hold morning services, be the bookkeeper, and to sing, with Momma, in the evening services.

So, we moved again. This time Momma and Daddy left to evangelize, taking our baby brother, David, with them. Jan and I went to Murphysboro to stay with Grandma Bessie and Grandpa Percy Wayman, Momma's folks.

Grandpa had only one arm. A farmer, he was out in the field throwing corn into the shucker one day when his shirtsleeve caught and pulled his right arm into the shucker. Wilbur, Mom's brother, went running to the house screaming. Grandma, eight months pregnant, ran to the field. She and Wilbur and Ralph, the oldest brother, somehow managed to get Grandpa into the back of the wagon. Grandma drove the team as fast as she could into town to Uncle Doc's. (I don't know Uncle Doc's name, he was Grandma's brother and we always just called him Uncle Doc.) Grandpa lost his right arm and Grandma lost the baby.

I didn't like very much living with Grandma and Grandpa. Grandma had been a schoolteacher and she made us obey everything she said. Grandpa would smoke cigars when Grandma wasn't there. I loved to stand by him at their church, Centenary Methodist, because when we sang "Bringing in the Sheaves" he'd always sing, "Bring them in, doodle-bug, Bring them in, doodle-bug, Bring them in from the fields of sin, doodle-bug...."

Grandpa's closest neighbors lived across the field, on the other side of the chicken yard. One day, the elderly neighbor asked me to visit them and play a song on their out-of-tune piano. After I played, the old lady said, "I think we should give Margaret Ann the candy we've been savin'." She handed me a box of chocolate covered cherries. The cellophane was missing, but I didn't care.

As soon as we arrived home, I opened that box, grabbed a chocolate covered cherry and took a big bite. I looked down—the half-piece of candy in my hand was crawling with worms! Little white, wriggling worms! Grandpa said, "Aw, a few little worms never hurt anyone." He reached over, took a piece of candy, and popped it in his mouth.

Grandma cussed once, and when Momma and Daddy came home for a few days between revivals, I told Daddy about it. "What did she say?" Daddy asked me.

"She cussed real loud!"

"Yeah, but what exactly did she say?" Daddy asked again.

I tattled, "Well, she was pullin' some cornbread out of the oven and she burnt her hand and she said, 'Darn it!'"

During the two years we lived with Grandma and Grandpa, Jan and I slept on a three-quarter bed with a quilt rolled up between us—to prevent Jan from getting on my side of the bed! During the summers we could travel with Momma and Daddy, because we were out of school then.

Sometimes Jan and I cried, especially when Grandma brushed the tangles out of our hair or made us practice our spelling words. But mostly we cried silent tears at night, wondering, "Does serving God mean you have to leave your family behind?"

*   *   *

Grandma's Fried Potatoes

INGREDIENTS

4 medium potatoes—Grandma always said one potato
  per person
1 medium onion
Lard or bacon grease—sorry, Grandma, now we use
  olive oil

DIRECTIONS

1. Cover the bottom of a heavy skillet with oil. Slice
   the potatoes and the onion; layer slices over the oil.
   Sprinkle a little salt on top.
2. Cover. Fry over medium heat until potatoes on the bottom are golden brown, flip potatoes over and continue
   frying until browned and potatoes are tender.

2

Moving Again

To Columbus, Mississippi and Pensacola, Florida
1952–1960

addy really enjoyed working with Roy Sherrill, the evangelist. They held tent revivals all over the southeast. Brother Sherrill, as we called him, would feel in his own body the pain of a disease, call out the symptoms, and the afflicted person would come forward to be miraculously healed. In meetings I attended, I saw tumors disappear, goiters vanish, cancers shrivel. One lady suffered with cancer of the lower lip. The pain was so intense that even after the lady was healed, Brother Sherrill continued to experience pain and swelling in his lower lip all the next day.

After a couple of years of traveling constantly, Daddy accepted a pastorate in Columbus, Mississippi. In the middle of the school year, I trudged up the steps to another new classroom to continue the sixth grade. My self-esteem dragged behind me like a soggy slice of French toast. Thick eyeglasses slid down my freckled nose. Overweight, every day I stood, ashamed, at the chalkboard as I struggled to learn how to diagram sentences.

But I sure did love the new, southern style of cooking: black-eyed peas, fried okra, fresh coconut cake, lemon icebox pie.

One evening while I babysat for a family from the church, I told them some "choice news" about their neighbors. Later that night

Daddy pounded on my bedroom door. "Margaret Ann, get out of bed right this minute, you have some apologizing to do!" Both families had gathered (ready to kill me—I was sure of it). I cried and truly was sorry that I had opened my big mouth.

Aunt Too was a schoolteacher (her name was really Thelma, but everyone called her *Tutor*, which I shortened to *Too*). She and Uncle Ed, Daddy's brother, came from Illinois to visit us in Columbus. I've loved them ever since I can remember. They lived across the garden from us in Patoka, near where I was born, and every summer they invited me to come and stay with them. They had lived in only two houses during all of my growing-up years. I had already moved eight times.

Aunt Too taught school for fifty years and had access, anytime, to Patoka's little open-once-a-week library. I could check out as many books as I wanted, so Nancy Drew and the Hardy Boys became my good friends.

Uncle Ed co-owned Patoka Hardware & Locker. The "Locker" was a very large walk-in freezer where farmers stored frozen food. They would bring their hogs or cows to the store, butcher them out back, cut them up, wrap them in white freezer paper, and store them in their own private freezer-locker.

Uncle Ed came home from work every day for lunch. We ate fresh vegetables from their garden and he would always read aloud a chapter from the Bible to Aunt Too and me. Their church didn't have as many rules as ours, plus I could go to Vacation Bible School at all three churches in town: the Christian Church (that was theirs); the Baptist Church (that was my other aunt's and uncle's); and the Methodist Church (that was Effie's church—Aunt Too's mother).

I loved the freedom I felt at Aunt Too's and Uncle Ed's house. They took me to my first movie, bought my first pair of shorts and my first bicycle, and taught me by their example that you didn't have to be "religious" to be a Christian.

One day, Aunt Too and Uncle Ed drove to Sandoval, a few miles south of town. Starting for home, they stopped at a stop sign. Suddenly, the back right passenger door opened and the "old goat lady" climbed into the back seat! She was so stinky! She never bathed; she dressed in raggedy, smelly clothes. She lived alone in a hut in the middle of a field where she took care of dozens of goats. The "old goat lady" didn't say a word until they had traveled a few miles down the road; then, abruptly, she grunted, "Get out here." As soon as she was out of the car, Aunt Too and Uncle Ed rolled down all the windows, but for days the car smelled like the "old goat lady." The moral of the story, Aunt Too reminded me many times, was: "Always lock your car doors because if you don't, the 'old goat lady' may get in the car with you!"

Besides Uncle Ed, Daddy had another older brother, Don, and a baby brother everyone called Mac. Uncle Mac was actually Cyrus McNichol Arnold, with Grandma's maiden name as his middle name. The McNichols came from the Isle of Arran in Scotland to settle in central Illinois. Daddy also had one sister, Aunt Ella, a petite, happy, patient person. When all the kids were young, Grandma Arnold would be gone for several days at a time as a mid-wife, so Aunt Ella had to learn to cook. The first time she made biscuits, they were so hard the boys played ball, tossing the biscuits back and forth across the table!—making Aunt Ella cry.

In the 1950s we moved again—from Columbus, Mississippi to Pensacola, Florida, when Daddy was chosen to be the pastor at Brownsville Assembly of God. We moved the last of August just before I started eighth grade. Brownsville Junior High was brand new, and there was no grass in the schoolyard. I signed up for the band, and when we practiced marching after school, the sand was so deep it would get in my new, white, penny loafers. But I loved playing tenor sax; I was "first chair." My self-confidence had improved a little as I grew taller during seventh grade, but I still saw a fat girl in the mirror.

One day the band director pulled me aside and told me she had selected me to be drum major. I was so excited! However, Mom was not so happy. First, she said I absolutely could not wear shorts. The band director agreed that I could wear long pants. Then Mom had a dream about snakes coming out of my saxophone and wrapping around my fingers. The interpretation, according to her, was that being a drum major was evil. She said that of course I could still do it, but it could ruin Dad's ministry.

My heart was broken. So many times I was told to "do this" or "don't do that" because it would ruin Dad's ministry. Guilt hovered just out of reach, ready to pounce on me for the slightest infraction of the unwritten rules.

When I was sixteen, Charles Greenaway, a missionary to Africa, was scheduled to come to our church for a missionary service. Dad was counting on him to help raise the annual missionary budget. On Saturday night, Charles called and cancelled — he had double-booked. But he could send his wife in his place. Dad agreed for Mary Greenaway to come, but he was really upset. Mary was like a quiet little mouse; Charles was a roaring lion of a preacher.

Mary spoke quietly on Sunday morning, with simple thoughts. Then she asked people to come forward who would be willing to do anything they believed God wanted them to do. I went forward and prayed silently, "God, bless all the missionaries." I paused, and a thought dropped into my heart, "What about you? Would *you* become a missionary?" And without a second's hesitation, I responded, "Yes, God, if You want me to be a missionary, I will."

All afternoon my prayer kept haunting me. After church that night, I went out with my boyfriend, a high school senior who played tight-end on the football team. As we sat in his car at the drive-in restaurant and ate our hamburgers off the window tray, I told him about my prayer. He thought that was very noble, and said he, too, would do whatever God wanted.

Mom was waiting up for me, and I told her about my prayer. She began to cry, saying that she had been desperate to have a baby after being married for three years. So she had prayed and told God that if He'd give her a baby, she'd dedicate that first baby to Him. She had felt that I would be a missionary, she said, but she wouldn't tell me until God had "called me" personally. This, she felt, was "the call."

Mom was, I've concluded, a product of sincere devotion to God mixed with a strong, dominant personality. When Mom was single, traveling and singing in churches, she was befriended by a pastor's wife from the legalistic Methodist Holiness Movement in southern Illinois. The legalism became so embedded that even on her deathbed, Mom was *hoping* she'd make it to heaven.

Dad was "absent" from our home—always off doing church work. He was sincerely serving God and loved the freedom of being on the platform. He studied hard for his sermons, loved using humor, and truly loved his congregation.

David, my brother, doesn't think Dad would have become a minister if Mom had not pushed him into it. Mother did push— him and everybody else—but I believe Dad was called by God to minister. Yet his legalism/works caused him to neglect his family. He never attended any of my brother's football games or any other school activity of his three children. He apologized to David later in life, but Dave has never forgiven either of his parents.

Faithfully I attended every church service, read my Scofield Bible daily, sang in the choir, took piano lessons, and participated as a member of the church youth group and girls' club. Only by all these good works could I be assured of *being good enough.* For God? Or so I wouldn't ruin Dad's ministry? Or to earn Mother's approval? It all mingled in my head. I feared failing and dreaded not measuring up to the diaphanous *should* that eluded me.

One day, sitting in English grammar class, I had finished the assignment and was waiting for the other students to finish. As I put down my pencil, a thought hit me, "You don't have to do all this religious stuff. You don't have to attend youth meetings. Why do you sing in the choir? Just refuse to do it! Dig in your heels!" Somehow I sensed that my choice was immensely important. I could rebel. I had the choice. I closed my eyes, oblivious to the classroom around me, and allowed God to "break my spirit." I surrendered to serve God because I *wanted* to, not because I *had* to. The "missionary call" and my decision during this prayer did not lessen. They sank into my core. I wondered if God could use me, somehow, to show his love to my generation. I determined to remain alert, to see if God would, indeed, direct my path.

College loomed and I was undecided about where to attend. I really wanted to go back north to college, but my boyfriend was going farther south, to Southeastern Bible College in Lakeland, Florida. I decided to follow him there. My best friend, Ingrid Black, went with me.

The very first week of college in September, 1960, Hurricane Donna came right through Lakeland! All of us students were ordered into the inside hallways of the dorm. We spent the night there, huddled in the dark, as the winds howled and the rain pounded. One of the students, a senior who worked at the college in maintenance, came down the hallway handing out milk cartons. "Come on, drink it up! It's just gonna spoil." When he reached a group of girls at the end of the hall, he sat down and started telling jokes. It was pathetic the way they laughed at him. "Joe, tell us another one," they simpered, their flashlights dancing around him.

That same Joe sat behind me in the one class we had together. He was obnoxious. He pulled my ponytail and said, "Ooh, look at all the cooties!"

Then, on Friday night at chapel service, he played a solo on his saxophone. It was beautiful. I couldn't believe he possessed any redeeming qualities! After service, he walked right up to me and asked me to go out. When I said, "All right," he told me, "Wait right here. I have to find us a ride."

How was I supposed to know the ride was with an old girlfriend? We went to McDonald's on Memorial Boulevard where burgers were only 19 cents. We pulled into the parking lot and stopped. The driver turned to us and asked, "What are you guys having?" Joe slapped his forehead, "Oh, no! I don't have any money!" I had only a dime. We ordered a coke with two straws. So much for a first date. (He has always said I didn't marry him for his couth or for his riches.)

We dated all during that year of college, and as we became better acquainted, we learned that each of us felt "called" to be a missionary. I had thought of India, but Joe wanted Latin America. I decided Latin America was good.

Joe was a graduating senior and I was a freshman, so when we parted for the summer, we did not know when we would see each other again. This would be his last summer to travel with the school quartet throughout the southeast to youth camps and churches. After that, he would have to find a job.

In July, Joe came to West Florida camp and the camp director asked him to lead the camp choir. Since I just "happened" to be there, Joe asked me to accompany the choir on the piano. We worked together during rehearsals and "trained" a four-part choir. We sang "Master, the Tempest is Raging," and it sounded like it!

The next week, Joe called the president of Southeastern to ask for more travel funds for the quartet, and the President said, "A pastor was just here looking for an associate. I recommended you. Give him a call."

So Joe called Tom Waldron, in Beckley, West Virginia. They talked for a while, then Pastor Waldron said,

"Joe, as I've explained, I am looking for a youth pastor—music director. But I have several preliminary questions to ask you. First, have you ever directed a four-part choir?"

"Yes." (It was several years before Joe told him he'd had only three days of experience with a youth camp choir.)

"Second, can you type? I would need you to type up the church bulletin."

"Yes."

"Third, are you married? I won't hire a single guy—too many problems."

"I'm willing to be. Could I call you back?"

My phone rang. "Margaret, I've just been offered a job as an associate pastor!"

"Joe!"

"In Beckley, West Virginia."

"Joe!"

"They have a little parsonage for the associate!"

"Joe!"

"It's furnished, too."

"Joe!"

"The pastor asked me several questions and I have to call him back. If I get the job, can we get married?"

33

"Joe!"

"If I don't get the job, we can't get married."

"Can you call me back tomorrow?"

That night I opened my Bible to the place where I'd left off reading in Isaiah 30. Verse 21 leaped out at me: "This is the way, walk ye in it." I just knew, then, that IF the job worked out, I should marry Joe.

Mom and Dad had no objection! They knew Pastor Waldron because they had toured in West Virginia during their years of traveling with Roy Sherrill. They knew the church was large and stable. I was eighteen and could decide for myself, they said.

Joe called back. I said "All right, let's go meet the pastor." We couldn't travel together unmarried, but Aunt Too was visiting Pensacola and was ready to head back to Illinois for another school year. Aunt Too said she'd drive me over to Palatka where Joe was staying with his parents. Then we would all three drive on up to Beckley.

We arrived in Beckley on Saturday afternoon, met with the pastor, and he asked Joe and me to sing a duet on Sunday morning. He introduced us as "Joe and Margaret" without a last name, since we weren't married "yet." We sang the only duet we had learned together, "Heaven in My Heart."

Sunday afternoon, Pastor Waldron told us we were hired. We had two weeks to go back to Pensacola, get married, and be back at work! The pastor broadcast a daily radio program and produced a weekly television program; he needed Joe to help with both. However, Ira Stanphill would be in Beckley for a two-week revival and could provide the music in the meantime.

I called Mom immediately and asked her to begin to look for options for bridesmaids' dresses and a wedding gown. We decided to print announcements rather than invitations. Fortunately, I was able to borrow a beautiful, hand-beaded wedding gown made by a woman in the church.

Joe went around telling all his college buddies we "had to get married." I teased him that he never did really "propose."

Joe and I bought our wedding rings on credit: $9.00 per month. AND, Joe went out and bought a new saxophone on credit, $11.00

per month, without discussing it with me. I was very angry! However, wanting to be a good Christian, I clinched my jaw, pursed my lips, and internalized my anger. I would not hear the term "passive aggressive" for twenty more years.

**Ingrid Black, Margaret's sister Jan, Margaret, Dad, Joe,
Joe's brother Kenny, Margaret's brother David
Joe and Margaret's wedding day, September 10, 1961**

So, two weeks after we were hired, we were married and ready to begin our ministry.

Even though our housing was provided, every month we made payments on a car, our wedding rings, Joe's college loan, and the saxophone. We had very little money left over for groceries. Somehow, God would find a way to give us a loaf of bread just when we needed it and "commodity" peanut butter and cheese when our cupboards were bare.

* * *

Aunt Too's Impossible Pie
350 degrees, for 40 minutes

INGREDIENTS

2 cups milk
3/4 cup sugar
1/2 cup biscuit mix
4 eggs
1/4 cup butter, softened
1 1/2 teaspoons vanilla
1 cup flaked coconut

DIRECTIONS

1. Combine all ingredients except coconut in electric blender, blend on low speed about 3 minutes. Pour into greased 9-inch pie pan.
2. Let stand about 5 minutes. Then sprinkle with coconut.
3. Bake at 350 degrees for 40 minutes.

3

Beckley, West Virginia
1961–1965

❧

I could see the little holes in the celutex ceiling tiles. What was taking the doctor so long? My back was aching on the hard table and my feet were cold in the stirrups. Brisk footsteps came down the hall.

"Mrs. Register?"

"Yes?"

"You do have a urinary tract infection. But, of course, we'll have to be careful which medication we give you since you're pregnant," said Doctor Merritt.

"What?! Pregnant? I can't be pregnant! I've only been married six weeks!"

"It doesn't take even that long," drawled the grinning doctor.

I couldn't believe it! I was stunned. Driving home, I started to cry. This would ruin everything. I was eighteen years old. I didn't know how to take care of a baby. How could I play piano for the choir? How could I teach those horrible nine-year-old boys in Sunday school? How could I attend every service? Every rehearsal? Every youth group meeting?

I was still crying when Joe came home from the church. He was happy we were going to have a baby. Unlike me! He suggested that I talk with the pastor's wife.

Maxine Waldron met with me the next day. She assured me that Joe was the one hired, not I, and that I would do just fine before and after the baby arrived. Only slightly less anxious, I trudged down the hill toward home.

Our little red-bricked parsonage was square: living room and kitchen/dining on the right, two bedrooms on the left. The back of the house opened out level with the grass. The front of the house faced down the mountain; the basement floor was ground level there and became the garage. A narrow little street went from the front of our house straight down the mountain, one block, directly into the church parking lot. We usually walked to church or slid down in a sled when we could!

Being newly married, I thought I had to cook a nice breakfast the first morning in our house. After all, Joe had been in college for four years and could eat a hearty breakfast every day.

My total pots and pans consisted of an electric skillet and a double boiler. So, I turned on the electric skillet, good and hot, and quickly fried the bacon. I had no idea it would pop so much! Then I cracked an egg into the skillet—whoosh, pop, crackle, brown egg lace danced around. Second egg, crackle, pop, brown lace.

I was just serving our plates when there was a knock on the door. Pastor Waldron came in and sat at the table with us. Joe tried to cut the rubbery eggs, then looked up and asked me, "Uh. Would you mind if I fried my own eggs?" He got up and, very slowly, fried two more eggs. I was so embarrassed. But at least he waited until lunch to say, "This weak tea isn't sweet enough, is it?"

Several weeks later, bacon sizzling *slowly,* nausea rising, I ran from the kitchen just in time. For days I cooked and ran, stirred and ran, flipped fried potatoes and ran to the bathroom with dry heaves and then lay down on the couch in the living room near the kitchen door until the nausea subsided. It never occurred to me that I didn't have to cook a big breakfast.

I did not have the faintest idea how to cook anything else. Growing up, I had finished my school homework and washed dishes, nothing more.

Up the mountain behind our house sat two white houses on a little gravel road. In the second house lived Helen and Roy Kidd with their teenage daughter, Judi. Helen was in her sixties, I guess, and she had befriended the previous youth pastors. When they moved away, she was so sad that she told everyone she would never ever become friends with the church's youth pastors again.

Every day, when the weather was good, Helen would walk past our house on her way to the store. I'd wave to her from my kitchen window. Then we started saying, "Hello," and then one day I asked her if she could show me how to cut up a chicken.

Helen became "Granny Kidd"—she was God's gift to me. She and Judi became my family in Beckley, filling the void in my heart where *alone and scared* resided. Granny and I walked together to Kroger's. She showed me how to choose meat, how to cook pinto beans, and how to make cornbread. She helped me through my pregnancy. She would never attend the church, though, because someone had hurt her deeply years before.

I tried to be creative with our meals on our very limited budget, like hot dogs scored diagonally with cloves in the "diamonds" (to look like ham). Aunt Too hand-wrote some recipes for me. So did my mother, Joe's mother, my grandma, and some of the ladies in the church.

One day we had no bread and no money, but we did have gasoline in the car, so Joe went to visit a sick lady. As he entered through Grace Bragg's kitchen door, he noticed two loaves of bread on the table. When he was ready to leave, Grace said, "Joe, have you folks tried this new batter-whipped bread? It is so light and fluffy." And she handed him a loaf of Sunbeam Bread to bring home.

Another time we had just $3.00 and no groceries. Joe had holes in the soles of his only shoes. It was raining every day. What should we do? Fix Joe's shoes? Or buy a few groceries? Joe left for the church and I knelt down to pray. I was still on my knees when someone knocked on the front door. Patty Gillenwater stood there with a box full of groceries.

I tried to eat a balanced diet, went for my regularly scheduled doctor's appointments, and bought a Dr. Spock book. Nine months had passed and I was ready to have this child! My due date came and went. A day passed. Another, and still another.

Toward the end of June, Mom rode the bus up from Pensacola, and we waited for the baby. On June 27, 1962, about 7:30 a.m., my back started hurting. Badly. Mom said, "Walk, Margaret Ann. Walk around the house. Once you get to the hospital, they'll just make you lie down and the birth will take longer." I walked. Joe paced. About 9:00 a.m. Joe said, "Let's go to the hospital." At 11:20 a.m., our baby girl was born. The nurses put a bow in her hair the first time they brought her to me. She was beautiful. We named her Crystal and called her Christy.

Mom stayed with us for about ten days. The morning she left, I stood at the front door as she and Joe walked down the stairs to go to the bus station. Suddenly, the weight of responsibility hit me. My body sagged, my chest compressed, I could hardly breathe. I was now responsible for the life of a child. She would die if I did not care for her properly. I could not do it! I did not know how! Tears ran down my cheeks, I felt alone, nineteen years old, hundreds of miles from family, how would I ever cope?

Once again, Granny Kidd rescued me from despair—she and Judi. Judi spent more time at our house than she did at home. She even volunteered to run the church nursery because she didn't want our baby cared for by just anyone.

Larry Meadows, a teenager in the choir and youth group, became my helper also. Larry was at our house when we heard the news that President Kennedy had been shot! We turned on the television and watched Walter Cronkite wipe tears as he told us what was happening.

After the first few church services there at Calvary Assembly in Beckley, Joe gave me a stern lecture: "Margaret, part of your job is to greet people. When you enter the church, don't just go and sit down by the piano. Shake hands with everyone and talk to them."

I dreaded the next service because—although I enjoyed playing the piano for rehearsals and church services—I was naturally shy and introverted. I forced myself to walk up to the first person; I stuck out my hand and began to talk ... Joe says I am now at the opposite extreme, talking too much to everyone I meet!

The first few weeks, I became angry and jealous because Joe was friendly to the girls in the youth group and choir. Joe set me straight on that, too! He said, "Margaret, that is part of my job. I love you. I chose you. You never need to doubt that. But I will be friendly with *everyone* in the youth group and the choir."

At first, Joe didn't keep a regular schedule during the week because now he was an adult and could "do what he wanted." While I was in the hospital with Christy, Pastor Waldron had a "come to Jesus" meeting with Joe: these are your hours, this is your schedule, and these are your specific duties. Since that day, Joe has been very structured in every ministry he has had.

Pastor Waldron was invited to Charleston, West Virginia, to speak to Presbyterians, Episcopalians, and Methodists who wanted to learn about the baptism in the Holy Spirit. That meeting changed everyone who attended, including Pastor Waldron. He told us, "I saw women with make-up and earrings praising God, tears rolling down through their mascara. They were receiving the Holy Spirit! Margaret, would you wear lipstick? I want you to wear it next Sunday and tell me how you feel."

I did. It felt great. Bro. Waldron announced from the pulpit that "the legalistic ban" was lifted from the ladies. This announcement even made our local newspaper. We were not only advanced for the Appalachian District, we were "way ahead" of the General Council of the Assemblies of God, of which our church was a member.

Having a robed choir was innovative, too. We had the typical mix of singers: good, fair, and terrible. Hazel, mentally challenged, stood on the front row, and always sang enthusiastically. She lived near the church and walked to every service. Once, we had a big snowstorm on the day of choir rehearsal. All roads were closed. School was cancelled. But about 7:00 p.m. Joe decided he'd better bundle up and walk down to the church just in case anyone had come. There was Hazel, standing in the sheltered doorway, drifted snow piled around her feet. She loved the choir!

One "rich" family attended the church. Since their tithes were the greatest, their daughter had to be allowed to sing a solo practically every other Sunday, or her mother would call the pastor and complain. Then he would talk to Joe and Joe would have to schedule the daughter again, and again, and again.

For the weekly live television show, we drove through the twisting mountain roads to the station in Oakhill. Joe planned two or three songs: solos, duets, the girls' sextet, the choir, or the Sharrett brothers' trio. There were no sound tracks, so I played the piano for everything. Pastor Waldron preached for about fifteen minutes. He was a good speaker with lots of colorful sayings, for example: "sky-blue, blood-red, stupendous, colossal."

The daily live radio program originated in a small radio studio just off the church platform. Pastor Waldron or Joe would play a cut from a music record and then speak. The program was so successful that everyone in the area came to know the pastor. After he resigned from the church, he actually bought the radio station, kept it secular, and made lots of money.

The youth group was a joy! Eventually it numbered about sixty kids who were also in Joe's Sunday school class. We bowled, skated, went to camp, performed dramas, and had a banquet each year for the high school seniors. After a high school basketball star began to attend church and accepted Christ, he and Joe organized a Christian league. Our team went on to become champions!

Ten of our sixty kids became active in full-time ministry: Ronnie West; Cheryl West Copeland; Eddie, Freddie, and Bobby Sharrett; Patty Ray Reese; Steve Fielder; Larry Meadows; Rita Meadows; and our youth camp soloist, Gloria Elliott. Other youth became successful businessmen—Max and Don Priddy each own large ACE Hardware stores; Herb Wheeler became an Air Force pilot serving several tours in Viet Nam. Joe's brother, Claudie "Cash" Register, lived with us for a few months; from Beckley, he joined the Army and, later, was wounded in Viet Nam.

A part of Joe's job that he really enjoyed was "visitation." He turned in a weekly report of the visits he had made: sick people, visitors to the church, and regular church members whom he visited just to stay in touch. When it was snowing the worst, he would go visit families on steep mountain slopes. He loved to slide around those narrow, gravel roads made of "red dog" (slag from the coal).

One of Joe's favorite people was Ben Wooten. Ben looked like he was 103. He was the church janitor, and sometimes Joe would sneak up while Ben was cleaning and unplug the vacuum cleaner. Ben had been a miner, and his face and arms were pocked with tiny black flecks of coal. He was as skinny as a rail, tall and lanky. His ears stuck out and he had a nick in the bridge of his nose that looked like someone had shot at him from the side. Joe loved him dearly.

Every so often Joe would go to Ben's house and sit with Ben and his wife in the rockers on the porch. Ben told him stories about "the olden days" when no blacks were allowed to set foot on soil near the mines. The miners would chase them off with a shotgun. Ben told how he had also chased his wife around the yard with a shotgun, shooting the ground near her feet to make her run faster and faster while he laughed at her. That was before he became a Christian. Many times, Ben and Edith gave Joe some of their food to bring home, what they called "commodity food" from welfare—delicious cheese, peanut butter, or butter. From their neediness, they blessed Joe and me.

One winter day, Joe visited Laura Vider, an elderly widow who lived alone with no relatives nearby. It was below zero, the snow was deep, the ice slick. She mentioned that it sure wasn't fun to go to the outhouse in weather like this. Joe came home determined to install a bathroom for her. He recruited an old man with a wooden leg to help him.

In Mrs. Vider's house was a closet the men could convert into a bathroom. They bought a sink, commode, shower stall, and water heater. They bought copper tubing and glue. They did the carpentry work and then slid under the house to connect the pipes. Now they had to "test" the water flow. Joe's helper stayed under the house while Joe went out to the street to turn on the water valve. All of a sudden, Joe heard screaming, "Turn it off! Turn it off!" The screaming was accompanied by a loud, rapid thump-ka-thump-ka-thump. The wooden leg came out from under the house first, followed by the rest of a very wet old man. Every joint of the new plumbing job was spraying water in every direction!

Another result of Joe's visitation was that one of the church families called and offered him a dog. Joe was really excited as he drove out to pick it up. An hour later, he came up our driveway with a huge boxer sitting in the back seat of our little, powder blue, compact Comet. The dog was so big his head hung over the front seat and drool slid down the seat cushions. I laughed until my sides hurt. Joe put the dog in the back yard for a few minutes, and during his very brief visit with us, the dog left us several presents the size of gigantic "cow piles"!

Just about every week, we were invited to someone's home to eat Sunday dinner. Grandma Meadows was a wonderful cook. She had nineteen children. Larry, my helper, was the baby. (One of her boys had been born in the "slop-jar." She "needed to potty" and before she could get up, *sloop…* here he came!)

We ate at E.W. and Louise Hill's home many times. Their house was on a steep "red dog" road with lots of curves—one of Joe's favorite winter places to visit. Also, the Gillenwaters, the Riddles, and Priddys were wonderful friends. So were Raymond and Ann Kidd. They were just a little older than we were, with two young children. The first time we went to their house, Ann wanted to impress us with a lovely dinner table, but when we sat down to eat, six-year old Dean blurted, "Momma! I have two forks! Why does everyone have two forks?"

Another church member I loved was Maxine Tolbert, who lived with Macel and Dallas, her two adolescent children, in a little frame house up a steep "red dog" road. Maxine had paid $20 for the house, which she had taken apart and reassembled, board by board, up on the mountain. In 2004 Joe and I visited her; she was in her nineties and had lived in that little house for over seventy-five years. (Throughout our entire missionary career, Maxine sent us $40 every month, money she did not have to spare.)

We became very close to a family with two young children; I'll call the couple Don and Elaine. Don, the church treasurer, worked at the *Raleigh Register*. He was quiet, with a shy smile and a dry sense of humor. Elaine went to the cemetery every day to visit the grave of their nine-year-old daughter who had died of leukemia the year before. Elaine had been sure that God would heal her daughter. When the child was not better after prayer at the local church, Don and Elaine took her to Charleston, to Dayton, to Tulsa, to anywhere a "healing preacher" would pray over her.

But the child died, and Elaine's concept of God's love became tainted with cold, gray disappointment. She became overprotective of her living children. Gradually, her Christian hope withered around the edges and shriveled into a hard prune of disillusionment. In 2004, Joe and I visited Elaine, then a widow. Her coffee table was literally covered with medicines for real and imaginary illnesses. Negative and reclusive, Elaine sat in disarray underneath her broken dreams. It broke my heart.

How I wished I had known, all those years ago, the steps of grief. I would have held Elaine's hand, and helped her acknowledge her anger toward the doctors, anger at the church, anger toward herself for what she "might have done differently," and anger toward God. I would have helped her cry, expressing deep sorrow for what "might have been." And I would have led her to accept the new reality, not what she wanted, but what "really was" so that one day she could have regained zest for life.

Ernest H. Hay, Joe's roommate from college, came to visit us. A grizzly old man, he had been a cook in the Army and a patient in the Milledgeville, Georgia mental institution before he attended Southeastern College on the GI bill. After Hay chased a roommate around with a knife, the Dean of Men asked Joe if he'd try rooming with Hay. Fortunately, Hay liked Joe and even bought a small refrigerator for their room and kept the fridge stocked with food. Joe thinks Hay liked him because Joe would listen without contradiction to Hay's tall tales—such as his escape with his buddy, Chase, from the Milledgeville institution through the Okeefenokee swamp, with hounds at their heels, in the coldest part of winter. Hay, being handy with a knife, taught me how to chop an onion by cutting it only two ways.

45

Joe's mother, Duckie, came to Beckley, too. She talked non-stop, even following me into the bathroom, still talking. She was a really good cook so I turned the kitchen over to her and just helped—until she yelled at me for peeling something "wrong"! To avoid conflict, I stayed out of the kitchen while she was there.

Aunt Too came every summer. Uncle Ed had passed away while I was at Southeastern College. Aunt Too loved Beckley, the cool evening air, and the mountains.

Once, when Mom and Dad came to visit, we had acquired another dog, a medium-sized, outdoor dog that would run and throw itself against the back storm door: *ker-blam*! Daddy said, "Joe, let's hot-wire that storm door. It won't hurt the dog, just scare him." So they did! *Ker-blam*! Yelp, yelp, yelp. *Ker-blam*! Yelp, yelp, yelp. That dog did not learn his lesson, but Joe and Daddy had fun. We later gave the dog away.

During that visit, Mom had a little talk with me about my ironing. "What is all this stuff piled in the closet?" "My ironing." "You do NOT leave ironing piled up. You iron it. You are a pastor's wife and your husband needs to look nice. Iron his hankies, too, because people will notice when he uses the hankies at church."

She also talked to me about our finances while we were folding clothes. "Look at all this new underwear!" "Yeah, Joe's underwear was pretty ratty so we went down to Montgomery Ward and opened a charge account." "What? You don't *charge* things, Margaret Ann. When you have a need, you pray. You ask God to supply your need. You don't just run out and buy stuff on credit!" We never did again.

Would I ever learn all the things I *should* do? Or *should not* do? How could I *do the right thing* if I didn't know what it was?

When Christy was about two years old, Joe and I decided we wanted another baby. After all, the Foreign Missions Board from Springfield, Missouri would allow us to have two children—we had checked on all the rules and regulations for becoming missionaries, and we had talked to Pastor Waldron about it. He was thrilled that we planned to leave from Beckley to go to the mission field as soon as Joe had fulfilled all the requirements to be ordained as a minister.

After several months, I was pregnant again. We were excited. We told Christy she was going to have a baby, a brother we hoped, and we'd call him Timmy. She talked incessantly about "My baby Timmy."

This delivery was not so easy.

In early December, 1964, my water broke. I called the doctor around 11:00 a.m.; he said he'd meet me at Raleigh General hospital. He wasn't concerned because it was almost my due date. By now my back was aching pretty badly. The doctor examined me and said the baby was breech. "There is something in the birth canal. I can't tell if it's an arm or a leg. If it's an arm, we will have to perform a Caesarian." Oh, no! I thought, we don't have the money for that! "But if it's a leg," the doctor continued, "you'll probably be able to deliver breech."

They wheeled the gurney into the hallway on the second floor between the delivery room and the elevator to the operating room on the third floor. My pains intensified. "Let's get her into the delivery room and have another look," I heard the doctor say.

I assumed the position… the doctor inserted his hand. "Still can't tell if it's an arm or a leg." He stood up and said to the nurse, "Call the interns, they need to see this." Into the room traipsed what seemed to me to be a dozen "boys" to insert hand, to *ummm*, to stand around shaking their heads and then to leave to bring back some more friends.

I was mellowed out "on drugs"; the contractions severe. I felt something warm hit my inner thigh and I heard a nurse exclaim, "There's a foot! Grab it. Don't let it get back inside!" Someone grabbed the foot; someone stood on each side of me, pushing on my lumpy stomach, trying to rotate the baby. Rotate, squish, push; hold the foot, rotate, squish, push.

Someone was holding a "gas mask" above my face. I stretched up as far as I could and took a breath as deep as I possibly could.

Our baby boy, Timothy, arrived at 4:18 p.m. Joe gave me a thank you card for presenting him with a son.

But postpartum depression hit me hard.

I lay in the front bedroom isolated from reality. I did not care if the world stopped. Tears ran from the corners of my eyes into my ears. I did not even wipe them away. I believed I would never feel better or be able to cope with life again. Despair drowned me.

Mother had been with us for several days but had already returned home. Joe called and asked her to come back. Meanwhile, Millie, an elderly black woman, came to live in to care for Timmy and to help Joe and me. Sammy and Patty Gillenwater took Christy home with them.

I cried, and the baby cried, and Millie comforted, rocked, crooned, and cooked. She said, "My little man jest hungry. I give him dis good broth. My little man feel good and strong in no time a'tall." She spooned broth into Timmy and into me.

One day while Millie was changing Timmy's diaper, he wet right in her face. "Dat's jest sweet water," she crooned as she wiped her face with a clean diaper.

Then, in January before Timmy was six weeks old, he was hospitalized with pneumonia. That winter we ran the vaporizer hour after hour. Slowly but surely, he improved, and so did I.

We welcomed spring that year, and Joe was officially ordained as a minister in Bristol, Virginia, at District Council, on May 5, 1965. We were ready to go and be missionaries! We sent for the "application packet," filled out all the forms, even answered such stuff as, "Are you afraid of contracting germs from door knobs?" "Would you be afraid to ride a motorcycle?"

The man in charge of Missionary Candidates talked with Joe on the phone. No problem. Routine. You folks have excellent recommendations. The Missions Committee meets next Tuesday. I'll call to let you know the good news.

He called. No. You've been turned down. At first, Joe thought the man was teasing. But he continued, "The Missions Committee is changing policy now and wants every missionary to be a pastor first. On your own. Not as an associate. Sorry. Contact us again after you have been a pastor for at least two years."

We were crushed! Confused! We thought God had called us to go and be missionaries! What on earth could we do? Everyone in the church knew we were just awaiting the final approval before going to the mission field. They were planning a big send-off. We were embarrassed. And we were bewildered. But that very afternoon, Joe began calling friends, district officials, pastors, and even family, asking if anyone knew of a church that needed a pastor. We resigned from the Beckley church. Pastor Tom Waldron was very gracious. We would not see him again for more than twelve years. But when we next encountered him, he would once again change *drastically* the course of our lives!

* * *

Granny Kidd's Pinto Beans
Allow at least four hours for simmering.

INGREDIENTS

Walk to the grocery store to purchase:
Two or three ham hocks, about 1 1/2 pounds
One package of pinto beans, about two pounds
(You'll need rice, onions, and cornbread, too.)

DIRECTIONS

1. Rinse ham hocks and place in a large cooking pot. Add about 12 to 16 cups of water (3 or 4 quarts). The beans will expand, so you will need a lot more water than you think.
2. Dump the beans into a large bowl. Sort through the beans carefully—you may find little clumps of dirt, half-beans, dried-up beans.
3. Fill the bowl with water and rub the beans with your hands, in the water, to clean the outsides of the beans.
4. Dip the beans from the bowl into the pot with the ham hocks.
5. Cover the pot and bring beans to a boil. This will take 15 minutes or more, because of the large amount of water.
6. Reduce the heat and continue to boil gently for about 2 hours.

7. Taste a bean to see if it is tender. Add a couple of teaspoons of salt. Add water to be sure the beans are covered with at least an inch of water on top.
8. Continue to simmer for several more hours. (The longer, the better.) The broth will thicken slightly and turn a dark color.
9. Serve over rice. Cornbread is a must, too! And chopped, sweet onions.

Joe and Margaret, Timmy and Christy
1965

4

Tavares, Florida
1965–1967

uff. Puff. Joe protruded his lower lip and blew upward, toward one eye, then toward the other. *The Gnat Blow.* I fanned the gnats out of my face. They were the only things moving in the still, stifling hot air. Joe was teaching Sunday school and I was poised beside the out-of-tune piano in the little, white clapboard chapel. Torn window screens hung open. A worn, stained strip of green felt carpeting ran from the front door down the center aisle. Nicked and scarred opera chairs faced the pulpit, which needed varnish. The steep roof and tall windows were the only elements of beauty in this little church.

When we left Beckley, we had moved temporarily to Pensacola to stay with Mom and Dad. They were the pastors of Brownsville Assembly and lived in a nice parsonage near a golf course. But four adults, a toddler, and a baby were a houseful! *They* began to pray earnestly, too, that we'd find a church to pastor. One Wednesday night, Joe attended prayer meeting with Dad and requested prayer for a pastorate. Jeanette Bedsole approached Joe after the service, "I'm here visiting my sister. We're looking for a pastor in Tavares; we have a little church with a furnished parsonage. If you're interested, call the chairman of the church board, Mr. Humphreys."

Joe did. And on that hot Sunday morning, the members voted us in as pastors, 100 percent...all fourteen members. Joe's Sunday school class in Beckley was four times larger!

Our salary was $60.00 a week. We never went hungry, but many times all we had to eat was macaroni. However, I knew we planned to stay only two years, to fulfill the requirement for becoming missionaries. Recently I'd read, "If life hands you a lemon, make lemonade." I wondered if I could make lemonade for two years. I parked my heart in neutral and plastered a smile on my face.

We moved our few belongings into the furnished, ranch style parsonage located in a nice neighborhood. I tried to hide the stains on the couch by dyeing it with a sponge. The dye made the couch scratchy and stiff and it looked even worse! For a living room rug, we asked a carpet store for samples, which Joe duct taped together to form a "beautiful" colorful rug. We placed it under the coffee table he made from a new, hollow core door (no door handle hole). A vinyl, swivel rocker looked nice, but was hard to get up out of, because the seat sank practically to the floor.

The old washing machine in the utility room off the carport actually worked, as did the clothesline in the large yard out back.

A window air conditioning unit was in the living-dining-kitchen area near the chrome dinette set, a table with six chairs. The three bedrooms contained a double bed, twin beds, and a rollaway-type bed. The master bath shimmered green with mold. It took me many hours to bleach and scrub the shower.

The walls inside the house were stuccoed. Joe would sit on the side of the bed, peel off his dirty socks, and toss them against the wall. The socks would stick and, according to him, form unique and interesting patterns.

One Sunday morning Joe announced from the pulpit, "We are glad to see so-and-so's husband here with her this morning, home from Viet Nam." Joe sat down and Brother Humphrey, next to him on the platform, whispered forcefully, "That man is NOT her husband, it's her boyfriend!" Joe was so rattled that he stood up and said, "Uh. Excuse me, that is not her husband sitting there beside her."

After a few months, Joe scheduled a Kid's Crusade, hoping to bring some new families into the church. We had been away for several days and arrived back in town on Saturday evening, just in time to welcome the children's evangelists who were to stay with us. We greeted them, showed them their room, and I asked what they'd like for breakfast. The man replied, "My wife and I would each like a poached egg, two slices of wheat toast—unbuttered, a cup of hot tea, and a bowl of oatmeal." I thought he was teasing! He was serious.

I noticed that my ankles were itching as we stood talking about breakfast, but we all went on to bed. The next morning all of us were covered with bites. Our house was infested with fleas! We had had a small dog but had given him away several days earlier. Obviously, his fleas didn't go with him. Since we discovered the nuisance on Sunday, no exterminator would come until Monday. The evangelists had fleas with their special-order breakfast.

Another Sunday morning, Joe's aunt and uncle surprised us by walking into the church service. I worried all through the service that Aunt Bootie and Uncle Rayford would go home with us for dinner. I was ashamed because in the refrigerator was one thing: a pitcher of water. Our cabinets were bare except for a can of tomatoes and a small bag of macaroni.

When church dismissed, Aunt Bootie said, "We want to take you out to eat. Where is a nice restaurant?" I ordered all the vegetables and fruits I could think of for both the children and myself. What a blessing!

Aunt Bootie was especially close to Joe. She was his mother's sister, a Garner. There were eight siblings, all of whom lived in the southeast: Carrie, Myrtie, Kitty, Claude, Bill, Duckie, Bootie, and Lola. Grandpa Joseph Garner came to Florida from Georgia, walking beside a covered wagon. He and Grandma Garner met in Florida, where they married and lived the rest of their lives. They owned extensive land in the Bloomingdale area of Brandon.

During World War II, Joe's parents, Duckie (Lillie Belle) and Ray, moved to Detroit to find work. They shared a house with Uncle Bill and Aunt Irma. They were not Christians, then, and drank and smoked pretty heavily. One day when Joe was about three years old, he went into the bedroom where Ray was passed out on the bed with a bottle of wine on the floor beside him. Joe came out of the bedroom a few minutes later, happy. He went back in. Came out happier. Back in. Happier. Drunk as a skunk—they say he threw up everywhere, even on his cousin Ann's doll....

After the war, the family moved back to the Bloomingdale area of Florida where they attended the Pentecostal Holiness Church and, later, Pleasant Grove Assembly of God in Durant. Aunt Bootie and Uncle Rayford, along with Uncle Bill and Aunt Irma, became "old time holiness," strict legalists. Duckie and Ray never "got their act together" and moved from place to place, always looking for the perfect job and the perfect boss. Aunt Bootie and Uncle Rayford and Uncle Bill and Aunt Irma stayed in Durant, raised their families in the church, and were a stabilizing influence for Joe.

When Joe was four years old, his father, Ray, owned a 1935 car, a coupe with a rumble seat. The doors opened backwards, a style that would soon be outlawed. One day, Ray asked Joe to ride along with him to a local bar, *Frenchy's,* and of course Joe went—even though Duckie had warned Joe *never* to go with Ray when he was drinking.

On the way back home, over the country roads made of slag (sharp rocks in tar), Ray growled impatiently, "Joby, quit sitting on the edge of the seat—sit back!" Joe reached over to the door, to push himself back on the seat. The door flung open—backwards.

The wind swooped Joe out the door onto the slag. He hit head-first, tumbling down the road on the sharp rocks. His little body rolled into a ditch, where he lay totally naked, his clothes ripped off, his scalp pushed back on his skull. Two elderly sisters, sitting on their front porch on Bennett's Hill, witnessed the accident. They went running to help.

One of the women picked Joe up and carried him to where Ray had stopped the car. Ray, shaking violently, climbed into the rumble seat. The other woman slid behind the steering wheel and drove to *Carrigan's,* the little corner country store. There, Mrs. Carrigan collected towels to try to staunch the bleeding from the unconscious little boy.

Someone ran across the road to look for the "hot rodder," Frank Emerine. If he could drive Joe to the hospital in his fast car, perhaps it would save the child's life. Frank happened to be home. They careened toward St. Joseph's Hospital in Tampa, about twenty miles away. A policeman caught them speeding and pulled them over, but when he saw the extent of Joe's injuries, he escorted them to the hospital, siren screaming.

For several days, Joe's life hung by a thread.

Concussion. Blood transfusions. Over 100 stitches in Joe's head. Two stitches in his knee.

Aunt Bootie donated blood and sat beside Joe's bed hour after hour. One evening she prayed aloud, "Lord, if this child would live to serve You, then please, let him live, heal him. But, if he would not serve You, Father, please take him home to heaven."

As Joe faded in and out of consciousness, he would cry, "Momma's gonna spank me. She told me not to go with Daddy." It broke Duckie's heart.

Ray murmured repeatedly, "If he doesn't live, I'll kill myself."

While Joe's health improved, fifteen boils developed on his back. The doctor lanced them all at once, with no anesthesia.

As he was recovering, lying in the hospital bed, Joe had his first audience. The nurses would gather around to see him make funny faces. He became a comedian!

Several years later, Duckie told Joe to take the trash out and burn it in the field behind their house. Joe liked to stack up cans and garbage and watch them tumble down, like Hitler's soldiers being shot by our troops. But this time, he forgot to keep careful watch on the fire, and it "got out" and started burning the pasture, heading toward the old barn. Duckie smelled the smoke, grabbed a croker burlap bag and beat the flames. Joe was nowhere to be found. Finally, when the fire was extinguished, Joe reappeared from way down in the pasture where he'd been playing the entire time. Duckie, panting, red-faced, and short of breath, glared at him, "Joby, when, uh, I get my breath, uh, I'm gonna, uh, tan your hide…" She did, too.

Ray was not a very kind man. He had a sharp sense of humor, but he usually used it in cynicism and bitterness. His mother had died when influenza swept the world in 1918; he never recovered from his childhood pain and remained angry at "life." One kind thing he did, though, was to buy, on credit, an old metal clarinet for Joe. Joe practiced for hours and joined the orchestra and band at school. Being in the band was extra special to Joe. His band director wanted him to try out for drum major, but Joe wouldn't because his friend, Donald, *really* wanted to be drum major.

Joe's parents, Ray and Duckie Register

Joe's best childhood friend was Johnny Giles. Barefoot, they would go off into the woods camping. Sometimes, they would drag home a snake they had killed. They cooked bacon, eggs, and potatoes in an old skillet over a campfire. Their tent consisted of a tarp tied between tall pine trees. Once, during a terrific thunderstorm, Johnny's dog crawled into the tent with them—he had horrible breath. Terrified, Joe and Johnny sat in the pouring rain, smelling stinky doggy breath, as they hugged some rubber boots. They hoped the boots would repel lightning and save their lives.

Being raised under "old time holiness," Joe and Johnny "got saved" every revival meeting. (Calvinists got saved only once. Armenians got saved a lot.) Finally, when Joe was a senior in high school, he and Johnny both realized they could "stay saved." A lady preacher "shook them over the pits of hell on a rotten stick" and they went to the altar for their final "salvation."

Joe had already decided he would go to Southeastern Bible College once he was "really saved," and he did. No one helped him with tuition; he worked at the college and at various part-time jobs to pay his own way. There were no scholarships back in those days, just government loans through the college. The day we were appointed as missionaries, the college forgave $600 on the bill — their policy if a graduate received appointment as a missionary. That paid Joe's bill in full.

Two families in Tavares became our life-long friends. Jeanette and Martin Bedsole owned the local hardware store. They would invite us to their house on Sunday nights after church for leftover roast or pork chops or meatloaf. Sometimes they took us to a cafeteria in Leesburg. I was *so* grateful, then, to be able to order fruit and veggies for the kids. Martin and Jeanette also took us in their boat down the Dora Canal to see the beautiful overhanging trees with Spanish moss cascading, fish jumping, and alligators sunning. The Bedsoles were our baby-sitters, too, since there was no church nursery. Martin actually taught Timmy to walk there, at the church. Timmy called him "Bedsoe."

Lucy and Arnold Wolfgong lived outside of town in a modest house. Lucy was a one-woman energy machine, the unpaid, unrecognized church associate pastor. She taught Sunday school, conducted children's church, sponsored Missionettes girls' clubs, organized VBS, cleaned the church, and visited sick members. Later, she and Arnold donated faithfully to our missionary work. We attended Lucy's 100th birthday party in 2007.

Lucy gave Christy her first opportunity to "perform." Reciting a Bible verse in children's church, Christy said, "What time I am afraid, I will trust in Thee. Psalm 50 cents, free." (Psalm 56:3)

When Christy was three-and-a-half, she went to the altar one Sunday evening. I could see her little body shaking with sobs. I left the piano and went to kneel beside her. "I want Jesus to come into my heart," she cried.

The summer Christy was four and Timmy one-and-a-half, the Humphreys let us borrow their foldout camper to vacation at Ft. Pickens, on Pensacola Beach. We set up camp and then went out exploring the old fort. Suddenly, Christy slipped down a sandy ledge and fell, hitting the bottom of her chin. The skin burst open. Joe took her into town to the emergency room for stitches. My dad, visiting his church members at the hospital, walked by the emergency room and saw Christy lying on a cot with blood all over her chest! He almost fainted!

That night, Christy slept toward the center of the camper; Timmy lay on the outside edge. The camper's beds folded out with the top tarp snapping in place under the edge of the bedside. We were drifting off to sleep when we heard *whoosh, ummph.* Joe turned on the flashlight. Timmy had disappeared! Joe went outside, and there was Timmy, lying on the soft sand, still sound asleep. Joe had forgotten to snap the tarp in place.

When my sister, Jan, and her new husband, Barry Hammac, came to visit us in Tavares, Jan brought clothes for the children. Mom and Dad came, too, and we all went fishing. Daddy caught a five-pound catfish, which Mom fried for supper. Delicious!

Several nights later, Joe and I were in bed asleep, the window open at the head of our bed with the attic fan pulling cooler air in through the window. All of a sudden, I woke up gagging. Retching. Smelling a *horrible* odor. Something had died. Under our window. I sat on the edge of the bed, still gagging.

Joe finally woke up. "What on earth is the matter?" he asked. "Don't you smell it?" I choked. "Smell what?" He could not smell anything! Turns out, he had buried the fish remains in the flowerbed under our bedroom window. A dog had dug them up...after a time of "seasoning." That's the night I learned that Joe can't smell; since then, there have been many opportunities to confirm it. (It actually was a blessing on the mission field.)

When Timmy was in serious potty training, I placed his potty-chair in the kitchen where I was working, and stripped him naked—except for his baseball cap, which was "glued" to his head. He walked around, humming, playing. Joe, in leisure shorts and tee shirt, worked in the utility room adjacent to the kitchen. I propped the door open between us. Suddenly Joe hollered, "What on earth?" I glanced in his direction. Directly behind Joe stood Timmy streaming a warm golden arch onto Joe's leg, watching it run into his tennis shoes. I died laughing. (I suppose I remember this incident so vividly because I did not have very many occasions to laugh during those two years. Timmy was sick repeatedly with respiratory infections. And I never had sufficient money for groceries—I tabulated the cost of every item as I put it into my grocery cart, but frequently at the check-out, I was embarrassed by not having enough money.)

That summer, before Aunt Too came to visit, she wrote to give us the train schedule so Joe could meet her. He left early to make sure she wouldn't have to wait. Several hours later, the phone rang. It was Aunt Too, "Where is Joe? I've been sitting here waiting." Half an hour later the phone rang again; it was Joe, "Where's Aunt Too? I've been here waiting. She wasn't on the train." I assured him she was there, to keep looking.

Aunt Too called again, "Where, exactly, *is* Joe?" I didn't know exactly, but I'd ask him the next time *he* called. Turns out he was in Orlando, Aunt Too in Leesburg. She teased him unmercifully and would never let him forget that he had left her stranded!

In 1965, Joe called to advise the foreign missions secretary that we were now pastors of a church. A year later, he called again. And again after 18 months. As the two-year anniversary approached, the man said, "OK, we won't hold you folks up any longer. Come on to Springfield for School of Missions." It was early summer, 1967.

Lucy Wolfgong cried as if her heart would break, "The first time we've begun growing as a church, and you're leaving. Couldn't you stay a few more years?" I felt guilty for not wanting to stay.

I borrowed some clothes from Jan for School of Missions.

Dad had his first heart attack that summer.

A new stage of life awaited us. We wondered, "What exactly is 'itinerary'?"

* * *

Typical Tavares meal

INGREDIENTS

Macaroni
Can of tomatoes
Salt

DIRECTIONS

1. Boil macaroni just until tender. Drain. Return to cooking pot.
2. Open a can of tomatoes, dump in with the macaroni. Add a little salt.
3. Enjoy. Be thankful there is something to eat.

We're finally on our way!
1967–1969

Remember to Pray for . . .

Margaret and Joe Register
Timmy and Christy

your missionaries to CHILE

Our first prayer card, 1967

5

i-tin´er-ar-y
n. 1. A detailed plan for a journey.
The dictionary has no verb "to itinerate";
no wonder it's so hard to do!
1967–1968

Her shoulders drooped; her footsteps were slow and measured. The twins scampered ahead of her up the three flights of wooden stairs. I called out, "Excuse me, you don't know me. But may I talk with you for a minute?"

She paused on the second floor landing, her hand on the stair rail. "Yes?" she said softly as she looked at me.

"My name is Margaret Register. I'm new here, just beginning, just wanting to be a missionary. And I've been watching you. All week. Here we are in this old, hot dormitory. I mean, I don't mind, being a new recruit and all. But you're a veteran. Why aren't you in the air-conditioned dorm?"

She looked me in the eye. Her shoulders straightened ever so slightly.

I continued quickly, "But you don't complain. That's what I wanted to tell you. I have admired you all week. I've heard some of the other women grumble and complain." I swallowed and spoke more slowly, "I've watched you go up and down the stairs, corral the twins, maneuver through the dining hall, sit in the sessions. And you smile. You greet others. Your attitude is gentle and kind. I guess you must not have suffered as many bad experiences as these other missionaries have."

Tears formed in her eyes while a smile curved the corners of her mouth. "Margaret, I'm Lois Stewart. I have lots of things I *could* complain about. We're in this dorm because we brought our nine-year-old twins, Sammy and Susie. We had no one to leave them with, like we were 'supposed to do' before coming to School of Missions. We've just returned from our second term in El Salvador." She paused.

"I just buried my baby there," she whispered. She took a deep, ragged breath and a tear began to roll down her cheek.

Softly, she continued, "I have to make a choice everyday. To become bitter and complain, or to accept what God sends—life with the good and the bad. I simply continue one day at a time, by God's grace."

Tears were rolling down my cheeks now. I told her, "Lois, when I grow up I want to be like you." Years later, when I was a veteran missionary and she was twice widowed and retired, I held her frail hand in mine, looked in her eyes, and said, "Lois, I still mean it, when I grow up, I want to be like you."

I was 24 that summer of 1967; Joe was 28. Christy and Timmy, ages 5 and 2–1/2, stayed in Pensacola with Mom and Dad.

It was our turn, now, to meet *The Committee.* Joe and I sat at the oval, polished wood, *official, sacred* table of the Foreign Missions Committee in the big, blue headquarters building in Springfield, Missouri. We were scared to death. The men kindly asked what country we wanted to go to. Joe answered, tentatively, "Perhaps Colombia?" "Sorry," they said, "we have recently appointed several families there. How about Chile or Peru?" When we looked bewildered, they told us to pray about it overnight and let them know the next day. Then they asked some more questions, and I guess we gave adequate answers because we were permitted to continue attending the School of Missions and given a schedule to fly to Chicago for our psychological evaluations.

That night we sat in the stuffy dorm room on our single beds at Central Bible College and prayed a simple prayer. "Lord, we really don't care where we go. Should we go to Chile? Or to Peru?" We didn't know much about either country, but Joe said, "Why don't we go to Chile? We'll trust that this is the right choice unless God definitely shows us otherwise."

The next day, sunshine streamed through the tall windows into the classroom where we missionary candidates, knowing absolutely nothing, were receiving our orientation class on Latin American culture. We had two hours to learn everything we needed to know. We were handed two books, *The Other Side of the Coin* and *The Ugly American.* Wow! We would learn a lot from those! Then missionaries stood and began to share anecdotes of what "not" to do—don't hold your hand with the fingers curved like this; don't motion for someone to come to you by crooking your finger. Joe raised his hand, "I think I'll just stand around with my hands in my pockets." They roared laughing, "That's bad, too!"

The information continued: Do take toilet paper with you everywhere you go; ladies, don't look boldly into the eyes of men; be assured that your North American space bubble is much larger than the Latino's space bubble. In fact, someone enlightened us, you can tell a new missionary because he's the one backed up against the wall. The Latinos keep getting close enough to him to feel comfortable, the Gringo feels uncomfortable and backs up again, backing up until he's against the wall. Plant your feet, they told us, and don't move. Let the Latinos set the space.

Later, after the evening service, we congregated in the college snack room. Veteran missionaries were telling stories in Spanish. They laughed and laughed, but we did not have a *clue* what they were laughing about. A couple walked over to our booth, "Mind if we join you?" Paul and Betty Brannan treated us like we were real people, not just "ignorant recruits." They translated some of the conversation for us. Several months later, Joe and Paul were in a missionary convention together and played golf. Joe called me, "Margaret, pray for me. I'm very uncomfortable around Paul. Today, on the golf course, he stood very close to me." *Duh.* Paul, a veteran missionary, had learned the Latino way of standing close. Besides, his hearing was poor and sometimes his hearing aides did not work very well. Years later, we laughed with Paul and Betty about Joe's worries! Joe insists it was *not* funny at the time.

I was amazed, at our first School of Missions, to see the missionaries pray. When the call to prayer was given at the conclusion of the evening services, men and women alike lined the altars and front pews. They didn't say a brief, quiet sentence. They prayed for half an hour or more. I had never seen such intense prayers. Some people knelt. Some stood. Some walked around. They called out names of people, names of nations in prayer. For the first time, I glimpsed what "to intercede" must mean.

I was also amazed at how old the women looked. The men didn't, just the women. Old and tired.

Dr. Richard Dobbins, one of the speakers, gave us a list of "Five Things a Wife Wants in a Husband" and "Five Things a Husband Wants in a Wife." We had never heard such wonderful teaching! Just in passing, he said, "You can overcome *anything* in your past. You can become who God wants *you* to be." As soon as that session concluded, Joe said, "I'll be right back" and he took off to waylay Dr. Dobbins. Joe came back with a look of awe on his face. "Margaret, he told me I *can* overcome my past—I can overcome my parents' immaturity and all the pain they caused me. I have never had that hope until today."

One morning, Philip Hogan, the Executive Director of Foreign Missions, held a question-and-answer session. The main topic of discussion seemed to be the missionary salary, it being too low. Various missionaries opined. Finally, Joe couldn't take it any longer. He raised his hand. "Yes, Brother Register?" I almost fainted; Philip Hogan *knew Joe's name!* "Sir, I just want to say that, to us, having been pastors of a small church, the salary seems more than adequate."

Of course, we weren't actually receiving a salary yet. In fact, the Foreign Missions Board did not give a candidate missionary one dime. "Approval" meant "You now have our approval to travel from church to church to receive offerings for your work." All funds, except for travel expenses, were sent to "Headquarters" to be distributed according to the budget set by the Missions Committee.

We had already received our "budget to raise": $800 per month. This covered the percentage "Headquarters" (The Foreign Missions Department) withheld for overhead, insurance, children's schooling, language school tuition, rent, utilities, and salary. In addition to the monthly budget, we were required to raise several thousand dollars in cash. The cash would be used to cover our School of Missions expenses, our transportation to language school, our airline tickets to Chile, and provide a cushion in case of inflation or in case the monthly pledges we raised in itinerary did not all come in as anticipated.

The trip to Chicago for our psychological evaluation was a hoot! We had never seen the "L" (elevated train) or ridden in an expensive taxi as it tooted and zoomed through death-defying traffic. The receptionist told me to go in, first, to talk with the psychiatrist. He began to ask questions, in general at first, and then about Joe. "What faults does he have? What does he do to annoy you?" I shook my head, "Excuse me? I'm not here to tell on Joe." The doctor interrupted, "Oh, so you think he has no faults?" "I didn't say that. I just don't think it's my business to tell you what they are." Later, I told Joe, "I wasn't about to tell him that you sit on the side of the bed and throw your socks up against the wall!"

In the Chicago waiting room we met a couple Joe knew from college, Bobby and Gloria Jackson. They were new recruits, too. They had completed their sessions with the psychiatrist and were ready to go back to the hotel. We decided to travel together on the "L." The "L" screeched to a stop, doors clanked open, people crowded all around us. Joe and I hopped on, Bobby followed, Gloria hesitated. The door began to close; we were panicking—Lord forbid! Gloria was going to be lost in downtown Chicago, all alone. We would never find her. We didn't even know the name of this stop. Bobby, do something! Hurry! Just in the nick of time, Bobby reached for Gloria's arm and pulled her inside. The doors closed; we sped down the track. We were sweating, our hearts pounding. We had survived our first fright as missionaries.

Little did we know that in Lakeland, Florida, thirty years later, we would be friends and neighbors of Bob and Gloria and Juanita

69

Cunningham Blackburn. We were all there at School of Missions that year, timid "candidates" headed to different parts of the world. But first, we all had to "itinerate" to raise our funds.

"No? But I'm a member of the Peninsular Florida District!"

"I realize that, Brother Register, but you cannot itinerate here this year."

"What?"

"You should have scheduled your itinerary this time *last* year."

"But I couldn't—we just received our official letter of approval from the Foreign Missions Department yesterday."

"Sorry, our policy is 'one year in advance.' We could schedule you for next year."

"Next …….. year?"

"Yes, we could probably work you in … *next year.*"

"But I hope to be in language school by then!"

"Well, if you change your mind, give me a call, but make it within the next few days."

Joe's face reflected his pain as he hung up the phone. We can't go to Chile … until we raise our budget. Suddenly, the Bible verse in Romans 10:15 became relevant, "How shall they preach except they be sent?"

I remembered an incident the previous spring. I had taken some women from Tavares to a women's rally in Oxford, Florida. The speaker was a veteran missionary. I was excited to listen to his stories, and I rushed to speak to him after the service. "I'm so happy to meet you," I gushed. "My husband and I want to be missionaries, too."

"Really? How nice," he said as he turned away to speak to someone else. Patronized and ignored, I stood there, wounded and seething. In my hurt I determined that I would never treat a hopeful missionary as he had treated me!

Surely someone would take us seriously. Joe floundered only briefly after learning that we could not itinerate in Peninsular Florida; then he began to make phone calls."Hello, Stan Lyon? Congratulations on being the new District Superintendent! Say, we've just been approved as missionaries ... yeah, to Chile, South America... could we come up there to Beckley, to the Appalachian District to itinerate? ... We can? Great!"

"Hello, is this the West Florida District office? Could I speak to O.L. Thomas, Superintendent? ...Brother Thomas, you don't know me, but my father-in-law is Pastor Carl Arnold, Brownsville Assembly, there in the Florida panhandle. We've just been approved as missionaries ... Could we itinerate there? ... We can? Thank you so much!"

Joe bought maps so he could coordinate our traveling from town to town: "Hello, Pastor? We're going to be itinerating in West Virginia in September, just a few weeks from now. We're going to be in your area and wonder if you have a Sunday morning open? ... Great!"

"Hello, Pastor? We have a Sunday evening free...."

"Hello, Pastor? We will be traveling through Georgia on our way...."

God opened the hearts of the West Virginia and western Virginia pastors and congregations to us. They would re-schedule their midweek service from Wednesday to Tuesday or to Thursday; or they'd have special Monday and Friday night missionary rallies, so that we could have services almost *every* night. From their scarcity, they blessed us. Many times the monthly pledge was larger than the offering.

Most of the West Florida churches were small, too. But they pledged and they gave offerings. A.E. Hall, a pastor and the district treasurer, and his wife, Bernell, the district director of the Women's Missionary Council, took us under their wing. Thanks to their help, sheets, towels, and dishes from West Florida women would grace our home in Chile.

Joe called old college buddies who were pastors and asked for services. Dave Norris, Cortez Frazier, Benny Rice, Dave Hunt, and Joe's cousin, Ed Blount, all scheduled us and they all gave offerings and monthly pledges.

Joe began to scan the letter we had just received from the Peninsular Florida District, and gasped. A stinging letter of rebuke from the district treasurer stated, "Brother Register, you have failed to send in your tithes since you resigned in Tavares. We are sending a copy of this letter to Philip Hogan, Director of Foreign Missions, to advise him of the type of character qualities you are displaying by not following the District mandate to tithe."

We were stunned. No congratulations. No blessings on being approved as missionaries. No questions about our income. The words and the tone cut us to the quick. Joe immediately called Philip Hogan. "It's true," Joe said, "that we haven't sent tithes to our district, because, as you know, we don't receive a salary during itinerary. Every offering goes directly to our missionary account. We only deduct travel expenses." Mr. Hogan soothed Joe, "I understand, but some districts are fussy. Just send them $20 a month and deduct it as an expense."

We did, but I was furious to think that we were required to send Peninsular Florida money from the missionary offerings of other, much poorer districts.

In retrospect, it is ironic that fifteen years later, the Peninsular Florida District became our largest supporting district. District officials blessed us with open arms, arranged itineraries for us; pastors opened pulpits and resources to us, and lay people became our cast and crew. Our off-the-wall, modern missions outreach was even based there. The very man who had told us "no" opened his church facilities and television crew to us. But I'm getting ahead of myself.

How could we conduct a missionary service when we had never been overseas and had never met anyone from Chile or who had actually been to Chile?

"Excuse me, do you have any 'foreign' slides?" Joe asked at the drugstore and the camera shop. We *had* to have slides—all missionaries had slides. Only God knows what countries' volcanoes and mountain lakes we actually showed.

We went to the library to read about Chile: almost 3000 miles long, never wider than 150 miles, bordered on the west by the cold Pacific, on the east by the rugged, majestic Andes Mountains. The northern Atacama Desert is the driest in the world; southern Patagonia is cold and rainy year 'round, so close to the South Pole. If Chile were placed across the center of the United States, the country would stretch from west coast to east coast.

In church services, I waved around a machete, put a poncho on a volunteer, and held up a little flat piece of wood about eighteen inches square that had been cut inside round and round. When picked up by the outside edge, the middle dropped down to form a basket. These $20.00 worth of curios were from Colombia, thanks to Floyd Woodworth.

During every church service, Joe announced, "Please see if there is an amount you'd like to spend, and take a Penney's or Sear's order blank with you." I had photocopied order blanks and picked out clothes for us for the next four years—dresses, slacks, sweaters, pajamas, underwear, jackets. Joe chose tools from the Sears catalog. I had filled in small amounts and large amounts, put our Pensacola address on the "to be shipped to" spot, and laid the order blanks on the front pew.

Joe chose 1 John 2:28 as his text, "Abide in him, (so) that when he shall appear, we may have confidence, and not be ashamed before him at his coming." Joe told how his mother would leave for work and say, "Joe, clean up this house while I'm gone. Get the broom and sweep the floor. Do you hear me?" Sometimes he would feel industrious and do what she said. Other times he would pick up the clutter and then take the broom and literally drag it one time through the middle of the floor. When he heard her car drive up, *if* he had done what he should have, he would be proud to see her. If he had *not*, he would be ashamed. When God comes "driving up," will we be proud? Or ashamed?

We tried to arrive from thirty minutes to an hour early at each church so we could set up our slides and curios and tune Joe's saxophone to the local piano for our piano and sax "duet"—usually the song, *The Vision* by missionary Oren Munger. Then we would be free to greet people as they arrived.

73

To raise the final $300 per month for our budget, Joe made a poster of "Gideon's Three Hundred" with small, paper pitchers over dollar amounts. He asked each congregation, "Who can give a dollar a month? Five dollars? Ten dollars a month?" Then he would take off the pitchers and hand them to the donors.

Sylvester, West Virginia, is a picturesque mountain village. High, tree-covered mountains crowd a narrow valley where a creek winds along, singing, over large rocks. On a space carved out of the mountainside sits a small white church. We arrived for our Monday evening service at the golden hour, when the sun sent almost horizontal streaks of golden light illuminating the little church nestled among the dark green trees.

As the service concluded, the pastor came to me and whispered, "Can you play the weddin' march on the pie-anner?" "Yes," I whispered back. He nodded toward the piano. I slipped over and sat on the round stool, waiting. He nodded again. I started playing, "dum dum de dum." In through the front door came a young couple, all of sixteen years old. She wore a shiny white street-length dress; the blue netting topping her head was held in place with a large ribbon bow. She carried a small bouquet of flowers from the garden. He wore a stiffly starched, white, short-sleeved shirt and a tie. They walked, tentatively, down the aisle.

"Oh!" I thought, "The youth are performing a drama." So enthusiasm dripped from my fingers onto the yellowed ivories. The pastor stood at the front, as if it were a real wedding. "Dearly Beloved," he began. And it dawned on me. This is no play.

I have the *Raleigh Register* news clipping: " __ and __ were married at 9:30 p.m. Monday at the Assembly of God at Sylvester ... The traditional wedding march was played by Mrs. Margaret Register of Pensacola, Fla...."

I lay in bed, wide-awake at midnight, wondering, "What is the crime rate in St. Paul, Virginia?" I heard another creak. Wood popped. Wind howled. There was no way to escape without going down three flights of dark, narrow, twisting stairs through the deserted church. Morning finally dawned on our nice, clean, *scary* apartment.

In another town, I was brushing dog hair off my sweater when the pastor said, "Uh. I forgot that we kept our dog in the church apartment for several days... I hope he didn't leave a mess."

In a small West Virginia town, we were invited to stay in a pastor's beautiful home. I was thrilled—large bed, our own bathroom. I snuggled into the sheets, reached my hand up under the pillow: a used hanky! These "clean" sheets were not so clean, after all.

In Matewan, West Virginia, the pastor announced, "Would Mr. Hatfield and Mr. McCoy come forward, please, to help receive the offering." Joe could hardly wait until the service was over so he could ask about "The Hatfields and McCoys." The next day the pastor and an elderly Mr. Hatfield took us out to the cemetery to see the graves of Mr. Hatfield's ancestors, the original feuders.

After a service in West Florida, the pastor invited us to his house. Joe carried our overnight bag into the son's bedroom where we were to sleep. I reached up to pull down the sheet: *filthy!* Streaks of dirt smudged the bottom sheet where dirty feet had dragged across it night after night. Black dog hairs covered the streaks. I began to gag. When Joe saw my throat start to open, he hissed sternly, "Margaret! Stop that right now! Don't you *dare* throw up!" I was so mad at him that I managed to swallow. Joe said, "I'll get the pastor and ask for clean sheets." Joe stepped out into the hallway and asked very sweetly, "Pastor? I don't think your wife had time to change the sheets. Do you have some clean ones we could use?" I didn't think I could sleep there even on the clean sheets ... but I did.

Another night, Joe went alone to a service. When he pulled back the sheet at that pastor's home, the bed was yellow and wet with urine! He called to the pastor, "You know, I just remembered, my cousin is expecting me, over in Tallahassee." And he packed up and left. Layne and Sharon Noble had told Joe they'd "be expecting him" any time he needed to get away fast!

Another time, Joe and I spoke on Saturday evening, taught a Sunday school class, and spoke on Sunday night at a large church's missions convention. The Sunday morning speaker was known as a "bell ringer." They forgot to tell us *how* the offering would be divided: to the bell ringer $3,000; to Joe and me, $300. We could not believe it! It was so painful and, to our way of thinking, unfair.

But those incidents are the exception—pastors and church members opened their homes and their dinner tables freely and graciously. I do not remember staying in one motel or eating in one restaurant that year.

One day Mother called us, crying, "Timmy is in the hospital and it is all my fault. You've got to come home. He is very sick and it is all my fault." She sobbed.

We walked into the hospital room to see a frail, pale little boy, less than three years old, under an oxygen tent, gasping for breath. The doctor spoke softly to us. "He has a severe case of pneumonia. We have done all we can and he is not responding to treatment. His life is in God's hands."

Mother sat beside the bed, crying softly. I said, "Mom, it's not your fault. You were taking good care of the children."

"Yes, it *is* my fault. I have not wanted you to go to the mission field. I didn't want my grandbabies to leave me, to leave the United States. God is showing me that they can get sick here, too, that He is the only one who can protect them wherever they are."

We called various churches to alert their "prayer chains" (the first person calls a second person, who calls another and another). This was Tim's third bout of pneumonia. Little by little, he began to respond to the treatments and began to pick up his little plastic cowboys and horses and move them around, slowly, under the oxygen tent.

Back out itinerating again, we received a phone call that Christy had fallen and broken her arm at a birthday party. By the time we returned to Pensacola, she was covered with a rash even down inside her cast. Measles, we thought. But it was an allergic reaction to an antibiotic. She hated to miss her kindergarten classes at Pensacola Christian School, where they had begun a new curriculum called "Abeka." Christy surprised us by being able to read street signs!

Every church we visited, large or small, had its distinct personality. I stood by the front pew every night praying, "God, help me to adapt to *this* congregation. Help me fit in *here.*" I tried to dress up or dress down to fit the socio-economic situation. I worried that I was being hypocritical, but then I'd remember what St. Paul said about "being all things to all men."

Pastors became our friends and shared their victories and their troubles. Wives of pastors cried on our shoulder. More than once, I thanked God that I was going overseas and did not have to pastor *that* church.

Sometimes I think that when we get to heaven, we "full-time-Christian-service" missionaries will be sitting on the front row, eager to receive our large rewards. Jesus will step to the microphone and announce, "This award goes to a person responsible for southern Chile hearing about me." I'll clear my throat, sit up straight, and get ready to stand. Jesus will continue, "You, there, on the back row. Yes, you, sir. You gave sacrificially from your coal miner's wages. Here, this big trophy is for you."

I think He will continue with special awards for "unknown" pastors of small churches and for MKs (missionary kids) and PKs, (preacher's kids) whose parents, like us, neglected them "for the work of the ministry."

By God's grace, we raised our budget in nine months. We became officially *appointed* "Foreign Missionaries" on April 8, 1968. We were ready to go to Chile!

But wait. We had to go to language school first, for a whole year. *Ayii, yii, yii.*

6

What did you say?

Guadalajara, Jalisco, Mexico
April 1968–April 1969

"*Do I dare take a deep breath* and relax slightly?" I wondered as the front wheels and then the back wheels bumped over the cobblestone ridge. The trailer wheels lagged, then bumped over, too. Whew! Perhaps I *could* breathe freely again, for a few hours. The brochure from the Mexican automobile insurance company stated, "In the event of an accident with injuries, the driver will be jailed. Lock your car; do not leave anything of value visible. Do not travel at night. Stay only in recommended motels."

The low, one-story adobe motel stretched on our left. A tin-roofed parking area protruded from the wall on our right. High walls topped with broken glass surrounded us. It was late afternoon, but now we were safely inside the courtyard of the little, *recommended* motel in Saltillo, Mexico in our white Volkswagen Squareback mini-stationwagon.

We could neither understand nor speak one word of Spanish. With gestures and dollar bills, Joe managed to check us into the strange motel. We had no idea how to order food even if we had found a restaurant, so I reached under the front seat and retrieved a can of tuna. Joe opened the hood-trunk and took out our suitcase along with a can of pork 'n beans. I ushered the children into the motel room. Thank God, it was clean!

The trip across the border had been harrowing. We left Pensacola two days earlier and spent the second night in McAllen, Texas. We'd had to buy the auto insurance the next morning and get in a long line of traffic to cross the bridge into Mexico. The U.S. border patrol waved us on through. When we pulled up to the Mexican customs area, the officer motioned to see our passports. Then he gestured for Joe to get out and open the little trailer we were pulling.

The Mexican customs officer spoke very broken English as he pointed for Joe to take out an item. Then another item, and another. Months later, we realized he had been waiting for a bribe. But he didn't receive one that day. We were too naïve and too scared. After Joe had unloaded about half the stuff, the poor guard just shrugged his shoulders and waved us on.

We had traveled a lonely, narrow road south from the Rio Grande, up and down hills, through a desolate desert area. What if we had a flat tire? What if the car broke down? What if one of the children became sick? We were alone, minute by minute driving farther south away from the safety of the U.S. border.

Occasionally we would view an adobe house fenced around with cactus, children playing in the sand nearby. Sometimes we would observe a man walking across a scrub-brush, arid mountainside.

The language school people had sent us a packet with a map and a list of things to bring. From a newspaper ad, Joe bought a little dog trailer and painted it white, inside and out, after he cleaned out the mess. We took a reel-to-reel tape player, electrical-voltage transformer, earphones, clothing for one year, and bedding. I added for the children a record player, records, books, and toys. Mom was sure there was nothing fit to eat in Mexico, so she tucked cans of tuna, pork 'n beans, jars of peanut butter and jelly, and packets of crackers in every available crevice under the seats, in the front trunk, and in the hatchback.

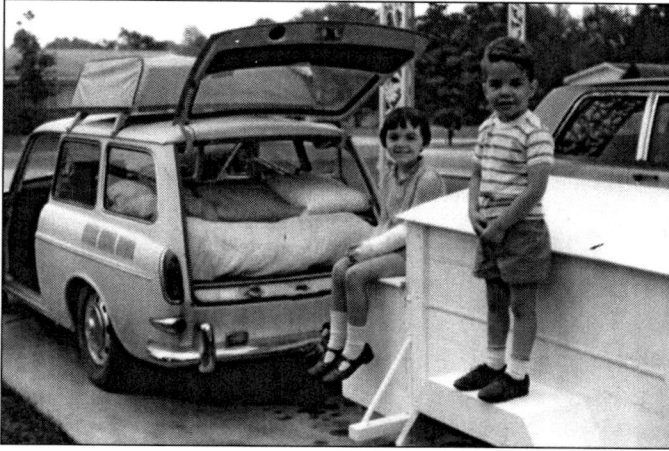

Christy and Timothy, ready to travel to Mexico

Joe had laid the back seat of the car down flat and packed stuff all the way from the rear window to the front seat. There was just barely room on top of the stuff for Timmy, three-and-a-half, to sit up. Christy, still five years old and still with her arm in a cast, was forced to lie down. Each one had a pillow and a small quilt. At my feet sat a red and white Coleman thermos with a spout (cup under the lid) filled with drinking water. The kids took turns sitting on my lap—no seat belts in those days and no air conditioning.

When Joe went from the Mexican motel back to the car to try to find the can opener for our tuna and beans, another car pulled in beside ours—a station wagon with a Texas license, the back piled to the top with "stuff" just like ours. A tall, skinny man opened the back hatch, caught Joe's eye, grinned, and drawled, "Howdy. Speak English?" Howard and Jerry Nutt and their three little tow-headed boys were Assemblies of God missionaries who were also on their way to *The Spanish Language School* in Guadalajara. Howard talked non-stop, saying they were from the West Texas District and assigned to Bolivia.

When I later went to their motel room to meet them, Jerry was busy making peanut butter and jelly sandwiches, but she looked as stressed out as I was and seemed ready to burst into tears. My first impression was that their hairstyles and clothing were old-fashioned; she wore no make-up.

81

Howard insisted that we caravan the next day as we headed even farther away from the U.S. border and safety. So we started out together, but Joe lost them after several hours. Later, they caught up with us and motioned for us to pull over. They had had a flat tire. I felt bad that we had gone off and left them. Initially, we didn't particularly like them; but uncertainty and fear linked us. We had no idea that in several weeks, after suffering language learning together, we would become very good friends.

Late afternoon of that second day in alien territory, we arrived in Guadalajara and pulled up to the gates of the language school. A student directed Howard to the "big brother" assigned to help them and directed us to another student's house. Joe got out of the car, walked up to the door, and went inside. A few minutes later, a woman in her thirties came bouncing to the car to welcome the children and me. She was smiling, she had a deep tan; she wore a sleeveless blouse and shorts. The man walked back to the car with Joe, giving him the key along with directions to our apartment. As we pulled away, I asked Joe who they were. "Lyle and Dorene Thompson, just finishing language school," he said. What a joy to meet Dorene, such an attractive, gracious person — gracious even after a year of language study. Plus, she did not appear to be legalistic — in her sleeveless blouse and shorts, no less. Thank you, Lord! I had hope!

*"!@##$%%^&**()())_," said the teacher.* Ten of us scared white Americans, with one brown, confident Mexican, were crowded around a table in a small narrow room. Nothing adorned the long, side walls except the plaster, painted white, over adobe bricks. At one end of the room, a window opened to a courtyard. At the other end, a door opened to the patio. The climate was perfect year-round. But our room smelled like sweat. And glistened with tears.

"!@##$%%^&**()())_," the teacher uttered again as she passed out workbooks.

"!@##$%%^&**()())_," she said as she opened a workbook and motioned to the drawings of two men walking toward each other, shaking hands, then walking away from each other.

"!@##$%%^&**()())_ ," she said as she pointed to her mouth and then to our mouths.

She turned to the student on her right, "!@##$%%^&**()())_."

She gestured to him, "!@##$%%^&**()())_." He repeated it, haltingly, "..#..#..**)...)_."She nodded brusquely.

Next student, "!@##$%%^&**()())_." He stuttered, "## ... $$$ ...%%%."

All the way around the table. "!@##$%%^&**()())_." Each of us tried and failed miserably to repeat the gibberish.

"!@##$%%^&**()())_ mañana," she said as she handed each family unit a reel-to-reel tape.

Finally, lunchtime came. Joe went to get Christy from her first grade class; I went upstairs to get Timmy from the nursery. By the time I was back downstairs, Joe had spread our quilt on the grass in front of the main building. All around us the other twenty families were doing the same thing in the open-air cafeteria.

A stubby, stocky toddler named Ralphie went running past, diaper so soaked that it dragged the ground. From our left, I over-heard, "I can't do it." A deeper voice said, "Yes, you can, Honey, you can learn it."

We opened our lunch basket: a can of tuna, crackers, and pork 'n beans, *again*, along with our thermos with purified water, and some bananas.

An hour later, we were all back in our classrooms. Another lady came and motioned to a student to follow her. We learned that she was the accent coach and grammar dragon imported from Costa Rica. Each of us had half an hour a day with her. Repeating, incorrectly, whatever she said. She would hold our jaw, all scrunchy, and make us repeat the word again. She would point to a word with a *d* in the middle and make us say it like a *th*. She would roll her *r's* and try to get us to do it. Then she would roll her eyes and sigh.

By 5:00 we were exhausted. My jaw hurt from trying to hold it differently. Why didn't they explain in English what we were "repeating"? We felt so silly mouthing meaningless babble. We felt like children. Worse than children. A three-year-old Mexican knew more Spanish than we did.

We struggled through the second day, the second week. Grown men cried silently, red-eyed, wiping tears with a fist. Grown women cried openly, sobbing as they jumped up and ran out into the patio. We could not learn this. It was impossible.

An upperclassman told us, "Just as a baby repeats what he hears, with no concept of what it means, you have to do the same. You'll see, it'll come together."

Little by little by little we began to recognize one word. Then another. Then one more.

The "profesora" (she pointed often enough to herself that we now had that word down pat) touched the table. "Mesa," she said. "Mesa," we repeated. "Silla," the chair. We tried our best to think of objects, now, in Spanish. To see a table and think "mesa."

The founder of *The Spanish Language School* was retired from the military, and he had "borrowed" some training manuals from the U.S. military—courses they taught in Texas and California. The principle was to repeat, memorize dialogue, then later learn grammar, i.e., the "why." The founder held a brief chapel service every day and a longer one each week. He actually spoke to us in the English language.

There were no supermarkets, only flea markets with vegetables. Chickens, plucked and dead, hung upside down, feet tied together, heads dangling. I pointed to a vegetable. "*Papas*," the woman said. She picked some up and put them on a scale. I motioned for more. "*Dos kilos de papas*," she said. I held out some money. She took what she wanted and put some change back in my hand. "Papas," I murmured, "papas, papas, papas." Next time I could buy potatoes and know what they were called.

I hated to go shopping those first weeks. Joe, knowing that it was the quickest way to force me to learn the vocabulary, made me go by myself, tears and all. The language was frustrating to him, too, but he had a better aptitude for it than I did.

One evening when we arrived home, Joe wanted to show off his Spanish by telling the maid (whose services were included in the rent of the apartment) that he was hungry. But in Spanish you say, "I have hunger." Hunger is *hambre*, man is *hombre*. Joe told her, "I am hombre." She looked startled, so he just repeated it, louder, "*Yo soy hombre*." "I am a man!"

I was proud of my new Spanish, too, as I hurried down our driveway in my housecoat just as a vendor arrived selling jugs of purified water. In Spanish, he asked, "Do you want water?" "No, I want a son," I replied in Spanish. His eyes flew open and he hurried away, thinking he was being solicited by a crazy gringa, one who didn't know how to say she was *searching for* her son.

Our first exam came at the end of the first trimester. Our teacher had prepared a little room with a tape recorder, ear phones, and a piece of paper and pencil. I went in, sat down, put on the earphones and started the tape player. I heard, "What is your name?" I wrote down, in Spanish, "Mi nombre es Margarita." "How old are you?" "Tengo 25 años." Half an hour later, I emerged into the sunshine. It was so easy! I walked over to some other students standing nearby and asked, "Why were the questions in English?" "What!" they exclaimed. "They weren't in English—they were in Spanish!" And for the very first time, I realized I had been *thinking* in Spanish! What a break-through!

Within several weeks, we were even dreaming in Spanish. Nightmares, actually.

It was time for a break! So one afternoon we headed to the wonderful, large swimming pool on campus. Timmy, who had never been swimming, went running toward the pool and jumped in. A Southern Baptist woman rescued him from certain death.

I loved the "social atmosphere" around the pool. Forty missionaries from many denominations, from different states, all sensing God's call, all frustrated with the language, were forming bonds of friendship that would last a lifetime. All of us, that is, except for some of the Independents. They did *not* wear bathing suits; the women did *not* shave their legs or wear long pants or shorts. They did not even *speak* to the pool people. They would walk past us pool sinners, giving us a wide berth, their noses in the air.

The language school campus had been a large, walled estate. It included the main house divided into classrooms, extensive grounds for a playground, the pool, and a patio with Ping-Pong tables and pool tables. Christy's first black eye came from a baseball bat on the playground; her second one came from a Ping-Pong paddle ... before the first black eye healed.

Behind the main building stood a two-room adobe dwelling for the caretaker and his family. Their only apparent joy was a tiny kitten, which Christy stole by sneaking it under her sweater. Joe "assisted" her as she returned the kitten and tearfully apologized.

The laundry consisted of five wringer washers in a row, each with an extra tub for rinsing. Clotheslines extended all the way to the back wall. We signed up for a given day and then stayed after class to wash clothes. We'd hang them on the line and collect them the next afternoon.

I never will forget one particular wringer washer that sat beside a creek out in the country. Mike and Karen Hines, who had already graduated from language school, invited us to their house. They had a generator but no running water, so Mike ran an extension cord down the hill to the washing machine sitting in the rocks at the edge of the creek, their water source.

Bob and Lynn Trout, ABWE missionaries (Association of Baptists for World Evangelization), became our good friends along with their three little children. Lynn introduced us to chocolate chip pancakes with peanut butter on top.

Ralph and Faith Leslie, another AG couple, came driving up to the school in an old, yellow, diesel Mercedes. They had two small children with another one due any minute.

Dave and Mary Hansen, AG, with their little children, Julie and Davie, came from New York State, headed to the Amazon head-waters in the interior of Peru. They, too, were expecting, and Mary gave birth in Guadalajara to a beautiful little girl.

Our apartment sat directly across the street from the front gate of the language school, an excellent location. Everything was fine until the first hard rain.

Three small apartments faced a cobblestone driveway; a wall topped with glass surrounded the small patio. On each side of us lived retired U.S. veterans, who could live very well on their pensions in Mexico. One veteran was a grizzly black man, who just sat, stared, and smoked one cigarette after another. The other was a loud, drinking, white man in a wheelchair. He had a very pretty live-in "nurse." We shared a long, red-tiled porch, about six inches higher than the cobblestones of the narrow, cramped, enclosed driveway.

One day heavy rain began to fall. Rain poured on our roof. It beat against the porch. Giant drops spattered the cobblestones. Rain sheets buffeted our car. Water cascaded from the drainpipes onto the porch; water bubbled up from the sewer drains in the street. Suddenly, little dark heads appeared in the murky water. Little black beady eyes stared at us as whiskers twitched. Rats, growing larger by the second (to me), began to scramble in every direction. Rats climbed up on the tires of our car and our little trailer with their rat tails hanging down from under the fenders. Rats ran up and down our porch trying to escape the flood. Huge half-drowned rats ran toward us. There was a big crack under our front door. Joe stood poised with the broom handle as I ran to get towels to stuff under the door.

During those days, Dave and Mary Hansen arrived in town, and we suggested they find *two* apartments—rat free. They found new, adjacent townhouses, unfurnished. Joe persuaded one of our professors to lease them, buy furniture, and rent to us.

I was so happy to move over there! I didn't even mind the wiggle-tails in the water from the kitchen faucet. Christy and Julie, Davie and Timmy became inseparable. They camped out in our large, walled-in back yard. They played ball and zoomed down the driveway on Tim's Playskool scooter. They were so adventurous they would walk all the way around the block. Once I sent them to the corner *tortillería* to buy fresh, warm tortillas. I told Christy to get a dozen. The lady laughed and laughed at her—you don't buy tortillas by the dozen, you buy them by the kilo.

The kids played hour after hour with Mitzi, a black, gentle, patient dog Mom and Dad had acquired for the kids in Pensacola. The kids dressed Mitzi in doll clothes, played church with her, danced with her around the yard. Calling out to each other, "Don't run into doo-doo land!" they ran around the back yard, nearing the corner Mitzi had chosen as her bathroom. But how did Mitzi get to Guadalajara?

We had driven up to the U.S.-Mexican border on August 17 to meet Mom and Dad. We were confident in our Spanish now; after all, we had finished the first trimester of language study and could say, in Spanish, "What? How much?" and "Say it more slowly, please."

When we met Mom and Dad at the motel in McAllen, Texas, almost immediately Dad said he needed something out of the bathroom. He walked toward it, then hollered, "What is this? Kids, come and see what I found in here!" In the bathtub was Mitzi! Mom would not allow a dog in the car, so Dad had built a little cage for Mitzi and attached it to the back bumper. They followed us to Guadalajara for a two-week visit.

When our time in Guadalajara was almost over, Mitzi zoomed past us one day, out the front door, into the street, and was hit by a car. Joe and Dave Hansen put her in the back of our VW and went to find a vet. But there was nothing the vet could do. None of us had ever cried so much in our lives. Mitzi died and we felt we had lost a member of our family.

Three guitars swayed side to side as the Mexican musicians sang loudly, their faces gleaming with Christian joy. The pulpit was small and draped with a velvet cloth. Fresh flowers in large glazed vases stood on each side of the platform. The little adobe lean-to was long and narrow. The congregation of about fifty people sang and clapped their hands, men on one side of the church, women on the other. Almost everyone had two books lying beside them on the slatted, wooden bench: their Bible and their own hymn book, a little red, half-sized book with just words, no music score. We bought both, too, since they told us the hymn book was used throughout all of Latin America.

The pastor's speech was loud and fast. We could scarcely understand a word. Then the pastor paused and said slowly, "*Aquí hay agua.*" Joe and I jerked our heads toward each other. We almost stood up and shouted! We understood an entire sentence! "Here is water." It must be the story of Philip and the Ethiopian.

Every morning and afternoon, as we went to and from school, Joe would watch a new house being built across the street from our townhouse. A workman dug a trough, stirred up the sand, poured in some Portland cement, and ran a water hose to it. He stirred the "soup" until it was just right to use. Then he mortared adobe bricks with this cement. The workman not only worked there, he lived in a tiny room out back, as caretaker. One day Joe decided to go talk to him, and after that, they talked almost every day. Joe was practicing his Spanish and the poor Mexican was probably learning some weird vocabulary, too! One day Joe came back, gleaming. He had explained the plan of salvation, and the man had prayed with him— our first convert in Latin America. Joe took him a New Testament and continued to encourage him. The man worked six-and-a-half days a week, so he couldn't go to church.

A trip to the "interior" was another story: The donkey's back was hard, bones protruded upward, toward Joe's jeans. Dave Hansen's donkey was so short that Dave's feet dragged the ground. Howard Nutt decided walking was easier than riding. The river, contaminated but still flowing, lined the side of the path to their right. It was a good thing Joe had his water purification kit. They passed fields of corn, small farmhouses, met people walking toward them. Finally they crested the low mountain and emerged on a path toward a large farmhouse. The whitewashed adobe home, with a thatched roof, stood in a cleared patio where chickens scratched in the dirt near a couple of pigs and several dogs. Dave and Howard greeted the owner; Joe asked if he could tell some stories. Joe's Spanish was the best, so the guys had appointed him to be the preacher.

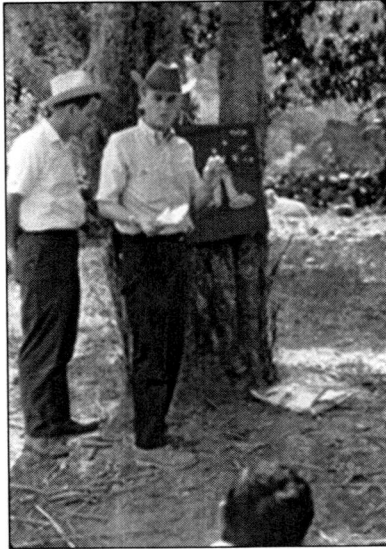

Dave Hansen, Joe telling the story

The flannelgraph board, tripod propped against the tree, was the focus of attention as Joe, in his faltering Spanish, explained the Christmas story. Neighbors, children, and the man and his wife leaned forward to hear the Good News, explained to them for the first time. Everyone repeated the sinner's prayer. Joe, Howard, and Dave packed the stuff back on the donkeys and headed home. The owner stared after them, knowing his life had been forever changed. Months later, Joe learned that the owner had formed a Protestant church, there on his farm. And he had suffered great persecution from his Catholic neighbors, even being shot at.

As the three new missionaries reached the highway where they had left the car, their guide took them to a hovel. They stooped to enter a dark, dank lean-to. An emaciated man covered with a filthy blanket lay on a wooden cot. Flies buzzed in his open mouth and touched down on his open, un-blinking eyes. Joe's heart broke as the three men prayed heart-felt prayers for a hopeless man. They prayed in English; God understood the language.

Joe's first missionary journey

Mexico had two faces. One face we loved. Beautiful flowers of every description lined broad avenues. Whitewashed rocks formed borders in park after park, where uniformed gardeners tended the green grass with rakes and wheelbarrows, clippers and a lawnmower with no motor—only twirling blades. Hundreds of fountains threw sparkling water high into the air; it cascaded back to earth in colorful rainbows of dazzling diamond drops.

Friendly people greeted us with an *abrazo* hug, a kiss on the cheek, a warm handclasp. Brothers and sisters in Christ welcomed us warmly, prayed fervently beside us, and sang enthusiastically in tune with us. The Latino sense of humor, shared simply and openly, delighted us.

Restaurants offered exquisite cuisine, our first *enchiladas*, first freshly made tortillas, first melted cheese dip. *Mariachis* serenaded our table, guitars, harps, and voices attuned to provide pleasure and the joy of laughter. Fresh fruit salads, strong black coffee, or creamy *café con leche* satiated our palates.

Birthdays brought colorful, swinging *piñatas* filled with candies for the children, who joyfully burst them open. Special occasions delighted even the neighbors with mariachis serenading outside the window in the early morning hours with the songs of the *mañanitas*.

Gigantic covered markets and tiny open air markets stimulated the senses with colors and smells of food raw and food cooking, of flowers fresh and flowers of crepe paper ten inches across. For a dollar or two, we could buy leather shoes and clothing of every need or description. Artisans displayed intricately designed glazed pottery and handcrafted jewelry. Vendors sold the sweetest pineapple we've ever eaten, the sweetest, juiciest oranges, papaya, melon, yucca, garlic, onion, varieties of bananas, and all the vegetables we'd ever seen and some we'd never heard of.

Many of the broad avenues intersected with multi-lane round-abouts. No stop signs with foursquare corners. No stop-dead-still rule. No yield-to-the-vehicle-on-your-right regulation. Roundabouts merge brave souls with their foot on the gas pedal and their thumb on the horn. Roundabouts push you into the flow, ready or not. Roundabouts spit you out, if you are on the outside lane, or suck you in tight if you are on the inside lane.

The roundabouts seemed symbolic of the other face of Mexico. The circular ethics, where nothing was really right or really wrong; flexible promises when *yes* meant maybe and *no* meant perhaps.

There was the circular time schedule, when time did not move in a straight line, but went round and round, saying don't worry, you'll have another opportunity *mañana*. A land where 8:00 meant 8:30 or 9:00 or even 9:30 or 10:00.

There were the very rich, snobbish, elite families; in contrast, literally against the walls of their lavish estates huddled the very, very poor peasants in cardboard or flattened-tin-can lean-to huts.

One of these peasants, a boy about eight years old, came to our house and asked if he could wash the car to earn a few pesos. Joe invited him in to eat supper—pinto beans, rice, and warm tortillas. Bewildered, the boy looked at the spoon beside his bowl. He had never seen silverware. Joe showed him how to use the spoon, but the boy rolled up a tortilla, bent over his bowl, and scooped food into his mouth.

Also, there was the roundabout way of looking at human life. Joe witnessed an accident between a bus, a dump truck, and two young men on bicycles. The bikers were holding onto the back of the bus, catching a ride, when the dump truck zoomed past them, clipping the back of the bus, knocking both boys to the pavement. They were gravely injured. A passerby walked over to one boy who had managed to crawl to his knees and kicked him back down into his blood. An observer, talking on a pay phone on the corner, just kept talking to his girlfriend and would not call an ambulance. We learned first-hand that *culture shock* is not a theory, it is a really disturbing emotional reaction.

We were absorbing the culture. Some of it we loved. Some of it appalled us. All of it was ours now.

April 24, 1969, the day of our graduation banquet, we dressed in our finest: Joe in his suit from his Southeastern College quartet days, me in a blue satin sheath dress, a hand-me-down from the rich family in the Beckley church. Joe was class president and graduated at the head of our class. I was close behind him, and we were proud that we could communicate now in Spanish.

Of course, I needed to have my hair and nails done, so that morning I went for my $2.00 *do*. As my hair was being "teased," a stylish lady breezed in, talking ninety to nothing. I did not understand *one* word. She stayed briefly, and when she left, I asked my beautician, "Was she speaking Spanish?" "Oh, *sí*, she is from Chile."

We were leaving for Chile the next day.

Language School – Assemblies of God Missionaries
Ralph Leslie, Mary and Dave Hansen, Margaret and Joe Register,
Jerry and Howard Nutt, Margaret and Bob Bowden

Post Script:

Ralph and Faith Leslie went to Peru, where little Vicky, born in Guadalajara, darted out into the street, was struck by a truck, and remains today in a vegetative state. The Leslies later moved to Lakeland, Florida, where both Faith and Ralph are teachers.

Dave and Mary Hansen spent two terms in the boonies of the Amazon basin, and then transferred to Guatemala, where Dave aired our very first television production (more on that later). All three children married Latinos. Dave and Mary now live in New Jersey; and Dave continues to travel into Latin America with short term missions groups.

Howard and Jerry Nutt went to Sucre, Bolivia, where Howard began a Bible school and built radio and TV stations. They, too, air our television and radio programs in Bolivia. Howard retired in Sucre; Jerry retired in Texas near their grandchildren. They commute.

Bob and Margaret Bowden arrived for language study just as we graduated. They would soon join us in Chile.

Lyle and Dorene Thompson went to Venezuela (where the church is extremely legalistic), then transferred to Colombia before returning to serve as manager of the editorial department at Life Publishers, International, in Miami, Florida. Later they served in Europe, where Lyle was European director of the International Correspondence Institute (ICI). Dorene died in her fifties of pancreatic cancer.

Mike and Karen Hines transferred from Mexico to Honduras, where Mike purchased a plane, fulfilling his dream of preaching from the air and dropping gospel leaflets. Years later, we produced a promotional video for him. Mike died in 2004 when his small plane crashed in Honduras. Karen died a few months afterward.

Bob and Lynn Trout went to Peru, then transferred to Paraguay and later to Colombia. We would be together, again, in both Paraguay and Colombia.

Brazil

Bolivia

PARAGUAY

CHILE

Viña del Mar •

Argentina

Temuco •

SOUTH AMERICA

7

Temuco, Chile—Arriving

(pronounced teh-<u>moo</u>-coh)
May 20–July 20, 1969

⸺⸙⸺

ach hand clutching a child, I stood on the train platform in the cold, drizzling rain. Behind me the train chugged, puffed, blew black smoke, and ambled on south. Stinging from the smoke and the rain, my eyes darted from person to person and toward the luggage piled at the other end of the wooden platform. Although it was 10:00 in the morning, I felt groggy because we had ridden the train all night, south from Santiago, Chile, to the little town of Temuco—so close to the South Pole that it is cold year around. I shivered in my red American coat. Christy, six years old, stood quietly, gazing at everything around her. Four-year-old Timmy danced in the drizzle, tugging at my hand. Joe told me to wait right there while he tried to find a taxi to take us to a hotel.

A man in a porter's uniform approached me, "*¿Pa'je?*" he asked. "*¿Mande usted?*" I asked. "*¿Pa'je?*" he repeated. I had no idea what "*pa'je*" was so I asked *again* in my best, most polite, Mexican Spanish, "*¿Mande usted?*" "What are you commanding me?" He shook his head disgustedly, closed his eyes and enunciated clearly each syllable, as if I were a dimwitted three-year-old, "*E-qui-pa-je, Se-ño-ra, e-qui-pa-je.*" Of course I knew *that* word: *luggage*. I had just learned three things: Chileans swallow syllables whole and without blinking; Chileans do not say *mande usted*; and Chilean intonation and expressions were *very* different from what we had studied in language school in Mexico. Then, as I gazed around me, I realized something else: everyone was dressed in blacks and browns and dark blues. No one else wore red.

As we sped away in the taxi, I looked out the windows at what appeared to be a western mining town—a movie set recreated with rain and cold and cobblestone streets. We stopped at a two-story stone building flush with the sidewalk. Heavy wooden double doors opened from the sidewalk into *Hotel Continental.* A square lobby, two stories high, formed the middle of the building, like a patio would in a warmer climate. Our room on the second floor, right front corner, held a double bed and two twin beds piled high with woolen blankets. Wind shook the windowpanes. Everything smelled of floor wax and damp wool. The room felt so cold, I touched the steam heater to see if it was working; it did feel slightly warm to the touch. Thankfully, we had a private bathroom complete with bidet and a huge claw-foot bathtub sprawled on a white-tiled floor. Everything sparkled with cleanliness.

We went back downstairs to the hotel dining room, where we learned that they served only "the menu of the day." After lunch, I tucked the children into their new beds for a nap. Joe and I were so tired; we just wanted to rest for a few minutes, too. But Timmy kept coughing. Hack. Hack. Cough. Cough. He moved restlessly. Cough. Hack. Cough. Tears filled my eyes. (Not for him, I'm afraid, but for me.)

Joe prayed, "Lord, we need some rest. Could you please stop Timmy's cough so we could all get some rest?" My hand was on Timmy's back. "*Please?*" I prayed, "Don't let him get pneumonia *again.*" As we prayed, his breathing slowed, he gave one lighter cough, and breathed slowly, peacefully, and did not cough again. Weeks later, Christy suffered from a bad cold, but not Timmy.

Joe left to try to find information about houses for rent. On the staircase, he met an American, Mr. Lester Vélez—a Puerto Rican from New York City—assigned to the embassy in Temuco. He had arrived with his family two months earlier, and he knew every available rental in town. Joe took a taxi and "previewed" houses, listing the "possible" ones for me to go see. The houses were not joined, like townhouses, as almost all of them were in Mexico. These houses stood alone and had a small yard with grass and a low fence at the sidewalk.

I walked into a two story, steep-roofed, little wooden house on Holandesa Street. Wooden floors creaked. A wide, wooden staircase led up to two bedrooms under the eaves, with steep, slanted ceilings. I felt at home. A college professor, traveling to the States to study for two years, wanted to rent his house, furnished, for $150.00 per month. Our budget allowed only $100.00. He would reduce the price, if we would pay him in dollars deposited to a U.S. account. The house would be available the first of July, in about three weeks. We signed the contract.

After a week at the hotel in Temuco, we worried about our money running low. Our shipment from Florida was due to arrive any day now at *Valparaíso*, the port in central Chile. We decided to travel back to Santiago to wait for the "stuff" and to pick up our car, also due to arrive by a different ship any day.

I dreaded going back to Santiago. We had spent two weeks there already. John and Lucille Mazurek and their two teenage sons had welcomed us warmly and taken us into their home. But they had just arrived back from furlough and their stuff had not arrived as yet, either. Both of our families were "camping" in their missions house, situated on the Bible school campus in a sea of mud. There had been no rain in Santiago for months, and all the grass had died. The street in front of the campus was under construction; thick heavy dust covered everything, inside and outside the house. Then, just as we arrived, so did the rain.

The old, stone house was cold and drafty. Our bed sloped so badly toward the middle that we clung to the edge of the bed to keep from falling into the wedge. We finally sacrificed a couple of blankets off the bed to stuff beneath the mattress, under the wedge, but then we were cold. At least the weight of fewer blankets didn't make my toes so sore. The kids slept on a hide-a-bed in the living room near a kerosene heater. It was warmer in there but it was smellier, too.

The Bible school chapel doubled as a church on Sundays. The doors were always left open and it was so cold inside we could see our breath, even though there was a small kerosene heater. When I wore the red winter coat the Beckley women had given me, a Chilean woman told me, "You must have more money than the other missionaries because they don't have anything as pretty as that."

On rare sunny days, the outside temperature rose to about 60, and we could see the snow-covered Andes Mountains from the front window of the house. People said "*Ja*" for "*Sí*"; "*Chau*" for "*Adiós*"; and the homes had steeply pitched roofs—all influences, we learned, from a heavily German immigration.

John Mazurek wanted to re-plumb the house with Joe's help, so this meant we had no running water for days at a time. We carried water in plastic buckets from a freestanding faucet in the back patio of the campus. There was a half-bath off the master bedroom for John and Lucille; the hall bathroom was for their two teenage boys and our family. Flushing the commode was a challenge. We decided to fill a bucket with water and leave it beside the commode. After we flushed, we took the bucket outside, filled it up and took it back to the bathroom for the next person. That way everyone on the campus knew when we had gone to the bathroom.

We learned to get around the city by bus, even venturing downtown to the post office. John borrowed a car from another mission one weekend and drove us up into the Andes to touch the snow on the gorgeous mountain peaks and drink some delicious, freshly squeezed apple cider at a roadside stand.

We worked every day to "Chileanize" our Spanish and learn about the food substitutes, like *zapallo* for pumpkin and *chancaca* for brown sugar. We became friends with Bible school students and their families and visited many of the churches in Santiago. We met the National Superintendent and many pastors, and we learned about the structure of the Chilean church, including youth groups and the Women's Missionary Council (CMF).

I was disappointed by two things: the extent of the national church organization (I wanted to be more "needed") and the large number of missionaries of various denominations both in Santiago and in Temuco. Again, I thought we would be more "needed." But

earlier missionaries—the Buenos, the Dowdys, and the Devines—
had laid the foundation in Chile. Now it was our job to build on that
foundation by teaching and encouraging believers.

Christy came running in one afternoon from the back yard, where she
and Timmy were playing with the Bible school students' children,
and asked for bread and coffee for their *once* (own-say) afternoon
tea. Christy's eyes sparkled, "I look just like the other kids!" She
wore mismatched sweaters and pants, layering everything she could
in order to keep warm. Through the open door, I could hear Timmy
trying to say "dog" in Spanish. He said *"pero"* and a little Chilean
boy said *"perrrrrro"* rolling his r's until Timmy said it correctly.
Timmy wore his PJs under his jeans to stay warm, but when he
stayed inside too long, he would dance around itching.

No water was connected to the old washing machine so I had
to wash everything by hand. Timmy's jeans were the most difficult
because the knees were caked and stained with red clay. One day
I asked what was wrong with the washer, specifically, and learned
that the water shut-off valve did not work. Well, I realized that I
could run a hose to the washer, and just turn the water off! The water
heater was lit once a week, every Saturday, so everyone could take
a once-a-week hot bath. (I am not kidding.)

I had packed some books and toys in the suitcases, so every
afternoon I read to the children, *The Bobbsey Twins*, *Alice in
Wonderland*. Tim asked for the story of Samson and the Flintstones
(Philistines). On especially dreary afternoons I gave the kids surprise
toys—a slinky, some little cars—given to us by the Milton, Florida,
Missionettes (a girls' club).

For Christy's seventh birthday on June 27, she wanted a piñata.
Timmy had gotten one for his birthday in Mexico, but she hadn't. So
Joe made a piñata out of roofing tiles and we filled it with candy and
covered it with colored paper. The ten Chilean children who came
to the party had never seen anything like it. Christy tried and tried
to break it, even taking off the blindfold and swinging at the piñata.
Finally, Joe gave Timmy the stick and he whacked it good.Candy
scattered everywhere, into the mud.

I placed two round layers of cake side by side and cut one a little smaller, forming a tail and two ears from the cut-off pieces. I covered it all with frosting and flaky colored coconut—a kitten! The Chilean kids were amazed at this beautiful birthday cake.

We boiled the drinking water and soaked vegetables in Bleach-water. Fruits and vegetables were abundant, thank the Lord. We learned how to eat artichokes and savored big, juicy peaches, oranges, grapes, watermelon, and bananas. The meat was tough; chicken was really expensive.

We had learned to love Chilean food while staying at our hotel in Temuco. On a typical day, they had served four meals with five courses for lunch and for dinner. Breakfast consisted of large, flat, cold, biscuit-like bread, with real butter, marmalade, juice and *café con leche* (coffee) or tea. For lunch there was, first, lettuce with lunchmeat, bread and butter. When the table was cleared, they served vegetable soup. Cleared the table. Served beefsteak with a fried egg on top and French fries. Cleared the table. Served a fresh pear. Cleared the table. Served a deliciously strong small cup of coffee or hot tea. Everyone drank water with his meal, or wine. To their dismay, we would ask for Coca-Cola or Fanta (orange soda). It was always served at room temperature. When we came back to the States for furlough, our kids wouldn't drink Coke served cold or with ice.

In the afternoons, at about 5:00 or 6:00 p.m., the Chileans always serve *once* (own-say) tea with hot bread (small French-bread buns— tough, crunchy, and fluffy inside), butter, marmalade, cheese, lunch- meat, and maybe some German *kuchen* (apple bread), along with hot tea or *café con leche* (coffee made with milk) or black coffee.

Cena, dinner, usually begins after 9:00 p.m. A typical meal could be: first course, homemade tomato soup; second, steamed clams in onion sauce; third, baked chicken in gravy with green peas, carrots and potatoes; fourth, caramel pudding, called *flan*; and fifth, with the table cleared, coffee.

Language was always a challenge. We ate at the home of some Chilean friends several months after we arrived, and each course was abundant and delicious. Finally, the hostess served *merengues* for the fourth course. Joe pushed back from the table, patted his tummy and said, "I can't eat another bite. My tummy is full." They died laughing, fell off their chairs laughing. He had changed one letter of a word and had actually said, as he patted his tummy, "I can't eat another bite. My *baby* is full." (*guatita* to *guaguita*)

A Presbyterian friend was asked to preach on his very first Sunday in Chile. When he announced his title, "God will give you comfort," heads snapped up. He thought, "Wow, they must really need this." So he said forcefully, "God wants to give you comfort, He wants *you* to have comfort." The congregation began to frown.

He continued, "You need never worry because day by day, God will provide the comfort you need." The people began to smile. "Don't run from your problems, sit tight, and God will come to you with comfort." Someone chuckled. Then another one. They couldn't resist—the entire congregation burst out laughing. Turns out there was only one brand of toilet paper in Chile—"Comfort."

"Comfort" came only in light blue and looked and felt like crepe paper. The Chileans have a national comic book featuring the national bird, the condor—*Condorito*, their Mickey Mouse. One cartoon showed the Air Force having problems with the wings falling off their planes, tearing apart at the rivets. *Condorito* came to the rescue by plastering the rivets with the perforations of "Comfort," because everyone knew "Comfort" would never tear at the perforations.

But I digress. We were in Santiago, waiting and waiting and *waiting* for our shipments to arrive. Before leaving Pensacola, we had found Navy half-crates and had packed sturdy boxes inside. Some of them we packed the year before going to language school and some during a quick trip back to Pensacola awaiting our flight to Chile. Every day, sometimes twice a day, Joe called the customs agent. "*Mañana*, the ship couldn't dock due to rough seas." "*Mañana*, your crates were underneath other items and the ship has gone down south to unload the top stuff. It'll be back soon." "*Mañana*, we need one more document."

Finally, on Friday, July 11, 1969, seven-and-a-half weeks after we arrived, our stuff cleared customs and was loaded onto a flatbed truck. Our Chevy Suburban was released, too, and although we had no lights, horn, or speedometer, the heater worked, thank the Lord. We headed south in the cold, blowing rain, on the two-lane Pan American highway (the only road to southern Chile). We hoped the truck had started south, too. The trip took two days; we stopped at a little motel (clean!) in the small town of Los Ángeles.

As we drove the unfamiliar road south, suddenly police officers appeared in the middle of the roadway, carbines slung overshoulders, gloved hands signaling "Halt!" The first of many police checkpoints. We showed our documents for the car and handed over our passports. The *Carabinero* examined the documents and nodded for us to proceed. Sometimes a *Carabinero* would give a quick tap on the back door, motioning for us to open it. He'd crawl in, sometimes with other people, and ride with us to the next checkpoint. The other missionaries had warned us never, *ever*, to offer a bribe to a Chilean police officer. (*So* different from the rest of Latin America.)

All of a sudden, through the drizzling rain, it looked as if the road ended at a deep fissure. Slowly, we hair-pinned down the deep gorge, in one-way traffic on a narrow, muddy lane; we stopped at the river below, went through a *Carabinero* checkpoint, crossed a low, wooden-planked bridge, and snaked back up the slippery hair-pins on the other side. A *Carabinero* rode in the "last vehicle" up the mountainside because the rain and fog were so thick and the mountain so steep that they couldn't see to signal each other when to start the traffic from the other direction. (They were building a bridge, which still was not finished years later when we left Chile.)

On Saturday morning at 11:00 we pulled up to #0933 Holandesa, our house; Joe went next door for the key and unlocked the front door. Just then, the truck pulled up, too. The truckers had driven all night. They helped Joe open the crates, unload our boxes, and carry them into the appropriate rooms. (I had numbered the boxes for customs with a list of what each box contained.) The customs officials had opened our stuff, but as far as we knew, nothing was missing. We had not examined the itemized list of taxes but had just paid the $480 charge for "duty" and had been thankful to do so. Later, I was sad to see that an inexpensive, cut-glass platter had been classified as "crystal"; we'd been charged $10 duty for it.

Late that afternoon, Joe went to see the Chilean pastor, to let him know we had arrived and would be in church the next day. We attended both Sunday services (about 60 people in attendance) and unpacked in the afternoon.

On Monday, Joe ran an additional electrical wire for the refrigerator we had brought, because there was only one electrical outlet in the entire kitchen. We were fortunate that the landlord had left the cabinets, the wall-mounted gas hot water heater, a gas range, and two gas tanks. On Tuesday, Joe started building a closet in the bedroom with wood from the crates.

Our first little house, Timmy leaving for *Kinder*

Wednesday was sunny, and I was so happy to be able to wash clothes in our little washer. It was on wheels and had two cylinders—one on the left to wash the clothes, and one on the right to "spin dry." I rolled the washer up to the kitchen sink, attached the water hose to the faucet and draped the drain hose over the side of the sink. After each load agitated, I moved the clothes manually to the other side to spin. Then back again to rinse, and back to spin. The "dryer" was a clothesline in the back yard.

Upstairs consisted of two bedrooms under the eaves of the steeply pitched roof. The kids shared one room with two single beds; our wonderful, Simmons Beautyrest double mattress almost filled the other bedroom. Downstairs were the bathroom, living room, dining room, and the little blue kitchen. Most kitchens in Chile were painted deep blue—it kept out the flies, they said. (If there *were* flies, just think how many more there would be if the walls were *not* blue.) The small back yard, surrounded by an uneven, unpainted wide-planked wooden fence, housed a two-room shed—a maid's quarters and Joe's radio room where he built a ham radio.

A wooden railing ran beside our tiny front porch with its terra-cotta floor. To polish the gleaming, highly waxed tile and wooden floors, the Chileans used a *chancho*, like a long-handled scrub brush (manual or electric). The walks were swept every morning.

That first Friday, Joe put together Christy's bike, and to our surprise, she took off down the sidewalk. She said she had learned to ride at her friend Lisa Medley's house. Timmy pedaled his little VW car so fast he would have to stop to rest his legs. The children played with Amiga, a German shepherd puppy we had brought with us from Santiago, since we had been advised to get a watchdog. That stupid dog never did learn to stay at home—time after time all four of us would run down the street trying to catch her.

The weather was in the 50s during the day and the 40s at night, with the sun in the northern sky and the coldest weather coming up from the South Pole. But we were snug with a kerosene heater down-stairs in the dining room and electric blankets upstairs on the beds.

* * *

Pineapple Upside Down Cake

Adapted from the *Jungle Camp Cook Book*, Wycliffe Summer
Institute of Linguistics, printed in Mexico, 1966

INGREDIENTS

3 tablespoons butter
3/4 cup brown sugar
One can of sliced pineapple
Pecan halves
Maraschino cherries

1 1/2 cups flour
3 teaspoons baking powder
1 cup sugar
1/4 teaspoon salt

2 eggs
About 1/2 cup milk
5 tablespoons butter, melted

DIRECTIONS

1. Melt together the butter and brown sugar in iron skillet.
2. Drain pineapple, save the juice.
3. Lay pineapple slices on top of sugar in skillet.
4. Fill "holes" with maraschino cherries and all other "spaces" with pecans.
5. Sift together in mixing bowl the flour, baking powder, sugar and salt.
6. Break the eggs into a measuring cup. Beat eggs with a fork. Add pineapple juice and top with milk to fill one cup.
7. Melt the 5 tablespoons of butter.

8. Add melted butter and egg mixture to dry ingredients. Beat well and pour the batter over the pineapple in the skillet.
9. Bake at 350 degrees for 35 minutes. Test with sharp knife or toothpick.
10. Remove from oven and run a knife along the edges to loosen the cake. Let cool about five minutes.
11. Invert onto large plate.

8

Settling In

Temuco, Chile
(teh-moo-coh)
July 20–August 31, 1969

In the Southern Hemisphere, not only does water drain clock-wise (in the sink and commode) but the seasons are also reversed. Summer is December, January, and February; winter is June, July and August. So the school year runs from March through November. We had arrived in Temuco in July, during a two-week winter vacation from school. But as soon as we could, we enrolled Christy in the *Colegio Bautista,* Southern Baptist School.

Since she would begin in the middle of the school year, studying in Spanish, we decided she should re-take the second half of first grade. We went shopping for her uniform: navy blue skirt, white blouse, navy knee socks, black shoes, navy wool jacket with logo, and white *delantal* apron to wear during class.

Christy's classes ran from 8 a.m. until noon. She loved learning to write cursive and loved learning to read the Spanish words she was already speaking very well. Her afternoons were free, so she and I began Second Grade in English from 2:00 until 4:00. I used the International School curriculum and Christy and I both really enjoyed studying together: Reading, Math, Phonics, English Grammar, Spelling, Science, Social Studies, and Health. She told me she wished there was school even on Saturdays.

Christy going to school, missing a tooth

About four houses down from us on our street, a German woman ran a *Kinder*, a German Kindergarten from 2:00–4:00 p.m. Timmy loved it. The children conversed in Spanish, but the lady also taught German customs and words. Timmy came home one day and told us he knew how to say "Goodbye" in German: "*Auf wiedersehen da me la mano.*" We laughed and laughed; he was repeating what the teacher said—*goodbye* in German, then *shake my hand* in Spanish!

Christy and Timmy played with Chilean children and also with MKs (missionary kids) from Christy's school. Many times they would play church, mixing English and Spanish.

The pastor of the church, Iván M., was quiet and "very consecrated," I thought. He was about 27 years old, single, and he lived in the back of the church. He came to help us move in and asked us to bring our accordion and sax to church to play along with his guitar. Iván sometimes asked Joe to preach on Sunday nights or to teach Sunday School.

No one else at the church owned a car, so Joe volunteered to take the youth to their first out-of-town rally. They were thrilled, and fourteen teens, sardined into the Chevy, traveled three hours north of town.

On July 29, missionary John Mazurek came to stay with us for a week to hold a revival at the church, emphasizing the Holy Spirit. Eighty-eight people attended the first service, which lasted from 7:30 p.m. until midnight. After we had sung choruses for about 55 minutes, my accordion arm ached, and Joe's bottom lip was sore from playing the saxophone. The people sang so enthusiastically that folks would stop on the street to listen and peer in the door.

John also fixed my new dryer—it would burn gas but wouldn't get hot. The Chilean women in Temuco always washed clothes on Tuesdays and dried them on Wednesdays. Because the weather was usually rainy, the women fashioned a rattan "dryer" shaped like a very large, upside down bowl. They would put a charcoal fire inside the "bowl" to dry the clothes, which they poked through holes in the rattan. The women needed to watch the clothes carefully, rearranging them frequently. The women ironed on Thursdays and went to market on Fridays or Saturdays.

A woman at the church told me her niece needed work as a maid and would work for me for 16 cents an hour, or, full-time for $22.00 a month. Demófila became part of our family. We called her Dema and she spoiled the children rotten, cooked, cleaned, washed clothes, ironed, and helped us chase the dog.

At the vegetable market, I bought some zapallo to make a pumpkin pie. The zapallos were so large that the vendor took a saw and cut off a chunk for me. I peeled it, boiled it, and mixed it with *chancaca*—the brown sugar substitute that is hard as a rock and very dark brown. Oohee!—the pie tasted so bad even the dog wouldn't eat it.

The beauty salon was located about three blocks from home and I went faithfully, every Friday, to get my hair shampooed and "teased" for 70 cents. Hair spray cost 20 cents extra.

August was a busy month, with Joe taking accordion lessons, me home schooling Christy every afternoon, and all of us attending church services Sunday mornings and evenings, Tuesday and Thursday evenings, and every other Wednesday. Also, I began to teach an English Conversation class at the Catholic University for future teachers of English.

And, we experienced our first earthquake! Late at night, we were all in bed when the house began to shake from side to side. It felt as if we were on a careening train. Timmy woke up and cried out, "That's a real earthquake!" but Christy slept through the whole thing and the next morning complained, "Man, I miss everything."

All missionary wives and female Peace Corp workers were invited to a tea at the American Embassy residence, about six blocks from our house. I was the only person there with a car and I was proud to tell them about our church youth raising money through Speed-the-Light so that *all* our missionaries could have vehicles.

Also, in August, my Dad suffered a serious heart attack. We did not have a telephone so did not know about Dad being sick until two weeks later. When we received Mom's letter, I went back to the Embassy residence and asked for their phone number, to be used only in case of emergency.

By the end of August, we had lived in Temuco for seven weeks and I wondered if we were "adjusting." Was I getting used to the inconveniences?

- Bread—purchased daily; it became very hard overnight.
- Vegetables—sold at the covered market. I spent hours talking to various vendors, buying veggies from one, then another, and another. Anything I didn't peel, I soaked in Bleach-water.
- Canned goods—bought at a little store, like an old Western store. We told the proprietor what we wanted; we weren't allowed behind the counter.
- Meat—hung from a hook in the open market. I would ask for a kilo from the side of beef and the butcher would take his big knife, whack off a chunk of meat, and plop it on the scales. Then

he'd wrap the meat in a piece of newspaper and I'd place it in the shopping bag that I always took with me.

- Water—boiled for drinking; but we could brush our teeth with the tap water.
- Milk—bought from the milk wagon. Fortunately, our street was on the milk route. A wagon pulled by a tractor came down the street daily, except for the days when it didn't show up. An old man dipped two liters from his milk can into my container. I had to boil the milk to pasteurize it, and the children wouldn't drink it at first. I bought butter whenever the milk wagon had it available.
- Range—how I wished I had known to bring a range with me. The little apartment-style gas stove had no pilot lights and only a tiny oven that worked "when it wanted to," sometimes leaving my cakes raw on one side and burnt on the other.
- *Almuerzo,* lunch and siesta—everything closed up tight from around 12:30 noon until 3:00 p.m.
- Mail—must be picked up and sent out from the only post office, downtown.
- Propane—we had to go to the company to order gas about every two weeks. They didn't have a delivery policy.
- Kerosene—same thing.
- Hot water heater—it hung flat against the kitchen wall and we lit a pilot light every morning. The gas would "catch" as the water was turned on and flowed through the tubing. If the water flowed too slowly, it became too hot; if it flowed too quickly, the water remained cold.

Anger became my adjustment gauge. If I was "aggravated" at something, I had not yet adjusted to it. If I performed without feeling annoyed (boiling the milk, for example), I figured I must be "adjusting" to the new way of life.

As I've mentioned, I played the accordion at all the church services, and the kids and I would take the bus to church if Joe was out of town. After only a couple of weeks, Pastor Iván asked me to teach children's church. I was thrilled!

Like the Pied Piper leading my children, I walked out the front door of the little church, turned right, walked alongside the building in the clumps of grass and dirt, or mud, and went into a small, windowless room with a solid wooden door. A bare light bulb hung from the ceiling, over a few back-less benches.

Soon there were so many children that we could scarcely close the door behind us. Kids squashed on the benches, stood in front of me, stood beside me, behind me, on my feet, under my elbows, inside the tripod of my trusty flannelgraph board. There was no heater and we could see our breath when we first entered, but soon the room was warm from our bodies, and damp from our clothes. It smelled of wet wool, dirty shoes, and runny noses, and it glowed with joy.

We sang, I taught them a Bible verse, and I told them a story. We memorized the books of the Bible, talked about the Old and New Testaments, and always closed with a simple prayer inviting *Cristo entrar a mi vida*, Jesus to enter my life.

Within a few weeks, I had more children in children's church than there were adults in the main service.

Sergio Hidalgo, about eight years old, was my favorite kid. He always managed to get a seat for himself and his little brother, Esteban, directly in front of me, where Sergio stared at me, transfixed. His big brown eyes, with long fringed lashes, looked intently at my every motion. And his smile! His whole face shone with his shy but radiant smile, showing his white, even teeth. He was always bundled up in a home-knit wool sweater with a dark gray wool jacket on top.

Although it must have been difficult for Sergio to understand my Mexican-accented Spanish, he hung onto my every word. I loved it! THIS was why we had become missionaries. My heart overflowed with joy. I could overlook the inconveniences of day-to-day living. I could suffer through the miserably cold weather. This was worth the travel of itinerary, the trauma of language learning. My heart connected to these children. My words and my life could make a difference in their lives.

Our congregation in front of the Temuco church

*   *   *

I had no idea then that when we would visit Temuco 28 years later, Sergio would be District Presbyter and both Sergio and Esteban would be pastors of thriving congregations.

9

Flourishing

Temuco, Chile
September–October, 1969

I was excited but apprehensive the first time we were invited to eat in a Chilean home. What if seven-year-old Christy and four-year-old Timmy would make "yucky" sounds when the food was served?

We traveled from Temuco south for half an hour on the Pan American highway, then turned east toward the Andes Mountains, bouncing on a gravel washboard lane for over an hour. Through the rolling hills we could see a volcano getting closer and closer. We rounded a curve, and there before us lay a scene straight from heaven: the tiny village of Pucón, composed almost entirely of wooden houses nestled between a mountain lake and a towering volcano, both named Villarrica.

The snow-covered volcano stood guard, while over its peak hovered its *sombrero*, a little cloud, hazy white against the deep blue sky. As we walked beside the pristine lake, the shiny, soot-black volcanic sand crunched underneath our feet. I picked up a handful of it and was surprised when it wasn't "dirty."

We passed the small *Gran Hotel* and drove around the Village Square. We saw only one bus and one taxi in all of Pucón.

As we drove up to a little unpainted house, Hermana Arancibia came to greet us through the tall, wooden, slatted gate. She stood shoulder high to me, a plump, smiling angel who welcomed us with a big hug and a kiss on the cheek. She led us through the dirt patio, hardened from years of sweeping, into the kitchen, separated from the rest of the house by an open walkway. We walked into the warm kitchen and walked back in time—wood cook stove, oilcloth-covered table, water pail with dipper, white enamel dishpan. Through the window I could see a privy, chickens, and a freestanding faucet, the only water source.

It was Thursday, the day when the Arancibia's held a church service in their home. Their son, René, a pastor in a neighboring town, had invited Joe to preach that night, and Mom and Dad Arancibia, in their 70s, had invited us for lunch and *once*, tea.

Mom Arancibia guided us into the other side of the house, to the dining-living room. She had set the table with an embroidered cloth and served at each place setting our first course: chopped boiled egg nestled in a bed of lettuce seasoned with lemon juice, *pan amasado* homemade bread, and home-churned butter. Mom A. did not sit at the table; she served us. She removed our plates and brought us the next course: a bowl of chicken broth with angel hair pasta and just a touch of cilantro; chicken and fluffy rice; half of a canned peach; and finally, the fifth course: coffee. Everything was delicious—the kids *liked* it. I was deeply humbled. Hermana Arancibia's love, totally undeserved on my part, enveloped me.

In the afternoon, Joe, René, and Pastor Iván (who had accompanied us along with two ladies from the Temuco church who had relatives in the village) decided we should drive up the volcano. Mom A. asked shyly if she could come, too, because although she had lived there for 25 years, she had never been up the mountain. She laughed when we told her we didn't have volcanoes back in Florida. She couldn't believe anyone lived without volcanoes rumbling and tremors shaking the ground night after night.

When the snow became too deep to drive any farther, we walked up the steep slope to the tree line. Panting, I had to stop and rest a couple of times, but Mom A. was never out of breath. The peak, at 9,338 feet, still seemed a long distance away. Mom A. said people hiked or rode horses up to the peak in the summertime (December, January, and February) when there wasn't as much snow.

The kids slipped and slid in the snow and laughed as the men built a *mono*, a snow monkey. We sat on a big boulder to eat the snack Mom A. had brought, crisp apples and juicy oranges.

Then it was time to get back for *once*. By 7:15 p.m., the little living room, with the table removed, became packed with people. I played the accordion as we sang choruses, Joe preached; we enjoyed a wonderful prayer time; René dedicated a baby; and around 11 p.m. we headed for home.

None of us dreamed that within two years, lava would spill out of the volcano Villarrica, slide down the slope we had climbed, begin to sizzle the edges of Pucón, and then swallow most of the village, including the Arancibia's home.

I usually didn't attend the Women's Missionary Council (CMF) meetings on Mondays at 2:30, but in her soft pleading voice, Hermana Nena, the mother of Sergio and Esteban, my two favorite boys, had asked me to give a little *enseñaza* teaching. Later, I learned that Joe was going out of town to Valdivia with Iván and a group of young people, so I wouldn't have the car or a babysitter.

Well, I could take the bus, for the very first time, *alone*, everyone else did. And I could walk the kids down to the Clarks, a really sweet, Independent Baptist missionary family from the Deep South with four boys and one girl who was Christy's age. The Clarks lived a good six blocks from our house, straight down the unpaved street dotted with large mud puddles. They received the children graciously, without previous notice since neither of us had phones.

Then I walked toward the bus stop. Because I always figured it would rain in Temuco, I carried a big black umbrella and a woven plastic bag—like all good Chileans carried—with my Bible, song-book, coin purse, and identification.

As I crowded onto the bus, I was scared to death for fear I'd go too far, or not go far enough, or get lost. I noticed people staring and grinning at my big umbrella, but the sky was overcast—how did they know it wasn't going to rain? The bus was *jammed*, so then I began to worry about how I'd be able to squeeze off the bus even if I knew where I was *supposed* to get off!

The bus drove into the center of town and almost everyone exited, much to my relief. The bus bumped along, a few people getting on and getting off. Finally I decided to ask the driver to tell me when we approached Valparaíso Street. A fat old woman overheard me and later announced, very loudly, that my street was next. As I exited the bus, I thanked her, even though she looked pointedly at my umbrella.

The clouds had thinned and the sun was almost shining through, so I tucked the umbrella inside my coat, hooking the handle on my sleeve, and stiffly walked the three long blocks to the church. I managed to unhook the umbrella from my arm and stand it in a corner just inside the church door without the women seeing (or maybe my back was turned).

Hermana Nena's calloused hands clasped mine as she kissed me on the cheek and asked me to begin the teaching. The little church building was so cold, the five women and I kept our coats on; we could see our breath. I began by teaching the arrangement of the books of the Bible: the Law, Prophets, Gospels, and Epistles. Then I told of the "Stream of Old Testament History" as Bashford Bishop had taught me at Southeastern College. The ladies were so eager to listen that I talked 45 minutes without realizing it. I felt humbled, *honored*, to sit with these ladies as their eyes glistened with eagerness for any tidbit of biblical truth I could share.

When we were ready to leave, I decided to pretend the umbrella wasn't there. But one of the dear sisters saw it and asked loudly, "Whose umbrella is this?" So, I confessed the whole story and they laughed and laughed and said I'd have to cut off the tip of the umbrella if I wanted to hide it under my coat because they had all seen it hanging down when I entered!

The doctor advised Dad to resign as pastor of Brownsville Assembly, Pensacola, due to his very serious heart condition. Dad was devastated and reluctant to do so, partly because of finances. I wrote to them, "Remember that God will provide for you or He's not the God you've taught me He is." Christy wondered if Papaw would still be a

Christian if he didn't pastor a church. Timmy thought Papaw should stand in the corner and put his face against the wall like Hezekiah did and pray.

One evening at supper, Christy asked the blessing very softly. Timmy wanted her to pray over again because he couldn't hear it. I said, "She's not praying for you—she's praying for God.""Why, is He sick?" Timmy retorted.

I sent Mom our Christmas list: for Timmy, a pullover sweater, size 4-6; for Christy, a white long-sleeved blouse for school, size 6; for me, a girdle (never mind the size); and for Joe, long underwear. And I asked her to cross the 7 in our address, "Casilla 570, Temuco, Chile," because our mail from her was going to Box 510.

About twenty American missionary families were stationed in Temuco—Christian and Missionary Alliance, Methodist, and various varieties of Baptists. We met for a monthly prayer fellowship and went to the American Embassy to see filmstrips of the Lunar Landing. But we did not have close relationships with any of these families because they were all too busy in their own missions.

One day, Joe came home from town smiling—a large crowd had gathered in front of the hardware store to stare at the test pattern on a black and white television set. The first television station in Temuco had just begun to broadcast one hour of test pattern daily. With no TV, we read, played games, and listened to records. Every evening I read a Bible story to the children and then a chapter from *Tom Sawyer* or another classic tale.

Joe was frustrated. "Here we are, *finally*, in Chile after itinerary and language school, and I can't travel around to the churches because the temporary tag for the car has expired." For two months he couldn't leave town. He had finished the "honey-do" list and had built a Heath-Kit Ham Radio. He'd even installed the gigantic antenna on the roof, with the help of the only technician in town. I'm sure all the neighbors thought we were CIA, because the antenna was so tall on our little house. But the Ham Radio license didn't arrive and neither did the car license.

So, in desperation for something to do, Joe began taking accordion lessons daily, for $5.60 a month.

Finally, the last of September, the new tag arrived and Joe was able to drive to a little town north of Temuco for all day services. In the church there were no musical instruments, so Joe decided to debut his accordion! He said people stopped in front of the building to listen to the singing. He even sang "He Touched Me" as a solo.

Joe arrived home at 1:30 a.m. and woke me up "rambling" about his day. "I know now it was the Lord." Sleepily, I asked, "What?" "Not getting the car tag … and learning to play the accordion. You'll never know what a difference it made—for me and for those people!"

Later, for a day-and-a-half, we hosted the five pastors from the Southern Chile Araucanía District at our house. I served lunch in courses and *once* tea. I was adapting! During one of their sessions, the presbyter asked Joe which type of missionary he would be: the kind who *mandar* (give orders) or the kind who *servir* (serve)? Joe assured them he was there solely to serve them in any way he possibly could.

Our family plus Pastor Iván and nine other people from church crammed into our Suburban to go to a three-day Sunday School Convention. Other missionaries would be there—even our boss from the States, Melvin Hodges! We drove for three-and-a-half hours—north, then west, to the Pacific Ocean, to an industrial town, Concepción. School was closed all week in honor of Chilean Independence Day and streets were beautifully decorated with the red, white, and blue Chilean flags.

The convention theme, *Ensanchad el Sitio* (Enlarge the Tent), implied continued church growth. The host church prepared all our meals from food we participants brought: live chickens, rice, pasta, butter, eggs.

We stayed on the second floor of a quaint, wooden hotel with narrow hallways that went up one step into a newer addition and down two steps and a little bit sideways into an older addition. But it was clean and warmish and we were near the missionaries who had flown in on a private plane: George Davis, Dave Scott, and Sam Balius. All three guys were a riot, and we laughed and bonded. I didn't realize how lonely I was for English conversation.

Christy was sick in bed with a really bad cold and high fever all three days we were there, so Joe and I took turns staying with her or walking the six blocks to the sessions. One afternoon, our boss, Melvin Hodges, came to the room to pray with Christy and to visit with us. We were really nervous about meeting privately with *someone so important* from our headquarters, but as soon as Brother Hodges entered the room, four-year-old Timmy saved the day. "Hi, I was born in the States. I have a dog. I go to kindergarten. I'm gonna be a lion-tainer. We're going back to the States one day, on a train I think."

We entered October joyously—thoroughly enjoying every aspect of ministry and personal relationships. We ended October totally devastated, isolated, told never to enter the Temuco church building again.

October began *so well*. The first week, Joe attended the International Council on Evangelism in Santiago. Juan Carlos Ortiz from Argentina was the speaker, one of the most eloquent speakers Joe had ever heard. We were the only missionaries whose car was cleared through customs, so Joe chauffeured all the "bigwigs" attending from our mission, along with the national superintendents from other countries.

That was my first week to be alone—left in Temuco with no car, no phone, a two-day drive from our other missionaries. My first night alone, I had trouble falling asleep. The house creaked. The windows rattled. I was really scared. Finally, I drifted off to sleep only to dream that a man was breaking into the house, climbing through the window at the foot of the stairs. In my dream, I went to the head of the staircase, saw his leg coming in over the windowsill, and called out, *"En el nombre de Jesús, le reprendo. ¡Vete!"* "In the name of Jesus, I rebuke you. Get out!" I was never scared to be alone again. Night after night, in the months ahead as Joe traveled extensively, I would picture angels sitting on the steep roof, guarding the front and back and both sides of our little house.

Then there was an attempted government coup! All mail was suspended, radios broadcast only government bulletins, soldiers with carbines on their shoulders stood guard on every corner. Within a few days, the army general who had attempted treason was arrested. Most of the soldiers left, but some remained on the principal streets, carbines ready.

Now that Joe could travel, he was invited to preach at a different town every Sunday. He loved it. His Spanish was becoming more fluent and a man asked him which Latin American country Joe's parents came from, because the man was sure Joe had been speaking Spanish all his life.

I was learning to say *pues* in the good Chilean way similar to an English "see" inserted at the end of phrases, as in "I didn't know, see, if it was the correct way, see...." Actually *we Chilean ladies* didn't say the entire word *pues*, just *pa* or just a puff of air. I also learned to say a word or two on an intake of breath, in the Chilean style.

One Sunday night, coming home from church at about 11:00, the children and I hurried in the dark, down a rough, uneven sidewalk. I tripped and fell, skinning my knee. Soon, the large scab (about 3" by 1–1/2") became infected. My beauty operator turned into my nurse by pulling off the scab and dusting the sore with sulfa and penicillin powder. I still have the scar.

My children's church grew from 40 to 100 to 142, and by mid-October, to over 200 children. As the children arrived, they filled the sanctuary; we had no other place large enough to meet. Pastor Iván decided to schedule only Sunday school on Sunday mornings. He said the 20 or so adults would enjoy the children's lessons also, so for me to teach in the sanctuary.

The adults loved the teaching; they, too, seemed to hang onto every word. An elderly woman told me as we walked to the bus stop that this was the first time she had ever learned these stories. I thanked the Lord that I had bought Spanish Child Evangelism Fellowship materials when we were in language school in Mexico.

One Sunday morning, as I taught, I asked everyone to turn in the Bible to the little book of *1 John* (toward the back of the Bible.) Even the adults began to open their Bibles in the front, at Genesis. So I announced I'd give prizes to those who memorized the books of the Bible. The Ladies Guild back in Beckley had sent me a packet of colorful bookmarks that I could use as prizes.

It was the last Monday of October when Iván, the pastor, came to our house. He and Joe went into the living room and Iván closed the door.

I heard Iván's loud, angry voice for what seemed like an hour. We were "under discipline." He gave no reasons, no explanation, only the conditions of our discipline: We could not speak to him. If he saw us on the street, he would turn his face away. We could not attend the church or have any contact with any church members. We had absolutely no idea why! We had never heard of being "under discipline"—a drastic measure in Chile, an assertion of the pastor's authority.

After only three months, three glorious, fulfilling months, my dream shattered. Tears soaked my pillow. How could my church children, my ministry, be taken away so abruptly? Where was God hiding?

10

Surviving

Temuco, Chile
November–December, 1969

The first Sunday of November I set up the flannelgraph board in our living room for my class of two, Christy and Timmy. Joe was not there; he was traveling with Demetrio, an evangelist.

We first met Demetrio Montero Méndez on October 21, 1969, in a little social hall that pastor Iván had rented for a week of evangelistic services. With no benches or chairs in that little building, 350 people stood shoulder to shoulder, back to stomach. People joked that if someone died during the service, no one would notice because he wouldn't be able to fall down. Iván opened the service, tentatively, and then Joe led the singing, playing the accordion. Demetrio walked to the front of the small stage. His deep voice resonated from the walls, penetrating deep into hearts. He was totally focused and authoritative. As he prayed at the close of the service, everyone prayed the sinner's prayer.

Demetrio's deep faith included divine healing. Thus, night after night miracles occurred. Deaf people could suddenly hear; pains of all varieties disappeared; so did tumors. We had never seen anything like it. Demetrio's extensive vocabulary complemented his professional and compassionate command of the platform.

This young, black evangelist, about 30 years old, slender, with a ready smile, stayed in our home and became a life-long friend. At first, I kept expecting him to speak English. He just *had* to be from Georgia or Alabama. But he came from the Dominican Republic. Though very few black people actually lived in Chile, the Chileans favored the "darkest-skin" member of a family.

Every night after service, Demetrio would unwind around our dining room table telling stories and jokes. He and Joe would laugh until tears ran down their cheeks. He told a joke about a guy who was *tan bobo*, "so dumb." Many years later, "Bobo" would come alive as the principal puppet character of our children's television ministry.

Joe lent Demetrio some long underwear and took him to the volcano Llaima, because he had never seen snow. Demetrio came back exhilarated and exhausted; they had climbed in the snow and sleet for an hour.

Demetrio asked Joe to play the accordion, lead the singing, open the service, do all the preliminaries for six more revivals in other towns in southern Chile. In language school, we had learned general vocabulary, but few religious terms. Now, Joe had the opportunity to absorb not only the words but also methods, such as how to call people forward, how best to pray with them for healing or salvation.

For all of November and December (except for Thanksgiving and Christmas) Joe traveled with Demetrio, who became his mentor. They stayed in Chilean homes with pastors or church members; Joe assimilated the language and culture.

The guys even traveled to the jumping-off place: to Puerto Montt at the southern end of the Pan American highway. Demetrio stayed there a few days for church services while Joe went even farther south.

Our Chevy Suburban at the church in Puerto Montt

Joe wanted to visit a small home-church in the village of Ancud on Chiloé Island, accessible only by ferry. The pastor and his wife, though *very* poor, treated Joe like a king. They even carried a folded rug-pillow from room to room so he wouldn't have to sit on a hard chair at the dining table or on a hard bench in the living room-chapel! Joe declared that the elderly hostess, who had no teeth, was a good cook even though there was no electricity or running water on the island. The next day the pastor and Joe drove the Chevy down the island as far as the only dirt road extended. Then they hiked, took a small boat to another island, hiked some more, and finally arrived at a "preaching point," another humble home. About fifteen people came to the service, and after Joe spoke, three adults committed their lives to Christ.

In another town, Chiguayante, Joe stayed with the pastor, Victor Burgos and his family. As Hermana Burgos bathed their small children one evening, Joe asked her, *"Hermana, cuando termine, ¿puede bañarme a mí?"* "Sister Burgos, when you finish bathing the children, could you bathe me?" Of course they rolled with laughter and they never let him forget it—he had said *puede* instead of *puedo*— "could you" instead of "could I."

Joe was traveling, ministering, and thriving. I was at home, barely surviving.

I saw pastor Iván one time near the post office. He abruptly turned his back to me and crossed to the other side of the street. Of the many new converts from Demetrio's meetings, Iván did not conserve even one. My children's church attendance had peaked at 200 on that final Sunday but I could not conserve even one, either, because the following day Iván had "put us out."

I reread the book *Broken Bread* by John Follette. Maxine Hurston, missionary to Korea, had given it to me before we left the States. I had read the book months before, but it meant nothing to me then. Now I cried on almost every page as I read that Jesus himself broke the bread and that until we are broken, we cannot "be useful." If we are like wine left on the dregs, and not poured out from vessel to vessel, we will remain with the same taste and the same aroma.

Alone for weeks at a time, I cried myself to sleep night after night. During the day, I stayed busy tutoring Christy, trying to finish second grade in English before her Spanish school year ended for summer vacation.

Now that the weather was more moderate, in the early summer I began a Saturday Back Yard Bible Club with nine neighborhood children. One week, I asked them, "How did Jesus die?" No one answered. "Was he hit by a truck?" They laughed. Then Timmy said rapidly in Spanish, "No, he was hit by a *horse.*" That really made them laugh.

Whenever Joe came home for a day or two, he went to a Western-style General Store to exchange money (dollars for *escudos*). The store sold hand-tooled leather saddles and all sorts of supplies for ranchers. Joe met a Chilean family there who invited us to their *rancho*. We arrived mid-morning, the day after Thanksgiving, and as the adults talked inside, the children played outside. The mother invited us to stay for a late lunch, and as soon as we agreed, she told her maid, "Go tell the men to get a lamb ready."

The servants went into the field, selected a lamb, led it to the back yard, killed it by slitting its throat, hung it upside down from a tree to bleed it, skinned it, built a fire and began roasting the lamb. Christy and Timmy witnessed the whole process and still to this day say they are traumatized!

Joe also met another Chilean family, disillusioned Methodists, who owned a large farm. Mrs. Brown invited me out for *once* tea. I drove toward the Andes Mountains, and there nestled in the rolling foothills sat a large ranch with horses, cows, oxen, sheep, and goats. Mrs. Brown graciously served me *once*, and as we visited, she asked if I'd like to take home some milk. Whole milk! I didn't realize how much water had been added to our milk-wagon mixture. (Later, I made scrumptious homemade banana ice cream!)

Mrs. Brown mentioned that she had built a small school for Mapuche Indian children, and she asked if I'd have any interest in teaching a Vacation Bible School for them.

A few weeks later, I drove about ten miles over rough, rocky, narrow roads into the Andean foothills to the little one-room schoolhouse. Eighteen Mapuche children stood waiting for me in the grass by the wooden building. Barefoot, the children wore hand-me-down clothing that smelled of wood smoke. The children were short and stocky with broad foreheads and thick black hair. Their freshly scrubbed faces shone with excitement.

Inside the building on a rough-planked floor sat about a dozen old-fashioned desks with inkwells. A wooden table served as the teacher's desk. Behind it, a black rectangle painted on the wall became the blackboard. There was a soccer ball in the corner and an outhouse out back.

The children were shy and respectful, but when I offered them candy, they got in line twice! The first day I held up a Bible and asked, "What is this?" No answer. "Is this the newspaper?" "*Sí, sí,*" heads nodded.

For five days we learned the stories of the colorful Wordless Book and each child made a little booklet to keep—a yellow page for heaven, black for sin, red for Jesus' blood, white for forgiveness, green for Christian growth.

The rancher, his wife, and their grown children came, too; they listened to the stories and prayed along with us.

The day after Christmas, we packed the Suburban for a weekend retreat. I was expecting the worst—"a retreat at a rustic ranch" the Talcahuano pastors, Leonardo and Sylvia Riquelme told us. We had met Leo and Sylvia at the Sunday School Convention in Concepción. Subsequently, they wrote asking Joe to speak to the youth and for me to speak to the children at their church retreat.

Man! What a totally joyous surprise! Leo and Sylvia were kindred spirits, a young couple, with a baby due in about two months. Leo was articulate and passionate about serving God. Sylvia was organized, efficient, and loving. Their church numbered about 150 and the kids from this church *knew* the Bible stories! Fortunately, I had taken extra material or I would have been embarrassed, too quickly finishing all my usual lessons.

Joe taught from a replica of the Old Testament tabernacle he had made; the youth and adults, knowledgeable in biblical history, devoured his teaching.

The *rancho* had a swimming pool, soccer field, and a barn-dormitory where Christy and Timmy stayed with their new Chilean friends. Joe and I slept in the main ranch house in our sleeping bags on cots.

The church women cooked soup over an open fire in two huge black pots. One soup had cabbage, the other did not. Take your choice. They were both delicious. We learned to eat *mote*, wheat kernels that had been soaked in ashes and water until the husks rubbed off easily. A tiny bit of sugar flavored the *mote* along with stewed, dried apricots. This time, I said "Yucky!" but under my breath, and I ate it anyway.

Sylvia and Leo asked us to stay an extra day for a local pastors' meeting. Four pastors attended and they invited us to move to their area, Concepción, to begin a night Bible school. We had said not one word about Iván, but apparently he was talking.

We were conflicted: why did we move to Temuco if we were not supposed to stay there? Temuco was centrally located for Joe's travels. We'd have to decide what to do before Christy's school began again in March.

Joe and I spent hours filling out applications for documents: for our identification *carnet* that must be carried with us at *all* times, and for our drivers' licenses. We went morning after morning for fingerprints, photos, and tests with questions such as, "How many meters should you park from the corner if it's a bus stop?"

Timmy turned five years old on December 4, and we invited our nine neighborhood children to his party. From a sheet cake cut into triangles, I formed a sailboat covered with colored frosting and coconut. The kids all gave Tim candy—later, the Vélezes, an embassy family, gave him a jar of stateside peanut butter.

Several days later, we went back to the country again, for horseback riding. We knew nothing about riding horses, so our host put Christy up behind him and told her to hold on tight. He took off galloping across the field. I watched Christy bounce up, fall sideways, and land face first in the hard-packed dirt. I was shaking, fearful that the horse had stepped on her. Her face was bloody, her lips already swelling, her eyes turning purple. Blood ran from her nose. Her two front teeth would have been knocked out, but fortunately, she had just lost them the week before. The doctor said she'd be fine. She looked like the losing prizefighter in an amateur boxing match.

That day, Christy chose two things from the "treasure box," a cardboard box filled with small toys and books. On especially dreary days, special occasions, or if they just needed cheering up, Christy and Timmy could reach in, and without looking, choose any one "treasure."

Earlier, for our first Thanksgiving alone, I had baked a chicken with dressing, mashed potatoes, gravy, and fresh green beans. I made Jell-O fruit salad and an apple pie. Perry Como serenaded us from a Christmas record.

That evening, when I put Christy to bed, she said, "Today sure didn't seem like Thanksgiving. It just seemed like a Saturday with no school and we ate just a plain old supper. Just a <u>plain old supper</u>, Mommy." She started crying and talking about Papaw sitting with the Chihuahua Twinkie on his lap in the big recliner and Grandma in the kitchen cooking. Sighing, Christy continued, "We didn't have as much to eat as Grandma always has." But she still was not satisfied with *why* it didn't seem like a holiday. Suddenly, she exclaimed, "I know what we needed—*people*!"

As Christmas approached, I asked about Christmas trees. The only ones available were a pole, like a broomstick, painted green with holes drilled in it. Into the holes were stuck brushes, like bottle-brushes, painted green. They were not angled; they just stuck out straight and were the same length all the way up the pole.

I decided to ask our *rancho* friends if we could get a tree from their property. Nope. Against the law to cut down an evergreen. But, they could cut off a big limb for us. So our first Christmas tree was a large limb, slanted—but with a real evergreen smell. Joe stuck it in a bucket of dirt and we turned it round and round in the corner of the living room trying to find the best and least-leaning angle.

Under the tree sat our Christmas-list box, which had arrived from Mom via APO. Also, she sent a second box with Cracker Jacks, popcorn, Dr. Seuss books and what would become the most treasured book of all—*Reader's Digest Classic Stories for Children.*

One of the pastors Joe had met in his travels invited us to spend Christmas Eve with his extended family down south, out in the country. The weather was cold, even though it was summertime. It was raining.

At midnight, we gathered at a long table in a lean-to kitchen for our meal. The wood stove gave off warmth, the food tasted delicious. After we finished eating, the hostess (who never sat down, but just served us) lifted a teakettle off the stove and poured hot water into a horn-like container. She added a pinch of sugar and handed the horn to Joe. A spoon handle stuck up from a pea-green, thick liquid.

Joe had no idea what he was supposed to do. So he stirred the stuff as he talked to everyone. He stirred and talked, stirred and talked.

Finally, someone said, "*Hermano José*, aren't you going to drink your tea?" "Oh, sure," Joe said, looking down at the spoon. The handle was hollow! It was actually a drinking straw! So he took a big sip. Suddenly, his mouth filled with bitter tea leaves. *Aaaach. Spit, spit!* Our Chilean friends roared with laughter.

We learned that the bottom of the straw served as a sieve; placed in the bottom of the horn were crushed green tea leaves called *mate* (mah-the). The smiling hostess took the *mate* cup, rinsed out the straw and handed it back to Joe. He drank promptly and handed the cup back to her.

She filled the *mate* cup with more hot water and handed it to the next person. He drank, handed it back, she refilled it. The next person drank, and the next. They had all been sitting there waiting for their *mate*!

The *mate* cup came all the way around the table to me. I happily shared mine with the children, and handed it back.

The hostess filled it again, and handed it to Joe. "Thanks, I've already had some," he said. Her face fell. Clearly he had hurt her feelings. He stumbled "Oh, ah, do you drink it more than once?" She smiled instantly, "Oh, yes, *muchas veces* many times." So it went around and around the circle.

Drinking *mate*

Twenty years later, in Tampa, Florida, we met some Chileans at church and went out to eat with them. They started telling funny stories and told about the poor missionary who didn't know how to drink *mate*...Joe confessed that he was the one! We tell stories about "them"—they tell stories about "us"!

We looked forward to January. We had been corresponding with a family in language school who were due to arrive on January 11. Bob and Margaret Bowden and their two girls were thinking of living in southern Chile and wanted to come to Temuco and stay with us for six weeks.

Also, Joe had invited his cousin, Roland Blount, to come to Chile and hold some revival meetings. Roland raised his money quickly and wrote that he, his wife, and two children would be arriving on January 9 for a three-month visit, staying with us.

My life was poised to change from isolated and lonely to crowded and smothered.

* * *

Dema's *Café con Leche*

INGREDIENTS

Per serving:
1 teaspoon instant coffee
2 teaspoons sugar
1 cup milk

DIRECTIONS

1. Place coffee and sugar in a coffee mug.*
2. Heat milk until the edges begin to bubble (in microwave or on stove.)
3. Pour milk slowly into mug, stirring constantly.
*4. For *batido* (froth), drop 2 drops of water into mug, beat rigorously until froth forms. Pour hot milk very slowly into froth, stirring constantly.

11

Hosting

Temuco, Chile
Summertime: January, February, and March 1970

"They're here!"
"Daddy's come back!"
"Momma, Momma, hurry! They're driving up the driveway!"

Gathered at the front window, all six children looked through the late afternoon drizzle toward our green Chevy Suburban stopped at the gate. Bob Bowden hopped out to hold the gate open while Joe drove inside the yard. Bob closed the gate while Joe led Roland Blount around the car and up the back steps into the house.

Under the grizzled chins and disheveled hair, the men's faces were radiant. Their clothes smelled like *fogatas*, campfires; and it was pretty easy to see that they had only had "spit baths" for a week.

Everyone started talking at once. "How was it?" "Did you have a good time?" "Did anyone show up at camp?" "Could they understand your Spanish?"

We gathered around the dining room table as Dema served us big bowls of chicken and rice along with salad and fresh bread.

Bob Bowden grinned, and sniffed the back of his left hand ever so briefly. "It was absolutely everything you could dream of! About 100 people from southern Chile attended the camp. Picture us in a big cow pasture. There's a small river on one side, trees beyond the fences on two sides, and a little dirt road behind the fence at the entrance."

"Being *gringos*, of course we arrived on time, which was a couple of hours early, Chilean time," added Joe.

"So we had our pick of where to pitch our camp tent," Roland stated.

"There was a clump of bushes, so we decided that if we camped next to the bushes, we would have a little bit of privacy," said Bob.

"Wrong!" exclaimed Joe and Roland at the same time.

"Problem was," Bob said, "everybody wanted to camp next to us, so they beat down the bushes and camped right beside us, all around us, in fact."

"Yeah, so even though Joe and Bob had strung up a tarp for a 'bathroom' on the back side of our tent, we could hear everybody VERY clearly, just on the other side of the canvas. I had to keep feeling of the tarp to make sure no one was watching me!" Roland lamented, comfortable in speaking of his blindness.

The men laughed loudly, openly, and freely, only as friends can who have shared common experiences. Joe added, "Everyone else answered nature's call by going into the woods."

Evelyn tried to change the subject. "Did you preach or sing?"

"Did we ever!" exclaimed Bob, briefly sniffing the back of his left hand again.

Margaret jumped in, "Where did you eat?"

"Well, we cooked a little bit on our camp stove, but mostly we ate with the Chileans," Joe said. "The women made vegetable or bean or wheat soup from the river water. We figured it boiled long enough to kill most of the germs."

"Yeah, and they served salad in a big red bowl!" Roland howled with laughter.

"Don't remind me," groaned Bob. "One of the women sprained her ankle and soaked her foot in the big, red, plastic bowl. Come suppertime, there was the bowl on the table with salad in it!"

"Where did you meet for church services?" I asked.

"Before or after the cows ate the roof?" grinned Bob. Joe and Roland chimed in laughing.

"The first afternoon," Joe explained, "the men cut and trimmed long, stout limbs into poles and built a 'brush arbor.' The ladies gathered branches, probably some of our 'privacy bushes' too, and laid them on top of the poles for a roof."

"But," continued Roland, "in the middle of the night, I woke up to hear 'crunch, stomp, crunch'—it was cows eating the roof!"

"And the services?" asked Evelyn again.

"Oh, man, it was incredible!" sighed Roland. "I played the accordion and sang every one of the nineteen songs I've memorized in Spanish. They loved it. They asked me to sing them again and again."

"Joe taught every day from his chart," Bob added, "strung between a tree and the brush arbor."

Joe teaching from his Bible time-line chart

"It was worth every peso I paid in Mexico to have that Bible chart painted," enthused Joe.

"Even when you get the words wrong," laughed Bob.

"Hey, all I wanted to do was point on my chart to the ball of fire and say in Spanish, 'All *sinful* men are going to hell.' But instead, I said, 'All *freckle-faced* men are going to hell.'" (*pecoso* instead of *pecaminoso*) The Chileans had roared with laughter and, of course, we did, too.

"Anyway," continued Joe, "I taught every morning. And Roland and Bob took turns preaching at night."

Roland picked up, "Joe translated for me." Roland grinned from ear to ear, "But he had to turn to me once and ask in English, 'Can you say that another way? I don't know how to say that in Spanish.'" The men laughed, reliving the moment.

Suddenly sober, Joe said, "We have invitations for revivals—all over southern Chile. More than enough to fill this summer while Roland's here. Bob and I even booked for March, April, and May, too. It seems as if every pastor wants us to come to his church!"

"And this morning," exclaimed Bob softly, his eyes misting with tears, "the *jóvenes* youth wouldn't let us leave. They blockaded the car. Made us get out and *despedir* say goodbye again. To *despedir*, they give you a big bear hug, pat you soundly on the back, and then shake your hand."

In the moment of silence that followed, each of us realized we were now "real missionaries." Lives had been changed in that little camp meeting. Chilean lives. And *gringo*, North American, lives.

Joe and I, with Christy, 7, and Timmy, 5, had driven to Santiago in early January to meet the Blounts and Bowdens. Then all twelve of us had wedged into our Suburban to travel for two days south to Temuco. We were "Aunt Margaret and Uncle Joe, Uncle Roland and Aunt Evelyn, Uncle Bob and Aunt Margaret" to the children.

"Documents out—police checkpoint ahead!" The hours passed quickly in the cramped van as the adults asked questions about Chilean customs and looked with fascination at the Chilean countryside. Bob and Roland kept us laughing at a new kind of jokes about "Polocks."

Bob and Margaret Bowden grew up in Covina, California. Connie was 13, Cheryl Jeanne (Jeannie), 11. Having just finished language school, they wondered what type of ministry to begin in Chile as well as exactly where to live.

Margaret was shy; language learning had been difficult for her. Unsure of speaking and hesitant to enter into a Spanish conversation, she was afraid to take the bus alone because of the language barrier.

Bob was just the opposite—a natural extrovert, with an amazing aptitude for language learning. He had conversed with every person at the camp. And he had already learned many Chilean pronunciations and *modismos*, such as, "I'm all ironed out," *planchado*, for "I'm broke." And *pu-cha-kai* for "good grief."

Though the Bowdens stayed at our house all day every day, they were able to sleep down the street at the Vélez residence. The Vélezes, gone to the States for a couple of months, had offered the use of their guest bedroom.

Roland and Evelyn Blount, from Durant, Florida, had recently served as pastors in Jupiter, Florida. Howie was 11, Carla, 4–1/2. Roland, though blinded from glaucoma as a child, felt God saying to him, "I want you to have a ministry in Latin America." So, he had written (more than once) to the Foreign Missions Board requesting appointment. The first reply was, "We do not accept handicapped people." The second reply stated, "Do not write to us again. You cannot ever become a missionary."

Therefore, when Joe wrote to Roland inviting him to visit Chile, Roland jumped at the chance—possibly his only opportunity to go to Latin America. A woman from Peru taught him phonetically some hymns in Spanish.

Evelyn suffered from culture shock in Temuco. Having been brought up to be very legalistic, she understood neither the religious rules nor the language in this foreign city.

The Blounts slept in our kids' room, their children on the floor. Joe and I slept in our bedroom, Christy and Timmy on the floor. Our house, approximately 900 square feet, had one small bathroom. The house quickly became claustrophobic and chaotic.

The three men had stayed in Temuco only a couple of days before they took off to the camp meeting. That set the tone for the summer. Men traveled. Women stayed home with the kids. The guys would come home for a day or two between revivals so we could wash their laundry. They'd tell us their exciting stories, and then head off again, in another direction.

When the sun shone, about one day per week, all six kids could play outside, usually staying in the back yard and playing near a little playhouse Joe had made from one of our packing crates.

But during the days of drizzle and cold rain, the children were underfoot all day long. Sometimes all six of them would slide down the wooden staircase on a blanket. One afternoon, after the kids had played games for hours, we heard, "Let's do a play—*Bonnie and Clyde!*" *Romeo and Juliet* followed, and then the children wrote original plays complete with sound effects and special costumes from towels, robes, and scarves.

Margaret, Evelyn, and I took the bus to the big downtown under-roof market. We took the bus to the post office and to the little stores downtown. None of us had any money to buy anything except necessities.

Under Iván's "discipline," we could not attend the church, so we women had Sunday school at home with our children. Margaret, tentatively, helped me with the Saturday Bible Club. Attendance jumped from 9 to 15! (with our guests) Evelyn, Howie, and Carla could not understand the Spanish, but they attended anyway.

Evelyn and I began to get on each other's nerves. We did not know that we were both passive-aggressive. We never "got angry." Oh, no. We were both good Christian women. And we both knew that Christians did not "get angry." We were annoyed, perturbed, worried, concerned, anxious, distraught, aggravated and nervous. But not angry. We never stomped our foot, or raised our voice—just raised our eyebrows and went "Hummph," softly, of course. She made me *most* "annoyed" by saying, repeatedly, "Howie, *other* parents may allow *their* children to do that, but *we* do not do that." I am sure she had a long list of things that "annoyed" her about me, too.

When the men came home for a day or two between services, Evelyn and I (unbeknown to each other) would literally cry on our husbands' shoulders, saying, "I can't stand it. I can't take another day with her." And our husbands would soothe and comfort us, saying, "It's all right. It's just for a few more weeks...days...then you won't have to see her again."

God, with his good sense of humor, had already planned that within a few years, Evelyn and I would become next-door neighbors and friends.

The middle week of February, all twelve of us took the train up to Valparaíso, the main port city of Chile. Valpo, as everyone calls it, is almost due west of Santiago, the capital. Valpo is an industrial city on a large cove; extending north around the cove sits Viña del Mar.

Viña del Mar is called the San Francisco of Chile—steep hills, picturesque houses perched precariously on the mountainsides, bumpy cobblestone streets. Beautiful, rocky, Pacific Ocean beach. When Bob and Margaret learned that there was no church in Viña, they felt "called"! They began to look for a house.

The reason for our trip was General Council, a three-day convention for all our pastors and laypeople. It was refreshing for us. We met the Superintendent, Raúl Morales, but didn't have an opportunity to talk to him about our situation in Temuco. The pastors from southern Chile bragged about the camp meeting and the revivals that Joe, Bob, and Roland were conducting. Pastors from the central region and from the northern region, a thousand miles from Temuco, wanted revivals, too. The Superintendent was thrilled and wanted to meet with Joe and Bob about becoming official nationwide evangelists. He said he would schedule a meeting with them within a month or so.

Roland sang at Council, and the people loved him! They asked him to return as a missionary, and Joe translated as Roland explained that he couldn't, that our Foreign Missions Department would not allow him to, because he was blind. Well, the national pastors decided, right then and there, they would do something about that. They drew up a petition and all signed it, mailed it to our headquarters in the States, and ¡voila! suddenly Roland *could* be appointed after all.

Roland and Evelyn stayed with us for nine weeks, leaving on March 10. Bob and Margaret stayed in Temuco for six weeks.

Just before the Blounts left, Bob drove back to Temuco in his new car, just like ours, fresh out of customs. He and Margaret had found a house they really liked four blocks from the ocean. He brought a new friend with him, Juan Toro. Juan, in his mid-twenties, lived with his parents and his sister, Gloria. The family attended the church in Valpo.

Juan was very close to his pastor, who also just happened to be our Superintendent, Hermano Morales. (We always called him by the respectful title *Hermano*, "Brother.")

While Bob and Juan were visiting us in Temuco, I mentioned that I had received an invitation to a women's rally the next Saturday, and I just knew that my friend Nena would like to ride with me to the rally, which was being held in a town three hours away. Bob and Juan said, "We'll go with Joe to ask her."

Nena was thrilled with the invitation, but her husband, Segundo, said, "I want her to go, but we have to ask Pastor Iván first. Come back tomorrow for the answer."

When the men returned for the answer, Iván was present and he was not happy. His face contorted with anger as he bellowed, "No! Nena *dare not* go with *Margarita* to *any* meeting!"

Juan was shocked! He had seen Nena and Segundo's attitudes, our attitudes, and then he saw Iván's temper tantrum.

"OK, level with me. What on earth is going on here?" he asked us point blank.

And we told him. He was the first Chilean we had said a word to about Iván.

"I will inform the Superintendent as soon as I get back to Valparaíso," declared Juan, outraged. And he did.

12

Confronting

Temuco, Chile
March–April 1970

I paced the floor at Bob and Margaret Bowden's house in Viña waiting for Joe to return.

True to his word, Juan Toro had informed the national Superintendent of the situation in Temuco. Within a week we received a letter from Hermano Morales: "I understand you are planning a trip to this area the last week of March to visit the Bowdens. Therefore, I have written to Iván telling him to travel to Valparaíso for a face-to-face meeting. Would you please be present in my office on Tuesday...."

The meeting lasted for four hours.

Iván stated that he had never requested a missionary; he did not want any "help"; no one had asked *him* before assigning a missionary to Temuco. Furthermore, he said, Joe had gone to Temuco with the express purpose of taking over the church. Iván read from a written list of grievances he held in his hand.

Grievance: Joe had suggested that a girl be allowed to sing in the choir during Demetrio's revival, a girl who had not yet been baptized. Hermano Morales asked if the girl indeed sang. "No," replied Iván, "I did not ask her to sing." Hermano Morales asked, "Then what is the problem?"

Grievance: Margaret gave away bookmarks as prizes to children and adults without asking Iván first.

Grievance: Margaret asked one of the youth to assist her during a service without asking Iván first.

And so forth and so on. All seemingly trivial.

Hermano Morales, a kind, soft-spoken, compassionate man with a gentle spirit, listened as Iván read his complaints. Hermano Morales commented on each one, gave personal stories of how he had overcome similar circumstances in his ministry, and for every complaint, asked Joe if he wanted to comment.

There was only one item on Iván's list that the Superintendent questioned. Joe had asked a young man from the church, Orlando, to travel to Santiago with him in order to see the Bible institute. Orlando was thrilled and immediately enrolled for the next term. Orlando was president of the youth at the church, an intelligent young man with real promise. But Iván became furious because Joe did not ask his permission before approaching Orlando.

Hermano Morales turned to Joe and asked if Joe thought he should have proceeded differently. "Yes, maybe," said Joe. "Perhaps I should have informed Iván. But, honestly, Hermano Morales, I knew that if I did, Iván would prevent Orlando from attending the Bible institute."

Hermano Morales did not deride Iván or belittle him. He did, however, make it very clear to Iván that he had no authority to "put a missionary under discipline" and that Iván should rectify the situation immediately. He told Iván to invite Joe back to church. Iván turned to Joe and mouthed the words.

On the outside, Iván had spoken the words. But it was as if a dull machete had whacked off a thorn bush at ground level. The root of bitterness remained hidden in the soil. Iván's jealousy of our spiritual gifts continued to deepen and widen. So did his envy of our "things"—our vehicle and even our typewriter. Of course, we did not know that yet—we would learn of it *painfully* in the coming cold winter months.

Joe and Bob met twice that week with Hermano Morales regarding their new Chilean Evangelistic Team. Hermano Morales wanted preparation of the local church congregation prior to the campaign, and he wanted follow-up. He knew a middle-aged woman, single, named Teresa, who had taught at the Bible institute. She would be perfect for this task.

They arranged the schedule: Teresa the first week, Joe and Bob for three Sundays (two weeks), Teresa the following week. Move to the next town. So Joe was home two weeks, then gone for two weeks.

In the very first campaign, the crowds were so large that no building in the town was big enough to hold the people. In those days, church auditoriums were small, and so were the civic centers. Joe and Bob concluded that they needed a tent. Our ham radio was up and running by now, so Joe asked my dad via the radio to contact the Valdosta Tent Company in Georgia. Dad did the negotiations. For $3,000, we could purchase a tent and have it shipped to Chile. Joe and Bob divided the cost and both wrote letters to their supporting churches to ask for special offerings to help cover the cost.

However, there is the extra, exorbitant cost of "customs" taxes. Joe and Bob approached the World Relief Commission (WRC) who helped all missionaries with their vehicles. "No," they said. "We do not help with tents." Joe wrote to Bob McGlasson at our headquarters. Mr. McGlasson wrote to the head of the WRC in the States. The head honcho flew to Chile and convinced the local leadership that indeed a tent could be allowed to enter duty-free.

We settled into a routine in April. Joe made a trip to central Chile for a two-week campaign, and the children began a new school year in Spanish at Colegio Bautista. Tim loved his kindergarten teacher, *Tía Lucy,* Aunt Lucy. Christy began third grade, accustomed now to kissing her Chilean teacher "good morning" and "goodbye." One of their projects was to knit *bombachas,* shorts to wear under their skirts. Since neither Christy nor I could knit, Dema knit a little bit every evening for "homework."

Speaking of Dema, our maid, she was an angel in disguise. Dema's monthly salary, in dollars, was only $16.00 because of the terrible inflation ($1 to 10 *escudos* when we arrived, $1 to 16 *escudos* now.) She worked so hard, especially when all the visitors were there. She spoiled the children rotten, picking up after them and even removing their dinner plates quickly when they'd give her a sign that they didn't want to eat the rest of their veggies. The children prayed for her every night and during the revival with Demetrio, Dema gave her life to the Lord Jesus.

Christy attended school from 8 a.m. to 1:00 p.m. Timmy went from 9 a.m. until noon. So Dema or I made four trips every day by bus to take the children to and from school. Christy preferred for Dema to accompany her because Dema would go into the classroom, unbutton Christy's jacket, help her into the *delantal* apron, and button it! "All the other maids do that, Mom," she explained to me with a big grin.

One day Christy came home fuming. "I had to tell the teacher in English class that you do not say 'peter pahter goe dee rah-een drohps.' Everybody knows it is 'pitter patter,' not 'peter pahter.'"

That evening as we sat down to eat supper, Timmy looked over the table. Leftovers. "We are going to get sores in our mouths because Christy studied in Health that you get sick from eating the same thing over and over." (malnutrition) Also, he let me know he liked cottonflowers but not coldslop. (cauliflower, coleslaw)

Mom mailed us some magazines: a *Time* for Joe and a *Good Housekeeping* for me. I hugged it to my chest—a beautiful, colorful magazine with pictures and stories in English. It was such a wonderful treat that I wouldn't let myself look through it all at once. I read only one or two pages per day.

I resumed teaching English classes on Wednesday mornings at the Catholic University, and I began to take conversational German on Tuesday and Thursday evenings with Carmen Vélez, just for something to do. It was lonely with only the rain to keep me company of an evening. I also continued the Saturday Bible Clubs, moving indoors because of the weather.

By the middle of April, the cold had set in—an unusually early winter, everyone declared. The temperature dropped into the 30's and stayed there. My feet were numb with the cold and began to swell and ache. My toes were swollen and inflamed. Standing up first thing of a morning was extremely painful, and by evening, my toes ached again. I could barely endure to have the bed covers touching them. Once when we had sunshine for three days straight, all the symptoms vanished. Then they returned with the cold rain.

One Saturday afternoon, a knock sounded on our door. I hardly recognized the gaunt, thin missionary standing in the chilly, blowing rain. "We are giving up—going back to the States. Is there anything we have that you would like to buy?" We had met this man and his wife in language school; they were independent missionaries. My heart ached for them.

After Iván's meeting with the Superintendent, we were allowed to attend the Temuco church again, twice on Sundays. But now, I dreaded it because Iván would greet us very coldly, averting his eyes. We were not asked to participate in any way; we just sat on the hard bench. Joe was in town only one Sunday per month. Surely Iván would not perceive him as a threat now.

Iván announced that Nena Hidalgo would prepare an *once* (own-say) tea for the congregation on Saturday afternoon. Surprisingly, we were invited to attend. Everyone was very nice and friendly. The food was delicious, except for some really strong fish mixture on crackers. I took one bite and almost gagged. I noticed Joe was eating his, so I said, "Oh, Joe loves this," and put my portion on his plate.

Several days later, Nena told me that Iván had informed the congregation that the *once* was our "coming-out-from-under-discipline" party.

But at least I could have some fellowship now with the church people. I asked one of the guys where his wife was—at least that's what I wanted to ask. Since the Chileans said *marido* for "husband," I figured *marida* was "wife." There is no such word! They laughed and laughed at me.

Speaking of language, I overheard a mom ask her little son something about drinking his milk. He answered, "Sa-ka-bow-yah." Oh, a new word, I thought, so I asked what "Sa-ka-bow-yah" meant. The mother looked at me really funny. "Sa-ka-bow-yah," she repeated. "I know," I replied, "but what does it *mean*?" Very slowly she said, "*Se acabó ya.*" "It is finished already." The kid had just run the words together, like we might say in English "G'eet?" "Did you eat?"

Existing throughout Chile were some weird Methodist-Pentecostal church groups. More than sixty years earlier, a Methodist missionary had received the baptism in the Holy Spirit, and this experience had spread to numerous congregations. The new groups had "seceded" from traditional Methodism, fracturing into 125 separate "denominations," and had floundered without any biblical teaching.

The preachers would not study for a sermon but would close their eyes, open the Bible, and point to a verse. Then they would preach on whatever phrase their finger first touched. If the Bible fell open to a blank page, then, obviously, the Lord had no word for them that day.

These groups had developed all sorts of "spiritual gifts." One was the "gift of the spool," the thread spool. To exercise this gift, a person carried an empty thread spool in his pocket. Then when he saw someone enter the church, he quickly pulled the spool out of his pocket, peered through the hole at the suspect, and discerned if he was good or evil.

There was also the "gift of operation" in which a sick person lay on the altar or a table. The person with the "gift" mimed cutting open the sick person, removing the diseased organs, then sewing the patient back up.

The Pentecostal Methodists were very evangelistic and would literally stand on street corners, hollering at the top of their voices, preaching to nobody. They reasoned that perhaps someone inside a house could hear well enough to cause the person to repent.

Our pastors and leadership tried for many years to reach out to these people. Finally, in 1977, the Bishop of the largest group asked for help. A veteran missionary from Argentina transferred to Chile, assigned to help them establish a Bible institute. They have changed considerably since then.

We attended a Youth Convention in Santiago in April at a very large church, Centro Evangelístico, pastored by Cyle and Helen Davis. The Davises were an institution in Chile, having been there 25 years, and had even, against "company policy," purchased a home there. Cyle and Helen were gracious to us rookie missionaries. Helen, who had just been elected national President of Women's Ministries, invited me to begin a national Missionettes program for girls.

Cyle suggested that we move to Santiago, so that Joe could continue to travel in revivals and I could be Cyle's assistant pastor. He was teasing me, but I considered it a great honor. He also encouraged us by saying that while he realized we felt quite useless in southern Chile, we had no idea what a positive influence our presence was to all the pastors there. The southern region had felt neglected by the church organization and now felt included.

Joe was invited to preach both at Cyle's church and at the Superintendent's church in Valpo.

At the Davises' church, I met Susana upstairs in the dining hall. As we sat together talking, she confided that she and Iván were engaged to be married in just a few months. I was shocked! Susana was sweet and gentle. I said, "Susi, do you <u>know</u> Iván?"

"Of course," she replied. "I met him at a youth meeting several months ago. I know his character is *duro* hard, but I will change him as soon as we are married." No amount of persuasion on my part could sway her. She was determined that she could change him.

Back in Temuco, one of my favorite people was José Carter, an ex-con. José was in his sixties, slightly hunched but still tall for a Chilean. He had a narrow black moustache that curved up when he smiled; he combed his thinning hair straight back. José was the self-appointed greeter at the church. Bundled in his old, woolen overcoat, he stood in the open doorway rain or shine, cold blustery wind or gentle breeze, his rough hands extended from frayed sleeves. As he shook your hand, he looked you in the eye, genuinely glad to see *you*.

Whenever Iván would ask the congregation, "What song would you like for us to sing?" José always spoke up, "*¡Soy Testigo!*"

Yo soy testigo	I am a witness
Del poder de Dios	To the power of God
Por el milagro	For the miracle
Que Él ha hecho en mí	He performed in me

Yo era ciego	I was blinded
Ahora veo la luz	Now the light I see
La luz gloriosa	The glorious light
Que me dió Jesús.	Jesus has given me.

Invariably, as we sang, tears filled José's eyes, ran down his lined cheeks, and dripped from his chin.

One day, Joe asked José, a carpenter by trade, to install a window in our living room. Day after day, as we became better acquainted, he opened up more and eventually told us his story.

José had been a drunkard who frequently beat his wife. He would abandon her, go live with another woman, then come home, and his wife would take him back. He did this numerous times. One night he came home so drunk that he beat her more severely than usual— he killed her. The next morning, sober, he turned himself in to the authorities and was sentenced to life in prison without parole.

When missionary Lowell Dowdy went to the prison for a church service, José could not believe that God would really forgive him. But he listened week after week and accepted Christ as his Savior.

José's conduct changed so dramatically that the prison commander let him practice carpentry inside the prison. Several years later, the commander even allowed José to have his own carpenter shop, there inside the prison walls.

José laughed as he told us of a supervisor visiting the prison. "You should not be allowed to have that ladder," the visitor exclaimed. "You might try to escape." José replied, "Well, I've had the ladder for ten years and haven't escaped yet." The prison wall was directly in front of José's shop door.

Then when a new governor came into power, he wanted to gain favor by freeing prisoners—and he pardoned José!

"And that's why my favorite song is *Yo soy testigo del poder de Dios.* I am a witness to the power of God," José told us softly, tears moistening his eyes.

No one knew that cancer cells were multiplying in José's frail body. We didn't realize then that during the long winter weeks of August, José would lie dying of cancer of the stomach. I visited him at the hospital on Thursday and Sunday afternoons, the only visiting hours. I held his calloused hand and cried with him. We smiled together, too, and looked forward to meeting again in a better place.

On September 11, 1970, I drove our Suburban in the cortege that followed José's casket to the cemetery. Everyone else walked behind the horse and wagon, but José's elderly mother needed to ride.

As I mourned his death, I mourned my pain also, for Iván had found a powerful ally. Just as the poison of Jose's cancer had killed him, Ivan's poison was slowly killing me.

13

Trying Again

Temuco, Chile
May, June, July, 1970

We moved on May 27, Dad's birthday. Not out of town, which I had been praying for during the past six months, but eight blocks away, closer to town. Within walking distance of the children's school.

Why?

During April, a man had knocked on our door—a man with the biggest nose I've ever seen. He was dressed in a tailored suit, a sparkling white shirt, a silk tie, and expensive shoes. He introduced himself as the *dueño* owner of a large house where Peace Corps executives had been living, but they had been transferred. He really needed to rent to North Americans as he desperately needed the U.S. dollars. The rent had been $350, but for us, it would be only $200. Joe thanked him politely, but told him we were not interested, as we were paying only $100 now.

The *dueño* said, "Let's just go see it. *Por favor* please go with me to tour the house. It can't hurt just to look at it. Maybe you will know someone else who would like to rent it." He added, "Oh, yes. For years I have been on the waiting list for a telephone. A phone will be installed in fifteen days."

155

We drove up to a "mansion" (or so it seemed to me, comparing it to our little bungalow). The house stood three stories tall, gray stucco with white trim, and with a full basement. Broad steps led up to the front porch and a beveled glass-and-wood front door. The grounds were *amplio,* spacious, all around the house. There was a detached shed for a garage. We entered the foyer. It was large, with a high ceiling reaching up to the attic. To our right, a door led into the maid's quarters, complete with a small bathroom. Farther down the hall, a swinging door opened into a large kitchen. On the back right corner, French doors revealed the dining room, where a sparkling chandelier hung over a beautiful table with ornately carved chairs for ten people.

To the left of the foyer was the *baño social,* guest bathroom, next to a large office. The back left corner, through French doors, included a large living room, nicely furnished, with a beautiful fireplace. More French doors led out to a back patio.

The upstairs consisted of three bedrooms, a large bathroom with an enormous tub, and the stairway to the attic, which was finished with two rooms under the eaves.

The basement seemed dry as could be with a nice cement floor; high, rectangular windows all around; and a wide entrance from the outside.

I walked away dazed! Although the house was gorgeous, I felt as if I would be pretending to be Cinderella if I lived in a place like that. I did not feel comfortable. Give me my cozy little cottage with its honeyed, warm, wood paneled walls, knotholes and all, and with its kerosene heater in the corner of the low-ceilinged dining room.

Joe left for a three-week trip to Quilpué, up near the capital. Home again on the first of May, he tried to spend extra time with Iván to assure him we were not a threat to him. "Please <u>tell</u> us when we do something you don't like," Joe repeated during many meals at our house. Iván, always moody, would be friendly one day, morose the next.

Even though we were trying so hard with Iván, we still prayed desperately for God to open a door for us to move. We drove to Concepción to look at houses. We drove to Los Ángeles to visit a home church where the leaders invited us to move there and for me to be pastor when Joe was away. A pastor farther south told Joe he planned to resign. Would Joe consider taking his church?

But nothing felt right. Nothing came together. Nothing gave us peace.

Then the *dueño* of the mansion-house came back saying he would take $150 per month for rent. Joe had been thinking and praying about the house as a possible Bible institute. If we did that, we could take the additional $50 rent out of our work account. The basement could be made into two classrooms....

Joe took Iván to see the house. Their enthusiasm grew — they could have classes on Monday, Wednesday, and Friday evenings, from 8 to 10 p.m. Iván could teach for an hour, then Joe. If Joe was away, I would teach.

Iván talked to his new church board (the Superintendent had insisted that he form a leadership committee). All three deacons were excited at the prospect.

Joe signed the agreement to rent the house.

Iván and Joe, along with the church board, set the opening date for the night classes: Monday, August 10. Almost every youth and adult in the church signed up to attend. These classes were not official Bible institute level; the people were way too unlearned for that. We would begin with Louisa J. Walker's *Nueva Vida en Cristo* and *La Biblia* ("New Life in Christ" and "The Bible"), elementary courses designed for local church use. They were excellently written and covered the basic tenets of Christianity.

The "mansion" Bible school, Temuco, Chile

When Joe came home at the end of June, he and Iván shopped for carpentry supplies to convert the basement into classrooms: lumber for studding, masonite for walls, electrical wiring, light fixtures, wood for the furniture.

No one was happier than our friend Segundo, one of the new deacons. The original congregation had formed in his and his wife Nena's living room, and he agonized over Ivan's treatment of us. But now, as carpenter, he skillfully built the desks and benches for the students. As he finished the furniture, sanding with care, he prayed for the students who would sit there and absorb the teaching.

One of our missionaries in Santiago even sent someone to help with the construction. Ron Robbins, a young intern with Missionary Placement Services (MAPS), hailed from Colorado. He worked really hard for the month he stayed with us.

One afternoon, the chandelier gleamed over the dining room table. Candles glowed. My best tablecloth provided a backdrop to the delicious goodies Dema and I had prepared. They included cupcakes dipped in whipped cream tinted in various pastel colors.

Ten women stood grouped at the French doors into the dining room. "Ooh," they gasped. A woman whispered softly, "It is just like the marriage supper of the Lamb will be in heaven!"

These women from church were so precious to me. They were considered "poor class," their coats were frayed and mended, their shoes had walked many a mile, their hands were rough, their nails uneven. Their clothes were clean, their hugs and kisses genuine, their love for me apparent through their shining eyes.

Whenever any kind of Women's Ministries event occurred in southern Chile, these women and I piled into the Suburban, eager to travel together. Sometimes we even stayed overnight, if the church was far away.

One Saturday, we went 'way down south to Máfil, a village with streets of mud, mud, and more mud. The little house where we met for the event felt cozy, with the kitchen woodstove serving both to warm the food and us. As was typical, the kitchen stove sat in the corner, away from the walls far enough to place picnic-style benches behind it. That's where we sat drinking our *mate* (mah-teh) green tea through the community straw. I didn't even try to wipe it off now.

Joe and I invited each of the rancher families over for dinner again. Also, we invited my beauty operator, Julia, and her husband. Julia had prayed with me in her shop, but that night after we finished dinner, Joe explained, clearly, the plan of salvation to her and her husband. Quietly, Julia asked, "Could we pray? I accepted Christ with my emotions the other day when Margaret prayed with me, now I want to make an intellectual decision." Her husband prayed, too, and while he asked Joe lots of questions, he was still a little uncertain about the reality of this new "salvation by faith."

Eight people came to stay overnight with us! Bob and Margaret were taking some American pastors from California on a grand tour of Chile. Margaret brought all the electric blankets she owned, and we had people "plugged in" all over that big house.

Dema cooked for fifteen people. Our money was really tight because we had paid the higher rent, bought all the Bible institute materials, and, in addition, we were feeding Ron and Iván. Dema figured that beef stew would probably be the cheapest. She could get a big bone to help season the broth, and potatoes, carrots, and onions were plentiful this time of year.

As the Californians left, Bob said, "We'll be back in three days, for supper and breakfast again."

I almost panicked. We did *not* have grocery money. Dema and I talked. The only thing we could afford was more beef stew.

Later, I overheard one of the men complain, "That woman fixed the same meal as before. Doesn't she realize she should have prepared something different?" He had no idea that some people did not have as much money as he did. He nonchalantly handed us $10 on his way out the door. I sure did wish he had given it to us after his first visit.

For Christy's eighth birthday on June 27, we invited the Missionettes for *once* tea. Christy also invited five girls from her class at school who would be sleeping-over. When Christy changed out of her pajamas Saturday morning, the girls noticed little red dots on her back and tummy—chicken pox! They call them *la peste crystal,* the crystal pest. (Timmy thought that was apt since Christy's name is really Crystal.)

Three weeks later, Timmy was down with chicken pox, too. Then we all took turns having a three-day intestinal virus.

I read to the children every night, but now, because they were sick, I read hour after hour. Fortunately, Mother continued to send us children's classics every month, this time stories by Hans Christian Andersen.

Joe's July meeting was 'way up north in Antofagasta in the Atacama Desert that extends into Peru; so close to the equator it is <u>hot</u> year around. The Chileans say it is so dry there the trees chase the dogs down the street! Joe and Bob stayed with Bruce and Audrey Manning, who had just returned from furlough, bringing with them a small black and white TV set for us.

Now Christy and Timmy could watch *Huckleberry Hound, Cheyenne, 77 Sunset Strip*, and *MeteOro*. The shows were dubbed into Spanish, but the theme music was the same. How on earth had the children stayed entertained for over a year now, in the rain, without television?

Joe and Bob alternated taking their cars to the revivals. So I could have a car sometimes! I was thrilled to drive to the post office. I pulled that big Suburban up toward the curb to parallel park. Most Chilean cars were Citroens or VW bugs. I backed in between two little cars, oops, pull forward, turn hard right, back in again. On my second attempt a crowd of men gathered to watch. On my third attempt, one man held up his hand in a "stop" sign, and motioned to his buddy. They opened the doors of the little car in front of my space, grabbed hold of the car frame, and scooted the car forward several feet. They dusted off their hands, and nodded to me. I parked, my face red. They were clapping and grinning. I guess taking the bus had its advantages.

In May, Joe and I filled out a volume of paperwork for our *permanencia* visa and sent it along with our passports to the government offices in Santiago. It would take three to six months for the paperwork to be completed.

It was a busy time. The Christian and Missionary Alliance asked Joe to speak for their Youth Week. Our neighbor boy attended and accepted the Lord. The Keswick Convention invited Joe to sing and play his sax. School chaplains Charles and Betty Alexander asked Joe to speak for Spiritual Emphasis Week at the children's Baptist school.

Surprisingly, Iván asked me to teach the Intermediate Sunday School class. Twelve adolescents trooped with me out the church door, down the gravel road, over the railroad tracks, across the canal, over the dirt street into the side room of a neighbor's house. Our room was furnished only with two backless benches against the walls and a bare light bulb suspended overhead. Thankfully the reverse side of my flannelgraph board was a chalkboard. The room was so cold I could hardly hold the chalk. My feet did not feel cold; they were numb as usual.

The class met me on Saturday mornings for "visitation" to other adolescents in the *barrio* neighborhood.

Iván also permitted me to begin two girls' clubs. The younger group was actually girls from my Sunday school class. The older girls helped me to implement ideas that I was diligently working on for the Missionettes handbook for the country. Any place I visited with our church women, I plied the local women for ideas. Mom mailed me material, too. By the end of July, the booklet was completed, and every women's group in southern Chile bought booklets, planning to form girls' clubs.

Iván was away one Sunday night and asked me to preach! I loved it. He asked me to speak at prayer meeting on a Thursday night, to the teachers on a Friday evening. Orlando asked me to speak to the youth on Saturday evening.

For the first Sunday evening of August, we planned a Missionettes initiation ceremony, with Iván's permission, of course. The girls were so excited. The nicest clothes they owned were school clothes, and for that reason they dressed in their knee socks, pleated skirts and blazers. Each girl held a candle. At the appropriate time, we would turn off the lights, the president would light one candle, and then, one by one, they would "share the light." We rehearsed and made holders for the candles to catch the wax. The girls memorized the Motto, the Pledge, and the Scripture. A couple of the girls practiced giving a brief testimony.

I didn't notice that Iván had not come in to tune his guitar just before service, as he usually did. Abruptly, at exactly service time, he rushed through the back doors and up to the front of the church.

"Are there any sinners here?" he asked in a loud voice. "I said, 'Are there any sinners here?' Raise your hand. Raise your hand if you are a sinner. If there are not ten sinners here, we are dismissing church and going out to the streets to preach."

One man actually, timidly, raised his hand. "See!" declared Iván. "Only one sinner. Everybody stand up. Church is dismissed. Everyone go outside to the street corner. We are going out to look for sinners."

My girls' faces turned pale; they were stricken, astonished. The unlit candles drooped in their hands; tears filled their eyes.

"Some of you stay here and pray," shouted Iván as he hurried out the door into the rain.

My mouth hung open. I could not *believe* what I had just witnessed! How could he do that to these girls? I did not budge from where I sat. I was so stunned, I couldn't even comfort the girls as they filed out one by one. I stayed seated and I prayed, all right. For "**a**" sinner. One stupid, ignorant, dumb, hateful, hurtful sinner. "God, are you listening? How could he do that! God, how could you let him do that to these girls!?"

When I arrived home, still fuming, I looked at the thermometer, 33 degrees, just perfect weather for a street meeting in the rain. Uuuuuuuh....

I felt like St. Paul shipwrecked on the island of Malta. The islanders had gathered near the bonfire to hear him speak. But there was a snake hidden in the firewood. We, too, felt shipwrecked, alone. We wanted to escape. But we didn't have a boat. We wouldn't know where to go even if we had a boat. We, too, found a snake hidden here, though we thought the snake had been tamed. On the contrary, it bit us. Again. These people loved and needed us. But the snake prevented us from helping them. The snake slithered just out of grasp, hissing, tormenting.

Our only Bible in those days was the King James Version, and my tears stained Lamentations chapter 3.

"He hath led me and brought me into darkness ... He hath hedged me about, that I cannot get out; he hath made my chain heavy ... When I cry and shout, he shutteth out my prayer. He hath enclosed my ways with hewn stone ...

"This I recall to my mind; therefore have I hope. It is because of the Lord's mercies that we are not consumed, because his compassions fail not. They are new every morning; great is thy faithfulness ... The Lord is good unto those who wait for him ... It is good that a man should both hope and quietly wait for the salvation of the Lord."

It was hard to maintain hope. It was hard to believe in God's faithfulness when God's hand was hidden.

The cold rain beat relentlessly against the big, cold house. The chill in my heart deepened as I slid in my emotions from joy to despair, prey to Iván's mood swings.

The month of August would be the month from hell.

14

Changing

Temuco, Chile
August 1970

❦

he winds of change blew across Chile. Presidential elections loomed. Of the three candidates for President, two were from the traditional parties, one of them with the slogan, "Go home, Yankees." He assured the public that as soon as he was elected on September 4, he would send the foreigners packing.

The third candidate was Salvador Allende, a Communist and a leftist. He was much more radical. His chant was "Death to the Imperialists." His campaign promise was that every Chilean would have a job, a house, and milk for his children. Allende ranted, "Rich land owners will own the land no more. You, the common man, will own the land. All wealth will be shared equally. Why should the wealthy have 'things' when you do without? Vote for me and we will take the riches from the rich. We will send the Yankees home."

For me, it was very hard to be considered "rich," but we were— —we owned a car, a refrigerator, and used a kitchen stove. My church friends had none of these. The women cooked over a *brasero* (charcoals in a shallow pan). One Monday, at our Women's Ministries meeting, I put the equivalent of a quarter in the offering. When the treasurer counted the offering, she called me over, certain that I'd put it in by mistake. To the other women, five cents was a large offering. They usually gave a half-cent or a three-cent coin. I was embarrassed to be so rich.

When Joe and Bob had been in Antofagasta (up north in the hot desert), they had stumbled upon a demonstration downtown. Youths were carrying a black casket on their shoulders, chanting, waving, and shouting. Joe could not understand exactly what was being shouted, and asked someone what was happening. "These are Allende's supporters. They are shouting, 'Death to the Yankee Imperialists.' The casket is to carry the dead Yankees."

Allende secretly told his followers to hoard things so that he could appear benevolent by providing great amounts of food to his constituents immediately following his victory. So, during August, suddenly there was a shortage of groceries. We went to buy flour. "*No hay* (pronounced no-eye), there is none." Cooking oil. "*No hay.*" Sugar. "*No hay.*" Potatoes. "*No hay.*" Cabbage. "*No hay.*"Dema could purchase only a very small amount of necessities by going daily, from vendor to vendor. Our menu consisted of whatever she found. (Being a *Yankee,* I could purchase nothing at all.)

Our landlord was scared. Our missionary friends were scared. If Allende were elected, how much time would "wealthy" people have before they would have to flee for their lives? The director of the children's school received anonymous phone calls in the middle of the night saying, "Go home, Yankees."

But we had to admire the Chilean sense of humor: a newspaper cartoon depicted a truck filled with large jugs of wine being unloaded into a man's basement. The caption read, "They say we must store necessities for the tough times ahead."

Another cartoon showed a man in a suit talking to a man in jogging clothes. The caption, "Is there anything to the rumor I heard about you wanting to leave the country as fast as possible?"

The children felt the tension. Christy's grades dropped: one B, two C's, and two D's. One of the D's was in math, which she found especially difficult, as everything had to be calculated in Spanish. She finally learned the multiplication tables: *tres por tres son nueve,* written 3.3=9. During August, she began long division, in Spanish.

Calculating mentally, the students wrote down only the remainder of each step. Christy began to study fractions, too.

Christy's other D was in History—Chilean history. She did not know the national anthem by memory or the meaning of the colors in the flag. Neither could she name the great liberators.

Timmy's teacher told Dema to send me in for a conference because Timmy was getting into fights at school. Joe had spanked him before leaving on a trip and Timmy was fine for a week, according to the teacher, but now, he had bloodied another kid's nose.

And both children began to lie. Doing this is common in Latin culture. It was not acceptable to us.

Just before a three-week postal strike, when we could not get our financial statements from the Mission or family news, Mom wrote that she was going to the hospital for a lumpectomy.

Mom also wrote that Grandma Bessie had died. (Jan and I had lived with her for two years, while Mom and Dad traveled in evangelistic work.) Christy composed a poem in memory of Great-Grandma entitled, "O Besy, O Besy, I love you, Besy." Timmy wrote a song, "When you walk to the mailbox, there is no letter."

Twinkie died, too. Mom sent pictures of her grave, and of the neighborhood children putting flowers beside a wooden headstone. Our children cried. They loved Twinkie, the Chihuahua.

When the postal strike ended, there was good news: Mom's biopsy was negative; Jan and Barry were poised to adopt a baby; and the house across the street from Mom and Dad was for sale. Dad had already made an offer on it, had been accepted, and had paid the down payment—for us! They would lend us the money until we could pay them back. In the meantime, Dad would find renters for the house, to make the monthly mortgage payments.

I heard a knock on the side door, and then Dema's footsteps as she came to get me. There stood a young man that I recognized from the week before. He had come begging and Joe had invented a job for him in the yard. Now, the young man said, "I came to finish cleaning out the basement as I promised I would." I didn't know anything about it. "But I promised your husband last week. He said he would give me a shirt, if I came back today to finish the job." I didn't know of any shirts that Joe would want to give away. "Please, señora, you don't even have to give me the shirt today, I will return for it. But I gave my word. I want to keep my promise to your husband."

I relented and opened the basement door. A few minutes later he was gone. So were as many tools as he could stuff under his coat! He had seen Timmy playing in the yard and had asked if his dad was home. When Timmy said no, the beggar knocked on the door. Later, through the years, we would have lots of con-artists come calling. But I had learned my lesson well!

Joe came home for overnight, just long enough for me to wash and iron his clothes before we headed to a Ministers' Retreat in Concepción. I was looking forward to the Retreat. For one thing, it would help take my mind off of last Sunday and the Missionettes' non-event.

We registered, found our room, and went to the dining hall. Sylvia and Leonardo Riquelme motioned for us to join them. We admired their new baby and talked and laughed together. Sylvia was my number one helper with the Missionettes booklet and we always "connected" on a true friendship level. The men wandered off, as Sylvia and I continued to sit, talking.

"Margarita," she asked, "when you go to the market, how do you know who the other missionary wives are?" I didn't understand what she was trying to say. "How do I know the wives from other missions groups?" I asked. "*Sí*, the other North American missionary wives," she persisted. I looked perplexed as she continued, "By their clothes, no? They dress like you do—old fashioned. Tacky. Anyone can recognize a missionary wife immediately because they look so pitiful."

I was shocked silent! "Margarita, you don't have to dress so unstylish. Here in Chile we have wonderful *modistas,* seamstresses, who will make for you very beautiful clothes for a very economical price. Please go to a *modista.* Let her measure you, let her make you modern clothes." For the first time, I looked at Sylvia's clothes and then at mine. She wore a woolen blazer, nice turtleneck sweater, and a straight skirt—above her knees. I wore clothes from high school and college days with a long, gathered skirt. I wore loafers. Sylvia wore stylish boots. "That's another thing. The shoes," she continued. "Go to a shoe shop. They will measure your feet and make you beautiful leather boots."

So much for non-stressful friendships.

At this Annual Ministers' Retreat I soon learned that "retreat" was not an apt term. "Advance toward the Registers" would have been a truer title. Because, the next morning, church officials convened a special business session. We were not included until a man came to summon us. "You are requested to appear at the meeting." Joe asked me to accompany him, in view of the fact that it was probably Iván-related. Joe told me to wait outside in the hallway until he called for me.

I sat on a cold bench against the wooden wall of a wide hallway. The meeting room had a transom, opened, so I could hear everything.

"Brother Register, we have called you to ask you questions," began the Superintendent, Hermano Morales.

Tomás S., an influential pastor of a large church in Concepción, (where Joe had not been invited for a revival) interrupted, "Brother Register is disrupting the work in Temuco. I know from my friend Iván that Brother Register is trying to begin a Bible institute. No one wants it. He is going against the express wishes of the pastor and the church members."

Hermano Morales replied softly, "The church board is in favor of the Bible institute. They have given their endorsement."

Tomás, loudly: "Then why are other churches not invited to send students? Why is Brother Register trying to keep it only for Temuco, who doesn't even want it?"

Morales, softly: "It is just a local church endeavor. A night Bible school. The distance is too great for other cities to be invited at this time."

Tomás, more loudly: "Why hasn't the president of the Bible institute in Santiago been down to Temuco to organize it?"

The president of the Bible institute spoke up, matter-of-factly: "This new school is on an elementary level. It has nothing to do with the institute in Santiago at this point."

A missionary colleague from Santiago, *C.*, said loudly: "Tomás is right! Joe should not be trying to start a school in Temuco. It is easy to see the church there does not want or need it."

I could not believe my ears! *C.* had endorsed the Bible institute when he had talked to us. He had even sent Ron down to help with the construction of the rooms! My world was spinning upside down!

C. continued, loudly: "Joe should just get out. Get out of Iván's town!"

C. had encouraged us to stay! He had told us how important it was for us to be in southern Chile!

Tomás continued: "We do not want Joe here. He should leave. He should give us his car. He should leave his typewriter to Iván. We do not need Yankees in southern Chile. We do not want Yankee missionaries here in the south."

Tomás turned to Joe, "I resent your foreign ideas. Go home, Yankee!" he yelled, spittle flying.

Tears ran down my cheeks, I shook from the cold and from the shock of it all. My teeth chattered, my knees danced up and down.

Tomás and Iván were allied against us. A missionary colleague had betrayed us. And our soft-spoken Superintendent was very soft-spoken that day—too weak to be able to help us.

As soon as we arrived home from the Retreat, we packed to leave for Santiago for the first Missionary Field Fellowship meeting. We would take the train up on Friday, have meetings all day Saturday and take the train back to Temuco on Sunday. The Bible institute classes were scheduled to begin on Monday evening.

Scarcely had the business meeting begun, when *C.* said forcefully, "Write in the minutes, 'It is unanimously agreed that the Registers should move out of Temuco.'" Silence.

Joe spoke up to explain that we would probably need to move at some point. We did not know how things would be when we returned. Joe continued, "Hermano Morales told me privately that he wants to remove Iván."

"No!" roared *C.*, "If he does that, all the Chileans will take Iván's side. There will be an explosion against all missionaries!"

My stomach felt tied in knots. I was glad to get on the train to head home to Temuco.

Monday morning dawned cold and rainy. Mid-morning, a knock sounded on the front door. There stood the three deacons. They wore solemn looks on their faces.

We invited them into the living room, where we had a fire in the fireplace, and offered them something to drink.

So softly we could hardly hear him, Segundo said. "We have sad news. Last night at church Iván announced a continuous revival beginning tonight. He said the revival would last for a minimum of five weeks. Then Iván said, 'No, the revival will last until Jesus comes. We do not need education. Sinners are going to hell and you people want to sit around studying. We do not need to study. My friend, Pastor Tomás, says we do not need education, we need only revival.'"

Earlier, when the deacons and Joe and Iván had made plans to begin the institute, there was one loophole: all classes would be suspended in the event of a revival.

Segundo whispered, "What do we do now? I have run interference for Iván for months, making excuses for him to church members. I am sick of it. I am through with him."

Joe suggested that Segundo call the Superintendent. He picked up our new phone. The Superintendent said he would come to Temuco for a meeting on Thursday evening at our house with the deacons, Iván and us. He said for Segundo to inform Iván of the meeting.

Segundo told us later that Iván was *furioso,* furious, when he was told to appear at the meeting. Segundo said, "He spewed venom all over me, telling me 'Don't you dare try to put me out of this church!' And, 'I hate the sight of the Registers. I am going everywhere telling everyone I meet about them. I will see to it that they never go anywhere, ever again, as missionaries.'"

Thursday came.

Once again, we met beside the fireplace. Hermano Morales asked softly, "Iván, will you leave Temuco?"

"No! A thousand times no. I was here first, I will not leave!" Iván exclaimed tersely, bitterly.

Joe spoke, "Hermano Morales, I will leave."

"I am sorry for you to have to leave," Hermano Morales said, "But the church will split if you stay."

Iván interrupted, "Tell him to leave me his things—his car and his typewriter. And to give me money." He motioned around the room, "This mansion he is renting for $500 a month—that much money would build me a new church!"

The deacons did not say one word. The meeting was adjourned.

Joe left for his next revival, up in central Chile.

I cried myself to sleep—as I did night after night after night. My heart seemed frozen in my chest.

I attended church on Sunday. Iván, of course, would not look at me.

Monday, I did not go to the women's meeting. A knock sounded on the front door. All the women had come to me! They came into the living room; they stood clustered around me, crying. Begging me to stay. To form another church. They would all attend. There was room, here, in the house. We could start Sunday. Please stay. I reached out to hug each woman. We formed a circle, arms around each other, and cried together.

Later that afternoon, the deacons came to apologize. I had been really disappointed in them for not speaking up in the confrontation with Iván. But they stated that nothing they could have said would have made any difference. Segundo cried, actually sobbed, telling me how much he loved us and how sorry he was for Iván's demeanor. He said the church people noted our attitude and admired us even more.

That night, after crying myself to sleep, I was awakened about three a.m. by a phone call—an obscene phone call. I was petrified. What if the caller knew where I lived? What if he knew Joe was out of town?

Scared, alone, I thought I would die of disillusionment—the deep disappointment caused by my destroyed ideal. All my aspirations crushed. My joy and hope for meaningful ministry buried underneath one man's hatred. I talked to God out loud and clearly,

"God, I will stay the remainder of this missionary term. But I will *never* return!"

August bled into September. In the Presidential election on September 4, Allende received the most votes but did not have a majority. The Congress did not know what to do. They decided to hold a special session on October 24 to make some kind of decision. The new president was scheduled to assume power on November 4 for a six-year term.

Wealthy people packed suitcases, preparing to leave quickly in the event the Communists took the government by force. There was talk of a military coup to prevent the Communists from taking over. People were scared. No one spoke on the streets. The newspaper called it "calm panic." Everyone believed there would be fighting. All air flights out of the country were booked solid.

Joe came home. He and Bob had cancelled the revival. It was too dangerous to meet publicly.

In case we had to evacuate, we told the children to choose a favorite toy or book to hand-carry. Joe told me to pack a small bag with essentials, all we'd be allowed to take in the event the U.S. military evacuated us.

Timmy had been sick for two weeks and had finished a round of antibiotics. But on September 6, I called the doctor. Timmy was still pale, listless, feverish, without an appetite, vomiting. The doctor said he would come to the house. His diagnosis: Timmy had viral spinal meningitis. The doctor prescribed gamma globulin and total bed rest. Christy became ill, too, but with a mild case. For Christy the doctor also prescribed a "tonic" to help her gain weight.

At 10:30 that night, the phone rang. It was Juan Toro. Bob had been arrested. Prepare to evacuate. The line went dead.

We were panic-stricken. We'd sent our passports to the government office in Santiago for our visas. We could not leave without documents. The children were sick in bed. I shook from fear.

Joe searched for the phone number for Melvin Hodges, our Missions Director, in Missouri. Should Joe call him now, in the middle of the night? Or wait until we had more details from Juan?

Had Juan called the other missionaries? Should we call our embassy friends tonight? Or wait until morning?

At 10:45 the phone rang again. It was Juan. Joe listened, shook his head, and said, "Juan, that is not *chistoso,* funny. This is not a funny joke." Bob and Juan were pulling a joke on Joe. Bob, laughing, took the phone, talked to Joe, and then he stopped his chatter. He apologized profusely for trying to joke about such a serious matter. He was truly sorry.

The next day Joe called the Superintendent to consult with him about our leaving Temuco as soon as possible and moving to central Chile near the Bowdens.

Then Joe left by train for Viña to look for a house.

It was during these days that José Carter died. I looked down at his body lying in the crude casket, eyes half-opened, stubble of growth on his chin, fluid dripping from a partially opened mouth. Just the way I felt. Stripped of dignity. Wretched. Cold. Lifeless.

The mansion became a mausoleum where I sat alone with my heart cold and my dreams dead.

15

Transition to Viña del Mar, Chile

(pronounced veen-yah thel mahr)
September, October, November 1970

The cold rain of Temuco blew in my face as I stood in the doorway with Christy and Timmy watching Joe and Bob load the last boxes into our Suburbans.

The children's viral meningitis was cured—thanks to the medication and to prayer. By "international long distance," which was extremely expensive, we had called Mom and Dad and they in turn had called everyone they knew to pray.

When Joe found a house in Viña available on September 25, he called to tell me to start packing.

Joe shoved the refrigerator one more time. It lay on its side, next to the washer and dryer in the back of our Chevy Suburban. With a grunt, Bob loaded the last box into his Suburban. John Mazurek had already left with a full load in his Suburban.

Everything we owned was in those three vehicles.

I walked out the door of the mansion-house, climbed up into the car and shut the door. I was relieved to be leaving Temuco, and yet I was deeply sad. The only thing I could compare to "being a missionary" was giving birth to a baby—no one told you the pain would be so intense. And even if they had, there was nothing you could have done about it.

There was no going away *once* (own-say), tea, as was customary. No goodbyes at the church. No closure.

"You are gonna love the new house in Viña," Joe said repeatedly on our two-day trip north on the Pan American highway. "You will be so happy there. The ocean is only three blocks away. Of course, you can't see it because of all the high-rises, but you can walk down there whenever you want. Everything will be great, Margaret, you'll see."

On and on he babbled, trying to assure me that I would soon be fine. I wanted to tell him to shut up. Things would not be fine. A different house would not heal my hurt. Moving would not erase my memories. Another town would not take away my sense of failure. Being near friends would not eliminate our enemies.

Being a missionary wasn't supposed to be like this. Leading others to faith in Christ was joyous for them and for me. The potential existed. The love in my heart existed. The opportunity existed. But the door had been shut. Tight. By human beings. Religious leaders. Men influenced by the political climate and by jealousy and envy and hate.

As I stared out the side window into the rain and fog, I prayed silently for God to "help me make it through the rest of this term. Just get me through this next year-and-a-half, Lord." The hope of not having to continue as a missionary consoled me. It gave me the strength to mark off one more day.

We arrived in Viña and I walked through the door of our new house. I did not love it. I did not hate it. I did not care. I was hollow. Brittle. Plastic. Some saint I'd turned out to be!

The landlady had met us with the key. Joe walked into the hallway with me, but then turned left into the living room. He exclaimed, "What on earth?! This is not the furniture that was here when I rented this house! You changed the furniture!"

The landlady said sarcastically, "Well, I couldn't leave good things for renters. And I cannot be out of the garage, either, for at least another month. My clients are counting on me for the uniforms we sew in there."

As she and Joe argued in Spanish, getting louder and louder, I turned away with tears in my eyes. I wandered through the dining room and kitchen and then slowly climbed the stairs. Upstairs I found four bedrooms and two bathrooms arranged around a large open hallway surrounding the stairwell. A door led to a flat-roofed patio over the garage.

I went through the motions of settling in. The weather was great, "Mediterranean," everyone said, warm days, cool nights. The scenery was beautiful, everyone said, the rocky coastline zigzagging against the roaring Pacific Ocean. I barely noticed.

The Bowden girls attended the British School, and Joe had already enrolled Christy there. Connie and Jeanne said it was "hard," that the British system was extremely strict, but they had enrolled at the beginning of the school year (March) and had adjusted well. There was a fairly strong anti-American sentiment, but once the teachers and students got to know you, they weren't too harsh.

Christy began classes the first of October with only nine weeks left before summer vacation. We met her British teacher, "Miss Margaret." She seemed to understand the implication of Christy's having attended an all-Spanish school for nearly two years.

From the first day, Christy hated school. The kids' cliques were well formed by then, even in third grade. Christy could not calculate math in English; her multiplication tables had been memorized in Spanish. She did not know English grammar rules. She began to cry and *beg* not to go to school. We figured she would soon adjust.

After several weeks, Christy would curl in a fetal position of a morning, lying on her bed, "Please, Mommie, don't make me go to that school today. Please. *Please.*"

Dark circles formed under her eyes. She would hardly eat. Surely she would adjust any day now. But every day seemed to be worse to her than the last.

Joe and I went to consult with "Miss Margaret" and she actually apologized to us in her British English! "I have been too hard on Crystal. I forced her to stand in front of the class to recite her multiplication tables. She could not do it in English. The children laughed at her and called her stupid. I was wrong."

But the apology came too late for Christy. Her self-esteem bottomed out. Her identity floundered in total confusion. We had forced her into a *Spanish* school and then, in the middle of the school year, into a *British* school. I feared she would have a nervous break-down at eight years of age.

Thankfully, summer arrived and, as she began to recover, we promised her she would not be sent back there next year. I would home-school her and Timmy. She would be in the fourth grade and Timmy in first grade.

Meanwhile, Timmy was having his own problems. He played with Juan José and Marcelo, two neighbor boys. One day Timmy came home crying his heart out. Marcelo had told him his name was stupid, that absolutely no one was named *Timoteo*, Timothy. Only cats had that name.

I asked Timmy what would be a good name. "Not *Timi* (tee-mee) but *Jimi* (gee-mee). Marcelo said *Jimi* is good. <u>Please</u>, can I change my name to *Jimi?*" So, in Spanish we always called him "Jimmy" (Gee-mee) and everyone in Viña calls him "Jimmy" to this day.

The political climate continued to crackle with tension. For forty years Chile had been the only country in Latin America to have a stable, multi-party political system. Allende had received only 36.2% of the votes; Alessandri, on the right, 35%; and centrist Tomic, 27.8%. Congress decided to honor the election, even though Allende had not won a majority of votes. This democratic election of a Marxist sent shock waves around the world.

Eagerly, Allende's supporters anticipated October 24, when he would be ratified. They planned an armed struggle if neces-sary followed by a nationwide celebration for his inauguration on November 3.

A deep polarization formed with all conservatives and moderates uniting to try to prevent Allende's Marxist party, the *Unidad Popular (UP)*, from assuming power. There was a botched kidnap attempt on October 22 when General René Schneider, the commander-in-chief of the army and military police, the *Carabineros*, was assassinated.

We were under curfew. Everyone was sure there would be more bloodshed. But we could not leave; we still did not have our passports.

Joe and Bob repeatedly visited the government offices in Santiago trying to obtain our passports and *permanencia,* permanent visa papers. Finally, the last of October, we received our passports back but not the visa.

Joe and Bob left for Vallenar on October 29 but had to cancel the revival after only a few tension-filled days.

All of the evangelical leaders in Viña and Valpo were invited to meet with the local *UP* communist party leaders. We were assured that we would not be forced to leave immediately if we did not get involved in any way with politics.

The U.S. Diplomatic Corps was poised to pull out of the country. The U.S. Air Force and Navy set a departure date for November 11 but were ready to leave at a moment's notice. Since many of the military personnel were stationed in Viña, we were able to buy canned goods, peanut butter, Crisco, and boxes of cereal from them, but we wondered if we would stay in Chile long enough to enjoy these goodies.

Meanwhile, Bob and Margaret were as nice as they could be. Bob had apologized profusely to Joe about the "joke" of saying he was arrested. So had Juan Toro. Of course, they had no idea when they told the joke that the phone connection would be cut before they could explain it.

When we invited the Bowdens and Toros over for dinner, we met Juan's parents, his sister Gloria, and his fiancée, Julia. We loved them all and they loved us.

Our relationship with the Bowdens was peaceful and reassuring. Joe and Bob had only one disagreement the entire time we worked together—and it was because they each wanted to cede a position of honor to the other.

Margaret would call and say, "I have some pinto beans and corn-bread. Wanna come over?"

I would call her and say, "There's a ladies' *once* tea on Saturday. Wanna go?"

Margaret was content being a "missionary's wife." She cooked and shopped and looked after her girls, Connie and Jeanne. I, on the other hand, was a **missionary** wife." I wanted to be involved in the work, teaching children, holding Bible clubs, forming girls' clubs, working with the women.

Christy loved to spend the night with Connie and Jeanne, and they spoiled Timmy rotten. The four of them, along with Timmy's friends, dressed up for Halloween and trick-or-treated at our two houses.

The men had scheduled a revival over Thanksgiving week, not realizing the date. So the kids and I went to Margaret's. Timmy thought Thanksgiving was a dumb holiday without either costumes or gifts. So the girls dressed him up as an American Indian.

We ate our chicken, dressing, mashed potatoes and real pumpkin pie (canned pumpkin from the military purchases). It was quiet and sad for Margaret and me, her first Thanksgiving in Chile.

The children, of course, did not have a Thanksgiving holiday from the British school, so they needed to make up work. We had to go to the school because the teacher would not give the girls their assignments.

Chilito (chee-lee-toe), a long, skinny puppy—a Miniature Dachshund—followed Timmy everywhere. We bought the puppy within a couple of weeks of moving—we'd had to leave the German shepherd in Temuco and the kids really missed having a pet. The Dachshund reminded us of Chile, being so long and narrow, so we named him Chilito, little Chile. Chilito's legs were so short, and he was so close to the floor that when he sneezed his chin would hit the floor, whump.

As we came in from church one night, I told the children to change into their pajamas. But when I went to check on Timmy, he was sitting on the bed playing with Chilito. I said, "I told you to get your PJs on," and I reached over and swatted him on the bottom.

Chilito lunged at me, snapping and growling; he jumped off the bed attacking me! I screamed and backed into the corner. Joe came running in to see what was happening. He stood at the doorway looking at me in the corner with the dog baring his teeth and snapping, and Joe burst into laughter. He laughed until tears rolled down his cheeks. I didn't think it was so funny.

After that, I could never discipline Timmy without first locking up Chilito. He followed Timmy around like Timmy was King and he was the loyal servant.

Chilito's favorite sleeping spot was underneath Timmy's blanket. Chilito knew he was not supposed to be up on the bed. He had his own orange-crate bed on the floor. But he would sneak under the covers and when he heard me coming, he'd try really fast to get out and jump into his bed. But he was so long that he couldn't make it before I came in fussing at both "boys."

The last of October, Bob came to our house bringing a baby duck named *Tito* (tee-toe). Bob put Tito on the floor, and Chilito smelled him. Timmy took a step, Tito followed, then Chilito. It was so funny—except Tito took a step and pooped, then step, poop. For three weeks the parade continued, never varying—boy, duck, dog— until we gave the duck away to Marcelo. Since he was so good at changing names, he could decide what to name the dumb duck.

Audrey and Bruce Manning invited Joe and me to Antofagasta for ten days, where Joe could preach and I could rest. Christy was delighted to stay at the Bowden's house and Timmy wanted to stay with Chilito and Dema at our house.

The Mannings were so sweet to us. Audrey planned a women's *once* tea to make me feel welcome. She wanted to begin Missionettes clubs for the girls up north.

Audrey and Bruce had three children—Becky, 13; David, 12; and Teresa, 9. The older two were adopted. One day the three kids were playing outside when Teresa, crying "big ole tears," came running to her mom. "They said you didn't choose me. That you *had* to take me. It's not fair. I want to be adopted, too." Audrey showed Teresa in the Bible where we are all adopted children of God, and Teresa ran back out to play. "Ha, ha, ha," Audrey could hear her say. "I'm adopted, too, ha, ha."

I felt sure that as soon as Joe and I left Temuco Iván would settle down. However, his friend Tomás was elected District Presbyter and the two of them called a special Southern District meeting to request that all Yankee missionaries be forced to leave the country immediately. Iván further stated from the floor that if any missionary should ever be allowed back into the country, he should serve under the local pastor for a minimum of one year.

Iván told the people at the meeting that Joe was not capable of being anything except an evangelist, that he had never pastored (not true) and therefore he had to travel around. "In fact," Iván said, "Joe and Bob think they are the 'Department of Evangelism' but they are actually the 'Department of Tourism.'" (*Departamento de Evangelismo, Departamento de Turismo*)

Hermano Morales, the Superintendent, attended the meeting. The fervor was so acrimonious that he subsequently wrote a letter to our mission, requesting that all missionaries leave!

This time, I was not the only one in despair. Joe and Bob were discouraged, both of them in low spirits. They were not wanted by the national church, not wanted by the government, the tent was stuck in New York and even if it could be shipped, how on earth could they use it now? Due to inflation and political fears, our salary purchase power had been cut in half. And at our house, we had school problems and demon-landlady problems.

We received a letter telling us to attend an International Missionary Retreat—the first of its kind, to be held December 28–January 1 in Buenos Aires, Argentina.

Though it was still a month away, we made plans to ride with the Bowdens across the Andes Mountains to Mendoza, Argentina, and on to Buenos Aires.

Melvin Hodges, our boss, would be at the Retreat. Would he remember us? Could we talk to him?

No one but Joe knew I still cried on his shoulder night after night. No one knew how hollow I felt. No one knew the hurt I harbored, the pain that still penetrated my heart. I smiled on the outside and went through the motions of living. But the cold remained inside me. The cold that could not be warmed by the warmer climate of Viña.

16

Transformation

Viña del Mar, Chile
December 1970

" *Hey, Mom, look at this one.* The green spray paint is more even." I looked at the only Christmas trees available—a broomstick pole with bottle brushes sticking out the sides. We decorated our "tree" and the kids made streamers to drape across the living room.

Christy opened her gifts—a pink, stuffed dog and a doll. Timmy opened his gifts—a navy blue windbreaker, and a figure-8 racetrack. (Joe bought it from U.S. military personnel who were evacuating.) I opened our five Christmas cards—from Mom, Joe's Mom, Aunt Too, Aunt Ella, and Anna Schloe, who sent one for the Women's Missionary Council in Pensacola.

During the hot December summer we celebrated Timmy's sixth birthday and the children opened a lemonade stand in front of the Bowdens' house. No customers, just lots of smiles at this "foreign" idea.

We received exciting news from home: after trying for seven years to have a baby, my sister Jan and her husband Barry decided to adopt. A friend at church had adopted a baby through an attorney specializing in "independent adoptions." Jan and Barry made an appointment.

The attorney pulled out several folders. "Let's see," he began, "here's a preemie … um … no, you don't want her. She's too expensive." He discarded the folder. "Here's another one—"

"Wait, wait a minute," interrupted Barry. "What do you mean when you say that one," he pointed to the folder lying on the desk, "is too expensive?"

The attorney tapped the folder with his finger. "This baby girl is a preemie. She weighed 2 pounds 4 ounces when she was born on October 2. She is still in Baptist Hospital here in Pensacola. But— and this is the problem—other families have wanted her, too, but her hospital bill is extraordinarily high."

"How much?" asked Jan. She could not believe the answer! That much money would buy several new cars!

"However," continued the attorney, "since she is almost five pounds, almost ready to be released, the hospital would probably be willing to reduce the bill, if you would make monthly payments."

Jan and Barry looked at each other, nodding. "We'll take her!" affirmed Barry.

"How soon can we get the baby?" questioned Jan.

"I'll call you as soon as the hospital lets me know she has reached five pounds," said the attorney.

Jan decorated a bedroom as a nursery; several women gave her a baby shower; and she called the attorney every day.

On December 11, Jan and Barry watched a nurse carry a tiny bundle into the waiting room. "It is the dress I brought," thought Jan. "This must be our baby!" She held out her arms to receive her daughter. It was their first glimpse of the baby.

The hospital nursery staff had called the tiny baby girl Becky, and they were sad to see her leave. These nurses had been her sole caregivers for ten weeks, since the moment of her birth when her biological teenage mother could not care for her. Without their love and nursing skills, this little girl would not have lived. Several of the nurses, with tears in their eyes, rode the elevator down with Jan and Barry and even went out to the car with them.

Kimberly Renee Hammac weighed exactly five pounds. Kimmy was so tiny that her new daddy, Barry, and my brother David could hold her in one hand.

I told the story to Christy and Timmy. Their eyes glistened; their faces glowed. They wanted to go to the States right then to see their new cousin. They begged me to tell them the story over and over. "Once upon a time, a tiny, little baby girl was born...."

Dema left us. Her parents were elderly and she used that as an excuse to return to Temuco, but I knew she was not happy in Viña. She was Mapuche Indian and they were "supposed to live in the south." Unfortunately, Dema felt the prejudice at the market and even at church.

Mestizos and Europeans lived in this central zone where the Conquistadors had radically altered the population; but the Conquistadors had never been able to penetrate the southern zone around Temuco. The Mapuche were very proud of never having been conquered by the Spanish, French, or Portuguese.

Without Dema, I felt as if I'd lost my right arm! As cook, house cleaner, and babysitter, she gave constancy and love to the children for almost a year and a half. I was never exactly "friends" with Dema; she was timid and not well educated. But she was like one of my kids and I missed her terribly.

Finding a replacement for Dema turned out to be a challenge. First I hired a nice, older, Christian woman, part-time. She was so old that she couldn't go up and down the stairs. Then I hired a young woman from an orphanage. She ironed my stockings, burning a hole in them. She scorched Joe's best shirt. And her cooking! I asked her to bake a cake—it turned out so bad, she hid it under the cabinet. I asked her to make slaw—she grated the cabbage and then dumped it into the dishwater to wash it.

Then I hired Isabel. She was 50-ish, made the children mind, and was a good cook. She had been a little snippy to me but I tried to ignore it. Until one morning when she came to me and said, caustically, "Did it <u>occur</u> to you, señora, to bring in the laundry last night, since it was supposed to rain?" I answered, "No, it did not <u>occur</u> to me, but it does <u>occur</u> to me that this is your last day. Good-bye."

Then Blanca came ... and she was a much better helper than the other three.

Allende's inauguration was celebrated riotously for two days, and then his UP party undertook the replacement of government employees one by one. Meanwhile, people waited anxiously for their job and their house that Allende had promised them. He reduced the price of milk, which helped the poor, but the farmers did not break even.

Squatters began to seize land. They would move onto a property, put up a Chilean flag, and proclaim it "a *toma*"—theirs.

As Allende began to socialize the economy, he nationalized the very profitable copper mines in the far north and ousted the American companies, Kennecott and Anaconda.

Owners of *fundos,* large farms, were nervous because farm workers became emboldened and threatened to take over. *Patrones*, landowners, fled the country, leaving a foreman in charge of businesses and farms.

We attended a specially-called missionary meeting in Santiago. All missionaries were scared and ready to evacuate at a moment's notice. We agreed that it would be extremely dangerous to mention politics in any way in any public setting and that we must exchange money only at the government banks and keep the receipts. Also, we must begin to pay rent only in *escudos*, not dollars.

Joe and Bob agonized over what to do about the tent. It was paid for and had been shipped to New York City. The Christian agency in Chile had been working with the prior government to clear the tent through customs and was now working with the Allende government officials. One day the guys were told, "Yes, bring it on in"; the next day, it was "No, wait." They knew that every tiny detail had to be correct on the paperwork before the tent was shipped overseas. Joe and Bob decided that if it was cleared on the Chilean end, and if the paperwork was completed in New York, they would go ahead and have it shipped. We realized that actually being able to *use* the tent would be an entirely different matter.

Joe and Bob taught a youth seminar in Santiago and then held a week's meeting at a Lutheran church in Viña for Pastor Joseph. The year before, Joseph's children had been killed in an accident, and a month later, his wife died. He really appreciated Joe and Bob and valued their friendship. One of the men who gave his life to Christ that week was a Carabinero (para-military police who always carried carbines). He and some Carabinero buddies came to our house to see Joe's saxophone and hear him play. They invited Joe to their Carabinero band practice!

I had been sick for several months, but the doctor assured me that another round of antibiotics would cure my fallopian tube inflammation. However, my left side really ached as I packed our clothes for the Missionary Retreat.

Joe and Bob spent hours filling out forms and standing in lines for the correct government paperwork involving permission to leave Chile by land and reenter from Argentina. Fortunately, we had our *permanencia* visa now or we could not have reentered Chile.

We traveled in Bob's Suburban, with Joe and Bob in front, Margaret and me on the second seat, and the four kids in back. The second day of our two-day trip was my birthday; I turned 28. Mom had sent us some six-track tapes and we listened to Andy Williams, Karen Carpenter and Mantovani for hour after hour as we rounded the hairpin curves up the Chilean side and then down the Argentine side of the Andes Mountains to Mendoza.

The Retreat was held outside Buenos Aires on a campground with rustic, but clean, accommodations. Missionaries from the "Southern Cone" were there — Argentina, Chile, Uruguay, Paraguay, Bolivia, and Peru. I tried to be friendly but could not relax because I knew that none of them were failures like us, run out of the very first town they had ministered in.

We had morning and evening services; the afternoons were free. "Who wants to go downtown?" asked Betty Jane Grams. Margaret Bowden told me that "we" did, so Monroe and Betty Jane took a group of us rookie missionaries to help us *conocer* (know) Buenos Aires. It was fascinating; there were modern, tall, office buildings, wide avenues with six lanes going each direction, modern shops with such things as cashmere sweaters, ostrich leather wallets and purses.

We stopped at a coffee bar for an espresso, my first. Uuh. It was so strong! And bitter! Monnie came over to me, "Did you put sugar in it?" "No," I told him, "I don't ever put sugar in my coffee."

"Well, you need to in espresso," he said, as he proceeded to dump three heaping teaspoons of sugar into my tiny cup. He stirred it and I tasted it, expecting it to be so sugary that it would be horrible. But it was delicious! It did not taste sweet! Just wonderfully delicious.

As we arrived back at the camp, men were just drifting in from a field where they had been playing touch football. Two men lagged far behind, both limping: Dick Ellis had seriously injured his hamstring; and Joe had a deep muscle pull in his thigh. At least Joe's injury wasn't as bad as in language school when, during a football game, someone had stepped on his toes and swiveled, removing a toenail.

Melvin Hodges, our boss, was gracious in a private meeting with Joe and me. He knew our names, he sympathized with our move to Viña, and he tried to assure us that everything would work out fine.

We had almost reached the end of the retreat. The benediction had been prayed at the last evening service. People began to gather their belongings off the slatted benches and were ready to leave the rustic chapel.

We had been standing, and I remained standing, my hands gripping the back of the bench in front of me. I could not leave the chapel.

I simply *could not* walk out. I could not go back to Chile without an encounter with God himself—without a sense of knowing that God still loved me.

I stood there, tears streaming down my cheeks. Joe stood beside me, his arm around my waist. Betty Jane went to the piano and began to play—although she was not the designated pianist. But she somehow sensed that this meeting was not yet over.

I began to sob. "God!" I shouted in my mind, "We played by the rules! We did everything we knew to do. I am disillusioned with the national pastors, disillusioned with a missionary colleague, disillusioned with the concept of what it means to be a missionary. My dream, my goal for my life is dead. Dead! Dead!

"I am angry at the men who caused this. I am angry with the politicians whose hatred of foreigners carries over into the church. I am angry with Joe for being 'fulfilled' while I sat alone in the cold rain with the children. I am angry with myself for not being able to 'take this in stride.' What else should I have done? How have I failed? There must be something wrong with me."

As I sobbed, I felt great sorrow for what might have been, for what could have been. I grieved for the potential that was wasted.

Yet, in spite of the circumstances, I believed in God. By the very act of expressing anger at Him, I realized that I was acknowledging His existence.

So, I relinquished it all to Him: all my dreams, all my anger, and all my pain. There was absolutely nothing I could do about any of it. I gave up, absolutely and totally.

As I did, a sense of God's goodness enveloped me. I knew He had not forgotten us. I *knew* God loved us. I knew, somehow, that He was with me. I worshipped Him for who He was—above and beyond my circumstances.

I was being "warmed" on the inside, from the inside out. The Temuco cold was thawing in my spirit. God's goodness to me, to us, was filling me up. God's presence was no longer external. He warmed my soul. I had found my identity in Him.

I asked God for strength. I asked Him for help. I asked Him for his peace, which surpassed human understanding. I believed He was good and that ultimately things could turn out for good.

I took a deep breath. I could do this. I could be a missionary. I could continue. I could look Iván and all his cohorts in the eye and know who I was in God. They could not touch that.

When I finally opened my eyes in that little, rustic chapel, Betty Jane was still playing the piano, and half a dozen other couples were there, too, praying just as earnestly as we had been.

I was not ashamed the next morning to stand and tell what had happened to me. And to my amazement, others told a similar story. Melvin Hodges decided that this first missionary retreat should begin a pattern for every country around the world.

In the future, Joe and I would be betrayed again, lied about, maligned, misunderstood, rejected, yelled at, and spit at. But never again would my sense of self-in-God be chaotic. Never again would I be shaken at the core of my essence. Never again would I doubt or question who-I-was-in-God.

I still had many lessons to learn. I did not yet know the difference between *being* and *doing*, or the difference between religion and relationship, or the ramifications of being passive aggressive, or how God was completely sovereign, or how His grace is so all-encompassing. But I had turned a corner of my life—a major corner.

This encounter with God was a milestone I would never forget. We called it "praying through," or getting the victory, leaving the burden at the altar, touching God, or pouring out our heart to God. This was the way we visited our Psychiatrist, the Heavenly One.

Many years later I would read these words by C. S. Lewis, "I know now, Lord, why you utter no answer. You yourself are the answer."

Temuco Post Script

A few months after we moved away from Temuco, Iván married Susana. Nine months later, she gave birth to a baby girl with severe, congenital heart defects.

While Susana was with the baby in Santiago to see a heart specialist, Iván had an affair with a girl from the youth group. When he was "caught" by Segundo, Iván left the country by bus with the girl and fled to Argentina.

Months later, in Santiago, I talked with a very repentant Susana and she begged me to tell girls that they cannot change a man's character, no matter how hard they try. She had suffered greatly at Iván's hand, from emotional and verbal abuse. She was haggard in her twenties.

The church people of Temuco scattered—confused and wounded. Only a very few continued to meet in a home to read a Bible passage and pray together. They met in the home of our dear friends the Hidalgos, Segundo and Nena (Guacolda).

A couple of years later, Juan Mella, a young pastor, and his family moved to Temuco. He is still there. He has a thriving congregation and has started numerous out-stations. He began a night Bible school in 1979.

In 1997, twenty-eight years after Joe and I left Temuco, Juan Mella invited us to fly back to Chile. The Temuco church paid our airfare! Unheard-of! We stayed for two wonderful weeks.

We were hosted totally by national brothers and stayed in a quaint, German hotel, spotlessly clean, just down the street from the "western hotel" where we had stayed when we first arrived. That hotel is still in operation and we considered moving over to it. The hotel managers even allowed us to look at our original hotel room, and it looked exactly the same. But it continued to be cold and drafty. Our newer, little German hotel was much cozier.

We drove by our small house on Holandesa Street. It looked unchanged, just a little softened with wear. The "mansion" is demolished now; a service station stands on that property.

The first thing we wanted to do was to see the Hidalgos. They are now in their 80s, in good health, and live in the same house. They invited us for lunch and we stayed through *once,* tea. Joe and Hermano Segundo hugged and wept. Nena and I held each other, crying.

Nena, a grandson, Segundo, Sergio (my favorite in children's church), and Joe sharing *once* tea with the Hidalgo family, 1997

Juan Mella told us that Iván had moved back to Chile and wanted to come down to Temuco to apologize to us. Would we be willing to see him? Joe said, "Of course," and that we had forgiven Iván long ago.

But Iván never showed up.

A personal note:

It was very painful for me to write about our days in Temuco. I had not revisited those emotions in all the succeeding years. Reading the letters I had written to Mom brought tears to my eyes along with the anger and the sense of hopelessness that I had felt at that time.

The cold of Temuco had seeped into my *ser*, my being. My identity became numb from the chill of rejection. My sense of self was shredded by hate-filled words from fellow workers. I questioned the essence of who I was as a person and as a Christian.

One day while I was writing this story, I took a coffee break, and as I stood in the kitchen grinding coffee, I thought, "At least this is one consolation of living in South America, good coffee." Then, with a start, I realized that I was in Florida and just "remembering" the terribly painful fifteen months in Temuco.

I am so grateful to God for His enveloping love at the Retreat in Argentina.

17

Summertime '71

Viña del Mar, Chile
January–March 1971

~·⬦·~

I turned off the paved road onto a cobblestone street to drive into the village of Quillota. Crossing a canal and rounding a corner onto a dirt road, I scooted up a steep, dusty hill and parked, setting the parking brake as firmly as I could. Margaret Bowden and I gathered the flannelgraph board, cut-out pictures, prizes, and the accordion from the back of the Suburban. Then we climbed uneven steps carved into the steep slope of the sidewalk that led up to houses perched precariously on the mountainside. We turned left, through a gate, into a walled patio.

The packed-dirt floor looked freshly swept under a "roof" of sheets suspended on ropes reaching from the outside wall to the adobe house to give us shade. A hand-embroidered cloth was draped across a small table flanked by two dining room chairs—special seats for Margaret and for me.

In front of the table sat the main attraction—54 children crammed together on low, rough benches. Every child's hair was freshly combed. Every face was expectant, and brown eyes were opened wide. How they looked forward to our Saturday story hour!

While I played the accordion, Margaret led us in singing. We used special pictures to illustrate the songs, and even a "stop sign" to hold up as we sang, "*Para. Voy a contarte.* Stop. And let me tell you." The children were so proud to know the words and sang them really loudly.

As I told the Bible story, my heart filled with gratitude. I did not take this opportunity lightly. During the hour's drive to Quillota, Margaret and I had been complaining about the government instability, the terrible inflation causing our salary to be pitifully inadequate, and the national church's anti-American attitude. But I was ashamed of my complaining as I stood there watching little lives being transformed.

Every Saturday morning, Margaret and I (sometimes with Christy, Timmy, Jeanne, and Connie) left home at 11:30 for this story time in Quillota followed by a picnic lunch, then another class at 2:30 in Villa Alemana and one at 4:30 in Quilpué. In Quilpué, we met in a partially finished church building, no windows yet, and just a dirt floor. But it was quiet and wind-free.

Joe helped with the VBS parade in Quillota

In Villa Alemana, our story hour was held in the open air on the side of a steep mountain. As we approached, children came running toward the van and Margaret exclaimed, "Careful! Don't run over a kid!"

The wind whistled down the hill so strongly that it blew my cut-out figures off the flannelgraph board just before the wind knocked over the *entire* board. So, we opened the tailgate and had our "platform" there.

The first week, I stood with my left side angled downhill as I began to play the accordion. Suddenly gravity yanked the bellows open—and I couldn't close them! I turned around and then set the accordion on the ground beside the car as I taught the lesson. Later, when I packed the accordion into the case, the keyboard was wet. I couldn't figure out why, until I saw a mongrel, male dog nearby. When I told the other missionaries about it, Cyle Davis quipped, "That's what you call tinkling the ivories."

One Saturday in Quilpué I suddenly felt the warm gush of a hemorrhage as I stood teaching the Bible story. Bewildered, I looked toward Margaret, requesting urgent help with my eyes and my expression. She came forward and finished the story while our hostess took me inside her house.

A few minutes later, I told Margaret she would have to drive home. "I can't!" she responded. "You know I'm too scared to drive in Chile!" "It's not an option," I told her weakly, "there is no other way to get home." I lay on the back seat as we headed down the mountain. (She drove confidently from then on, after this initiation-by-force.)

The hemorrhage had eased by the time Margaret dropped me off at my front gate. (Joe and Bob had gone to Bolivia for two weeks, so Margaret drove our car on to her house.) I managed to get in the door and up the staircase, where I collapsed onto the bed. Hemorrhaging heavily, I called loudly for Christy to bring me bath towels. She helped scoot them under me and I soaked one right after the other.

It began to get dark. The kids found something to eat for supper. Once again I felt all alone and I began to cry. I couldn't get to the phone downstairs. Even if I could, what could Margaret do on a Saturday evening? There was no "9-1-1" or "emergency room."

I lay on the bed, praying, "God, please help this flow of blood to stop. God, please help me not to hemorrhage to death."

After a few minutes, I reached for the mail lying on the night-stand and opened a church bulletin from Beckley, West Virginia. I read, "Please pray for Margaret Register in Chile. She is experiencing health problems."

Peace filled my heart! I was not alone after all. Immediately the hemorrhaging stopped. Then I remembered that I had written to a friend in Beckley, asking her to pray for me.

I stayed in bed for five days with piercing cramps. If the children even touched the bed, making it move ever so slightly, the pain was excruciating.

When I was finally able to get to a doctor, my gynecologist said both fallopian tubes were inflamed and infected. She gave me more antibiotics and scheduled me for "heat" treatments at the clinic. I have no idea what they were—I went for an hour a day for ten days. I lay on a metal table, like one used for an x-ray, and a nurse put a square metal box about the size of bathroom scales on my tummy. She plugged it in and left. I guess it worked, because my health improved.

Juan Romero, a Mariachi evangelist, came to Viña the last of January. Juan's English was heavily accented but he laughed heartily along with us at his mistakes; and he complimented Joe on his good Spanish.

Juan stayed with the Bowdens while he held a revival in Valpo. We went every night. On Friday night, when Juan Romero gave the altar call, Timmy, (now "Jimmy") leaned over to whisper to me, "I need to go forward—I need to ask Jesus to come into my heart." "All right," I replied. "Will you go with me?" he asked. "You can go by yourself," I told him, trying to see how sincere he was. He said, "OK. I'm going." And he did!

For the entire month of February, Joe went to Lima, Peru to attend the *Instituto de Superación Ministerial* (ISUM)—for an intensive month of studies toward a master's degree in Spanish.

Sitting in class, Joe felt a sharp pain like a knife in his back. Then, after several grueling hours of writhing in pain, he passed two kidney stones.

Howard Nutt (from language school, now in Bolivia) was one of the fifty students who attended. Howard warned Joe that the female student who kept wanting Joe's counsel actually wanted more than just counsel. Howard was a true friend.

While Joe was away, the kids and I went with the Bowdens and Juan Toro and his family to camp meeting. A real camp meeting! We pitched our camp tent by a gentle, shallow river. Bob and Juan and "Jimmy" slept, as did the other campers, under a blanket stretched between a tree and some limbs stuck in the ground. Margaret and I and the girls got the tent.

There was a wonderful swimming hole, and the kids had a great time. Juan had informed us that we could take the dog, too, so Chilito faithfully followed "Jimmy," protecting him from danger by day and sleeping with the guys at night.

More than 100 people attended the camp meeting. We had morning services in a brush arbor; the afternoons were free; and there was a bonfire at night. The church women set up the kitchen: a wooden table, two big cooking pots over gas burners, and an oval washtub for salad. One pot held rice or pasta, the other pot held the soup or sauce of the day. Each of us took a plate, bowl, cup, and silverware, washing them off in the river.

One of my favorite salads was made with fresh green beans sliced diagonally. They were dropped into boiling water just until tender, then drained and cooled. The cook added chopped tomatoes and onions along with oil, vinegar and salt. Delicious.

The last morning, Margaret awoke with a splitting headache. She groaned, "I am getting up. I am plastering a smile on my face. I am going to walk around the camp and smile at everyone if it kills me." "Why?" I asked. "Because if anyone finds out I'm sick, everyone will be here with their special herbal tea remedy, and then I will get sick." I laughed and laughed because it was so true.

The last week of February, we drove down to Concepción to the annual national General Council. Juan Romero was the speaker, so the ten of us (Joe was still gone) rode together in the Bowden's car and we all stayed at a nice hotel with the other missionary families. Christy and "Jimmy" made friends quickly and played outside during the services.

To my surprise, I was elected vice-president of Women's Ministries. Audrey Manning was elected as president. We planned all sorts of good things for the coming year. And Audrey put me in charge of preparing another booklet for the girls' clubs, as well as one for the women.

Later, Margaret helped me with a Vacation Bible School in Quillota for 100 children; one in Villa Alemana with 40 kids; and a teachers' workshop in the big church in Valpo. Also, I spoke frequently to women's groups at devotional meetings or *onces*.

"Jimmy" ready to ride on shining rims

Christy still rode her small-sized bicycle that we had brought from the States, but the tires had worn completely out. There were no replacements of that size in Chile, so she and "Jimmy" just rode on the rims, clanking down the sidewalk.

The children took turns riding around the block, and one day as Christy rode on the side of the block farthest from home, a man stood watching her. When she came around the block the next time, he was waiting. *"Niña, venid. Necesito tu ayuda."* "Come here, little girl, I need your help." He convinced her to walk up a driveway with him to "help" him ring the doorbell. He said he wanted her to look nice, so he tucked her shirt in and "found" a bug on her pants which he proceeded to brush off. He said, "Let's go over this way now." As they started back down the driveway toward an empty house, Christy darted ahead, hopped on the bike, and pedaled as fast as she could for home.

Joe went running around the block to try to catch the man, but of course, the child molester was gone. Joe went to the police station, too, but they said there was nothing they could do.

Years later, Christy told me, "The man was an adult and all children were taught to obey adults without question. The entire time I was with him, I didn't know there was anything wrong or dangerous. I did not fully understand his Spanish, so I didn't follow all that he was pretending we were to do. It wasn't until we were back out on the sidewalk, and he was taking me Lord-knows-where to do Lord-knows-what, that all of a sudden I felt something like hot oil pouring down from my head to my toes and an over-whelming sense of 'This is wrong! Dangerous! Get away!!' It was instantaneous and overwhelming. By the time I arrived home, I was crying—maybe more from fear and relief than from feelings of violation."

She continued, "'Jimmy' saw me crying and reacted in such an angry and protective manner! He was ready to go beat up whoever had hurt me. 'Who hurt you!? What happened?' he asked over and over. But I was so confused and embarrassed and overwhelmed, I couldn't give him a straight answer.

"Even now I remember this incident every time a person mentions a bug crawling on someone, and says a 'Let-me-get-it' kind of thing. Though it's not traumatic now, it is a very sad feeling."

Christy paused and sighed, "It still makes me angry to know there are creeps out there like that, so evil that they would harm a powerless, innocent child."

We had strong earthquake tremors every day. If we were walking or riding in the car, we didn't notice. But sitting or lying down, it was exciting to shake from side to side.

One day Margaret went to an art exhibit downtown and found a beautiful oil painting of the seaside. As Bob talked to the artist, he realized that the artist attended one of our churches in a neighboring town. Joe and I bought a painting, too—a sunset viewed from the end of our street looking over the Pacific Ocean toward an old Spanish fort and the Valpo peninsula.

When the kids and I walked the three blocks to the boulder-strewn beach, the water looked *deliciosa,* delicious, as they say in Spanish. We went running and waded in. Uuuuuuh!!! It was so freezing cold it took our breath away. We did not know about the Humboldt Current that swept up from Antarctica, keeping the water about 58 degrees (15 Celsius) even in the summertime. "Jimmy" ran along the edge of the waves until a big one came, capsizing him; Christy was sure she rescued him from certain drowning.

When Joe came home, he bought the kids a wading pool, probably eight feet in diameter, and put it on the roof above the garage. The children would sneak the dog in for a swim, too.

School began in March. Christy was now in the fourth grade, and "Jimmy" was in first grade. I home-schooled them every morning and prepared their lessons as well as my Saturday Kids' Clubs lessons in the afternoons.

Joe and Hermano Morales, our superintendent, who pastored in Valparaíso, began a night Bible school in the Valpo church. The church attendance averaged about 400 people on Sunday nights, and Joe formed an evening choir there. The singing was enthusiastic, though a little lacking in good sopranos.

Also, Joe taught two days a week at the Bible institute in Santiago. One day, about half an hour after he left on the sixty-mile trip, the phone rang, "Marg, I am at the government checkpoint up in the mountains and I forgot my wallet. They are holding me and the vehicle 'prisoner' until you can get here with my documents." I called a taxi and went speeding up the mountain road toward Santiago. Joe paid a fine and was "released."

Another day, as Joe finished his class and started home, a government official was assassinated in Santiago. All transportation was halted into and out of the city. Joe was the last car through the checkpoint before the city was shut down for 24 hours.

The transition to Allende's communist rule was fairly peaceful, but farm and factory workers began to plan insurrections, and poor people continued to seize land.

Tomas, takeovers, became the norm. One was *Campo Salvador Allende* near our house, where people erected makeshift tents in a large field as they staged a *toma,* a takeover of land. During the summer months, the people were content on their new property, but when the autumn rains began, people stole some government-built, pre-fab wooden shacks, called *media agua* half-roof (because the roof pitched only in one direction). Soon, Allende gave everyone who asked for it a *media agua.* Thus, on hundreds of *tomas* the shacks stood crowded together with each shack proudly flying a Chilean flag.

Milk became scarce. Powdered milk was imported and a great quantity of fish meal was added to it—not to stretch it, according to the propaganda, but to give it greater nourishment. Our kids would drink it only with lots of chocolate or vanilla. Joe and I could not drink it for the strong taste and smell.

As district elections loomed, a radio commercial appeared: "Mamá, are Communists bad?" "Your father and I are Communists, Dear, are we bad?" "No, Mamá." "Drink your milk, Dear."

Announcer: "If you love your country, you'll vote Communist. This party keeps its promises. For a better, healthier Chile, vote Communist!"

Our big tent had been shipped from New York City, but to travel and conduct revivals now was out of the question. How could Joe and Bob use the tent?

* * *

Chilean Stuffed *Palta* (Avocado)

INGREDIENTS

One ripe avocado for every two people you'll serve
One can Bumble Bee white tuna, drained and broken
 apart
Or, one can chicken breast, drained and broken apart
Two eggs, boiled and chopped
1/4 cup sweet relish
1/3 cup mayonnaise
Salt
Pepper
Dash of Tabasco

DIRECTIONS

1. Tuna or chicken salad: Mix ingredients well. Add more mayonnaise if it seems too dry.
2. Cut avocado in half, remove seed. Score the skin and remove.
3. Place the halves on serving plates and fill with chicken or tuna salad.

18

La Carpa Llega—The Tent Arrives

Viña del Mar, Chile
April–June 1971

"*I will be back here tomorrow* with my lawyer! You, sir, will be the one to move out!" screeched our landlady, standing so close to Joe that spittle sprinkled his face. "You'd better start packing your stuff right now or I'll throw it out on the street!"

"I repeat," said Joe, not very softly, "next month I will pay you in *escudos*, not dollars, and I won't pay you at all until you move your things out of the house and garage."

Every month when Joe had paid the rent, he had asked the landlady when she would move her things out of the garage, the walk-in closet and the maid's quarters. "Next month" was her standard reply. By now she had been saying that for over six months. She employed about five people to make insignia for military uniforms; the employees took their breaks under our kitchen windows—every person, it seemed, smoking the strong, acrid cigarettes used in Chile. Plus, the employees would enter our house at random, to get supplies out of a locked closet. In addition, the landlady had an extension phone installed in the garage and would take ALL daytime calls—and was rude to people calling for us.

Joe found an attorney and explained the situation. "Don't worry," she said. "If the landlady shows up with her attorney, just call me. Her threats are unfounded; the law is on your side."

The landlady did not return the next day and she moved her things out within a few weeks. Joe had already decided that he would not confront her again. We would move first. But thankfully, we didn't have to.

Now I enjoyed the house. It was cream-colored stucco with a red tile roof and white window frames. It sat on a corner and there were wrought iron fences on the street sides, walls on the back sides. The gate was set diagonally at the street corner and the sidewalk curved toward the front door. A beautiful bird of paradise plant sat by the stoop. A tangerine tree and honeysuckle vines were in the side yard. In the back yard, by the garage, geraniums grew taller than my head.

The downstairs windows had decorative wrought iron bars. The upstairs windows opened out like shutters. There were no screens and no heater or air conditioner. In the summertime we fanned, and in the wintertime, we layered our clothing.

The extra bedroom became a guest room, with a private bath across the hall. That bathroom doubled as a laundry room with our portable washing machine installed there.

In the side yard, a little wooden shed sat low to the ground, and one day Chilito got stuck under it. The children were so distraught that they determined to maintain a constant vigil until he was freed. "Jimmy," the neighbor boy, Marcelo, and Christy took sleeping bags, food, and water and lay alongside the building as they talked to Chilito to comfort him. They begged Joe to "Do something!" Joe said, "He got under there, he can get out." After about five hours, Chilito wriggled free.

The children had always slept in twin beds in the same room—in Beckley, Tavares, Pensacola, Mexico, and Temuco. Now each of them could have a room. Christy put posters and cut-out pictures on her wall. She told "Jimmy" he must not enter her room without knocking first, and then he must wait for permission to enter. "Jimmy" had the largest room, across from our bedroom. It was also the schoolroom and Joe's ham radio room. But at night, Chilito stood guard over "Jimmy's" bedroom.

The children kept us amused. One of the tourist attractions of Viña was horse-drawn carriages. Often they clip-clopped down our street, and Marcelo taught "Jimmy" how to run behind them and jump on the back for a free ride.

During April, a terrible smell began to emanate from upstairs. It seemed to be centered in Christy's room. She confessed that she had decided not to throw away the Easter eggs but to keep them under her bed....

One day, "Jimmy" was looking through the Bible Story Book and came to stories about Abraham and his nephew Lot. "Oh, look," he said, "here are Abraham and Field."

Christy wanted a friend her age. She didn't even care if the new friend would be like Heidi, our neighbor in Temuco who had a runny nose all the time and carried a soppy hanky. So we prayed, "Jesus, please send Christy a friend." A couple of days later, Dolores, a woman from the Valpo church, came to see us. When she turned to leave, she asked Christy, "Would you like to go with me to meet Carolina? She lives down the street and is just your age." Christy, holding Dolores' hand, skipped down the sidewalk. Suddenly, she turned to call back to me, "God is giving me a friend, just like we prayed!"

Joe and Bob talked to the Superintendent at length about the political situation. President Allende was forming strong ties with Cuba, North Korea, North Viet Nam, China, and Russia. Political relations with the U.S. were "frosty"—unfriendly, but not openly hostile yet. Hermano Morales knew that people were on edge, and he said it was just too dangerous for "Yankees" to travel for the purpose of conducting religious campaigns.

"Could we possibly use the tent here in Viña?" Joe and Bob asked Hermano Morales. "Could we try to begin a church here?" Hermano Morales believed it would be safe to try.

Joe and Bob then began to drive around looking at vacant lots. They wanted a lot in a busy area, on a bus route, preferably at a bus stop. It was essential to be able to see distinctly inside the property because nonchurched people would not enter a Protestant building—to alleviate fears, people needed to be able to see easily what was happening. There was no need for parking spaces, as few people owned cars; those who did could park on the street.

As the guys drove down the street called *Calle Quillota*, they spotted the perfect location, #575. This wide, deep lot walled on three sides had a nice wide gate and an open-style wrought iron fence in front.

Now Joe and Bob needed to find the owner of the property. They wanted to rent with an option to buy. They also would have to get permission from the city to erect a tent on that property. And they needed to contact our mission for permission to begin this project.

The tent had arrived, and the aduana officials assured Joe that it would be released on April 26. It was not, although Joe spent the entire day at the *aduana* (customs office) at the port in Valpo.

Finally, a couple of weeks later—in fact, it was the day after our landlady vacated the garage—the tent was released and Joe, Juan, and Bob took both Suburbans to pick up the large canvas bundles and store them in our garage.

On May 3, they were able to track down the owner of the Calle Quillota property. No, he would not rent—the property was for sale: $3000.00 U.S, non-negotiable. Joe wrote to Posey Rhodes (the "rich" family in Beckley, WV) asking for a loan.

The following week, the property owner called, "*Muy bien.* I've changed my mind. You can begin renting with an option to buy." That same day a letter arrived from Mr. Rhodes, "Where should I send the money?"

The next step was to clean off the lot, because everyone threw trash on vacant lots. Juan organized a group from the Valpo church to come and help. It took more than a week to clear the trash, rake, and level the rocky ground.

As the men stretched the canvas pieces of the tent across the dirt, the pieces reached almost from side to side, wall to wall. Oh, no! That meant the tent was too large for the property because guy-wires had to be extended to hold the tent upright and taut. Despair descended! Then one of the helpers said, "I have an idea. Let's set some posts next to the walls, and tie the guy-wires to them, high in the air." It worked! The tent was just a little sway-back....

Joe and Bob took turns sleeping on the property until a young man in his thirties, Hermano Funes (fooh-ness) from the Valpo church came with his wife María as the official caretakers. They qualified for a *media agua*, which the government would give to anyone who "squatted" on property. That soon became their house.

The city connected electricity to a pole near the front of the lot, and from there our guys strung a cable to the *media agua* for a single light bulb. From the light socket the Funes family could run an extension cord if they ever obtained any electrical items. In addition, the workers laid plumbing for a free-standing water faucet near the *media agua* and ran a sewer line to the back of the house.

For pews, Joe bought lumber—a half-dozen 2x8s—to make a few picnic-style benches. The men also constructed a short, square platform and strung three or four lights inside and outside the tent.

People stopped on the street to look at these crazy people erecting a tent in downtown Viña. "Must be a circus," they told each other. "Hey," someone shouted, "Will there be elephants? When's the circus coming to town?" Joe shouted back, "June 26. Be sure to come!"

The curiosity of the pedestrians was wonderful, but we wanted an even larger audience, so we printed handbills and ran ads in the newspaper.

Joe and Bob began daily, fifteen minute radio broadcasts, live, on two different stations. They played a song by Juan Romero and just conversed, always including humor. Sometimes Juan Toro was on the air with them. They would relate one of Jesus' stories of healing, stressing his compassion. In every broadcast they emphasized, "The Bible says Jesus is the same yesterday, today and forever." Then they would invite people to *la carpa*, the tent.

A radio station manager had never seen anyone so relaxed about religion and he told the men the programs were "terrific."

The guys also had a huge banner made to stretch across the street—they actually got permission to do that! It said, "*La Gran Campaña de Fe, Cristo salva, Cristo sana*" "The Grand Campaign of Faith, Jesus saves, Jesus heals."

Joe and Bob placed another huge sign like a billboard on the property. When they were trying to hoist it up, one corner fell and hit Joe on the back of the head. He literally "saw stars." It was scary, but after a few minutes he seemed to be fine. The board said the same as the banner, and added *"Cada noche desde el 26 de junio, a las 20 horas"* "Every night at 8 p.m., beginning June 26."

Connie Bowden and Margaret at the tent

As I walked briskly along a downtown avenue, a man stopped me. *"Corazón* (Sweetheart)," he said. *"¿Qué?"* "What?" I replied. I wasn't frightened; we were on a busy sidewalk. *"Corazón,"* he said again, this time pointing to his left wrist and motioning to mine. Then seeing the puzzled look on my face, he pronounced it more slowly, *"¿Qué horas son?"* "What time is it?" Man! I had thought for sure he was impressed with my new leather boots and the new, fashionable clothes the *modista* had made for me!

I had written several times to Mom and Aunt Too about coming to visit us. Mom wrote back, "We'll come on one condition—that you let us bring Christy home with us." Later, she offered to take both children, but I knew "Jimmy" and Chilito were inseparable, and two children plus a dog would really be too much for Mother to handle.

Christy had not fully recovered from her ordeal at the British school. The Brownsville church in Pensacola had begun an elementary school, Five Flags Academy, and Mom wanted to enroll Christy there. Mom had already talked to the fourth grade teacher. She would give Christy special attention.

Joe and I prayed about it for several weeks. Our furlough was coming up in the spring. Possibly I could leave at the end of December, and Joe could stay on through February. We talked to Christy. She was ecstatic! She wrote a list of why she "needed" to go home with Grandma:

1. Baby Kimberly; 2. Grandma and Grandpa; 3. Aunt Jan, Uncle Barry and Uncle David (my brother); 4. TV; 5. Cereal (We had none in Chile.)

When I questioned her about #1, Christy began to cry, "Mommy, I <u>have</u> to go home to take care of baby Kimberly."

"Why?"

"Because Grandma wrote in her letter that they are leaving Kimberly <u>all by herself</u>."

"What do you mean?"

Christy sighed, "Grandma wrote that Kimberly is 'sitting alone.' I need to go be with her!"

19

Bajo la Carpa—Under the Tent

Viña del Mar, Chile
July 1971

I didn't see him at first, standing in the cold drizzle. Then he lurched sideways just at the edge of the tent. His damp, tattered clothes reeked of nicotine from a thousand acrid cigarettes. His breath fanned my face as he puffed; the scent smelled of cheap Chilean wine.

"Señora," he slurred, glancing sideways at me through blood-shot eyes, "how long ya gonna be here?"

"Every night," I replied.

"*¿Mañana?*"

"Yes, *mañana* and every night."

"I'll be back." He staggered, stumbling toward the street.

Our opening day, Saturday June 26, dawned overcast. By mid-afternoon, cold drizzle fell continuously and the temperature dropped into the 30s.

We wondered if anyone would come to *la carpa*, the tent. The little light bulbs barely dispelled the darkness; the mist swirled with cold that seeped through our coats and sweaters and into our bones.

I stood just under the edge of the tent to greet people. But only a half-dozen people came in from the rain—people from the Valpo church who had promised to be there for opening night.

Twenty to thirty people stood on the sidewalk out front, waiting for the city bus. They peered through the fence. A few of them ventured cautiously onto the property, staying well back, near the gate, so they could escape quickly.

They believed the false stories that Protestants had a statue of the Virgin Mary at the entrance and every person had to spit on her before entering. Protestant girls, they heard, all had sex with the priest in order to become members.

But they could see no statue here to desecrate. There was no priest soliciting favors. Just a *gringo,* a foreigner, singing with an accordion on a little stage:

Jesús, yo te amo	Jesus, I love you,
Jesús, yo te amo a ti,	Jesus, I love you, I do.
Porque tú me has salvado,	Because you have saved me,
Porque tú me has sanado,	Because you have healed me,
Jesús, yo te amo a ti.	Jesus, I love you, I do.

After the music, another *gringo* with blond hair stood up with a small book. He read a story about Jesus healing a little girl who had died. He retold the story in his own words, and then he said, "Let's all pray together. I'll pray a phrase, and you repeat it."

"Jesus, you loved the little girl in our story. You love me, too. The Bible says you are the same yesterday, today, and forever. Touch me. Forgive me. Take away my sins. Amen."

No one repeated the prayer, except the *gringos* and the people seated on the benches. Everyone else kept their eyes wide open, just in case something weird was about to happen.

The man continued, "Now, place your hand wherever your sickness is—if that is not possible, place your hand on your heart. Repeat this prayer with me: Jesus, the Bible says you are the same yesterday, today and forever. Touch me. Heal me <u>now</u>. Amen."

No one repeated the prayer, except the *gringos* and the people seated on the benches. Everyone else kept their eyes wide open, just in case something weird was about to happen.

"See you tomorrow," the *gringos* said.

The people walked away in the rain.

Sunday, June 27, dawned with a heavy overcast. By mid-afternoon, cold drizzle fell continuously and the temperature dropped into the 30s. Again. Certainly no one would come tonight.

I stood just under the edge of the tent to greet people. But only a half-dozen people came in from the rain—just the friends from the Valpo church who had promised to be there for the second night.

I shivered in the cold rain. Then I saw him. He looked not quite so drunk. He stood unsteadily just outside the edge of the tent. Rain dripped on his head, ran down his grizzled chin onto the unraveled red sweater under his scruffy, wool overcoat. He appeared to be in his forties. His face revealed the puffy, dissipated look of an alcoholic.

"*Hola*," I greeted. "Want to come in out of the rain?"

He shook his head no. But he focused on the platform.

Joe led the same lively chorus.

Bob read the story of Jesus healing the blind beggar. Then he prayed the same two prayers.

No one repeated the prayers, except the *gringos* and the people seated on the benches. Everyone else kept their eyes wide open, just in case something weird was about to happen.

"See you tomorrow," the *gringos* said.

The people walked away in the rain.

The rain stopped on Monday. It was still cold, but the sun shone on the mud of the property and dried out the canvas of the tent.

He came back that night. He was not *tomado*, drunk. He ventured under the tent. He sat tentatively on the back row. He kept his eyes wide open. His lips moved ever so slightly during the first prayer.

I shook hands with him, "See you tomorrow?" I asked.

He nodded a curt yes.

Tuesday he was back. He shook hands with me, his eyes clear, his handshake firm. "Name's Daniel Pozo," he said. "I'm two days sober."

Daniel came every night. He moved closer and closer toward the front. He prayed openly now.

One night as he entered, I could tell the muffler around his neck was stretched "fatter" than usual. He avoided my eyes. I walked up to him, "*Daniel, ¿qué te pasa?*" "What's wrong?"

"Oh, I have the mumps. They sent me home from work. The doctor said to stay in bed for a week."

"Daniel! The mumps are dangerous! You could get serious complications from them! You need to go home right now!"

He shook his head no. "Daniel, go up front right now and talk to Joe."

He ambled up to the platform. I could see them talking, see Joe talking *seriously* to Daniel. I saw Daniel's head bow. Then I saw him look up at Joe.

"*Hermano José*, please don't send me home," his eyes filled with tears. "I have no family, no living relatives. I have never had a brother or sister until here—here in *la carpa* are my brothers and sisters. *You* are my family now. I slept passed out on this property many nights—drunk. But now I have hope. Now I have love. Now I have a family. *Please* don't send me home."

Daniel came every night with the mumps. His jaws swelled bigger and bigger. Then they began getting smaller. He had no complications and no one contracted the mumps from him.

Joe and Daniel

July 8, 11:03 p.m.

Joe kept shaking the bed. Where was the dust coming from? It was sifting onto my face. I pulled the sheet up over my head. Why does Joe keep shaking the bed?

"Margaret, wake up! It's an earthquake!" Joe gasped.

The windows banged open. Plaster cracked, large chunks fell, skidding across the floor sending plaster dust flying. Tiles slipped and slid on the roof, and then dropped, to crush on the ground two stories below.

"Margaret, go to Timmy! I'll go around the stairwell to Christy's room. Get him and stand in the doorway!"

We jumped from the rocking bed onto the shifting floor and ran to the children. Timmy was still sleeping but Christy was screaming.

Dolly, our Argentine guest, was yelling, "*¿Qué pasa, qué pasa?*" "What's happening? What's happening?"

The house creaked and rolled, cracking the plaster on every wall. Pictures fell from their nails. Books tumbled from shelves. Knick-knacks splintered as they fell to the floor. Lamps tilted and crashed. Dishes rattled and tumbled from open cabinet doors.

It felt as if we were on a boat rocking from side to side, or as if we were riding on a very bumpy road. The air was so saturated with dust we could hardly breathe. The windows slammed shut, flung open again. Slammed. Opened.

Finally, with a great shudder, the earthquake slowed. Then ... nothing. No noise. Heavy darkness. Silent fear. Stifling air too heavy to breathe.

Joe came with Christy in his arms. Dolly came down the hall crawling on her hands and knees. Timmy was still asleep, dreaming of flying on an airplane.

It was pitch dark. Where was the flashlight? I knew where a candle was. What about matches? Joe stumbled in the dark through the debris. Where were his pants? Where were his house shoes?

He located the matches in the overturned nightstand. Hands trembling, he struck a match, lit the candle. Oh, no! What about the gas? He blew out the candle and fumbled to find the flashlight.

"I'm going to try to go down the stairs. I'll see if I can turn off the gas," Joe disappeared, leaving us in the dusty darkness.

Dolly reached out to touch me, not letting go of my arm. Timmy, awake now, thought this was fun. Christy sat on my lap, shaking and crying softly.

A strong tremor shook the house. We gasped! We were cold. All the windows were open. Christy crawled into bed with Timmy. In the darkness, I tried to find blankets for Dolly and me. We sat together on the foot of Timmy's bed, huddled in our pajamas, shivering from fear.

The quake registered 7.5 on the Richter scale. In a forty kilometer swath villages were destroyed, roads buckled, homes demolished.

One hundred thirteen strong aftershocks sent everyone screaming into the streets where they hoped a building would not collapse on them.

As soon as it was daylight, Joe said he was going to go check on the tent, if the streets were passable.

The tent stood tall and strong, as sway-back as always—with the benches overturned. One person, arriving even before Joe, stood under the tent. Daniel stood there in the gloom, his new *New Testament* in his hand. His little rented room had been totally destroyed, but he wasn't worried about that—he just wanted to make sure *la carpa* still stood.

20

Family

Viña del Mar, Chile
July 1971 (continued)

All day Friday, July 9, as strong tremors shook the house, we scrambled to stand in a doorframe because the lintel helped to protect us from falling debris. Cracks widened in the walls and plaster continued to crash to the floor, sifting a new layer of dust on everything. More tiles tumbled from the roof into the yard—already littered with broken tiles and chunks of stucco.

The landlady came to check on the house. Her hands were trembling. "How are you? Is anyone hurt? How badly damaged is the house?" She stood on the sidewalk and looked up at the ragged roof.

We assured her that we were fine and led her inside to survey the damage. "Don't worry, I will have everything repaired. I'll get someone started on the roof first, and someone to make sure the house is structurally sound."

She was worried about the chimney, which was leaning precariously toward the master bedroom. "Pull your bed out from that wall." She wrung her hands, paced, and took short quick breaths. Finally she looked at me, "Señora, how can you be so calm? We all could have died!"

Just the opportunity I'd been waiting for! She was so brittle and hard-hearted that we had not been able even to hint to her of God's love. "I'm not afraid to die, Señora," I replied. "God's peace fills my heart no matter what occurs around me." She looked penetratingly into my eyes, pursed her lips, then sighed and walked away.

By the time roofers were ready to replace the broken tiles, rain began. We covered things inside the house as best we could and prayed for the rain to stop.

Though we had no phone service, within a couple of days we did have electricity. Bob and Margaret did not, so they came to use our ham radio to contact their families in the States. As word spread that Joe could contact the U.S. by radio, strangers came for Joe to "patch them through." Our house was like Grand Central Station for several days.

A trickle of water flowed through the kitchen faucet, so I sat pots under it to catch as much water as I could. We boiled it to drink and also used it for "spit baths."

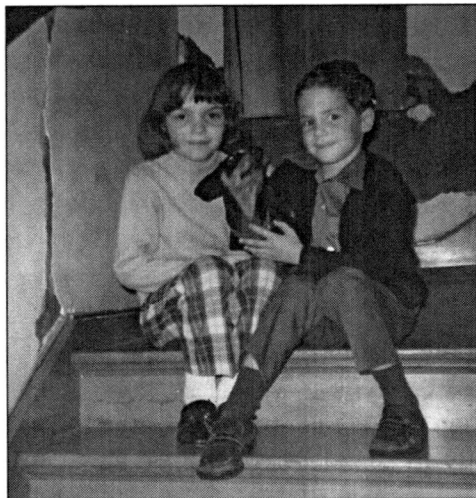

Christy, Chilito and Timmy by earthquake-damaged walls

Dolly stirred the mashed potatoes in a big pot. "Let's see if they have enough salt," she murmured, picking up the wooden spoon and aiming toward her mouth. She gave the back of the spoon a big lick,

"*Sí, perfecto,*" she said as she plopped the spoon back into the pot and stirred some more. So much for Dolly's "secret ingredient" in mashed potatoes Argentine style!

During early June, Bob had made a quick trip to Argentina to speak at the Bible institute. He brought back two graduates who wanted to be missionaries: Francisco (Pancho) Buono and Dolly Cándido. Pancho stayed with the Bowdens; he was tall and slim and looked like a Texan. Dolly was about 5'9" with naturally curly reddish hair. She looked like an Iowa farm girl. But neither of them spoke a word of English—just their Argentine-Italian-accented Spanish. They pitched right in to help with the tent campaign. They walked the street in front of the tent every evening, giving out hand-bills, inviting people to come inside the lot, and talking to people afterward. Both of them had a great sense of humor and we loved working with them.

Many North Americans looked down on the national people. I tried to instill in Christy and Timmy that "It is OK to be different. There are things 'they' know that we don't. Just because 'they' do things differently doesn't mean 'our' way is better. In fact, it is not 'them' and 'us'—we are all 'us.' And living here is an adventure!"

Attendance at the tent increased. Since the earthquake, people were scared; they had faced death. When a strong wind blows, or there is a terrible rain storm, the ground is still firm beneath a person's feet. But when the earth itself is unstable, moving, shifting—it seems like the end of the world. It is a terrifying experience.

Now, more people came inside the lot to observe, inside the tent to participate, praying openly.

These people had never held a Bible in their hands—never touched one. Only the priests were allowed to have a Bible. We bought a case of "*Dios Llega al Hombre*" (Good News for Modern Man) New Testaments. We were told that we should sell them along with the chorus sheets—not for much, but just so the people would appreciate them. The people covered the backs of their new Bibles in colorful paper to protect them and carried them proudly.

Bob decided to preach systematically through the Gospel of Mark. He announced the page number: page 76, a story of Jesus having compassion on Peter's *suegra*, mother-in-law. The next night: page 77, Jesus healing the paralyzed man let down through the roof tiles. The following night: page 79, Jesus healing the man with the crippled hand. And always Bob read from page 499, "*Jesucristo es el mismo ayer, hoy y siempre*," "Jesus Christ is the same yesterday, today, and forever."

After the prayer for healing, Bob asked if anyone had been healed. Tentatively, a man spoke up, "I had a terrible pain, here at my waist, in the back. It went away last night when we prayed." Heads nodded. A woman raised her hand, "Me, too. I had an awful pain here, at my waist on my left side. I've had it for days. It's gone now." A man said, "I have been deaf in my right ear since birth. I can hear from it now." A young woman said, "I've had a pain in my waist, here in front, but it disappeared earlier when we prayed."

There was no hoopla, no sense of "this is sure unusual." We prayed. God answered.

People told their friends about being healed at *la carpa,* the tent. By the end of July we were running 60 to 70 every night. But there was a big turnover. The people did not know each other. As soon as the meeting was dismissed, they all left, barely nodding to each other.

One evening, Joe told them, "Tonight, when we are finished, turn to the person next to you. Introduce yourself, shake hands." It was amazing. Within a couple of weeks, no one wanted to go home! They talked, compared healings, and compared prior lives. They were being transformed and united.

Everyone continued to pray the sinner's prayer. After about a month, Bob said, "If you know that Christ lives in your heart, if you have that assurance, you don't have to continue to pray that prayer. You can simply agree with others who are just now coming to Christ." I watched Daniel. He held his head up, a big grin on his face, as he looked at the "newcomers" praying.

At home in the living room, I sat on the area rug to play "Sorry" with Christy and Timmy. We usually played "Whoops," a game Mom had sent: spin a dial and do whatever the dial points to—clap your hands, hop on your left foot. The first one to accomplish it and ring the bell won. But today, they wanted "Sorry." As we played, little black bugs jumped onto the board. I brushed them off. "Must be something as a result of the earthquake," I thought.

The next morning, Blanca helped me make the bed. It was still pulled out into the middle of the floor. As we tightened the bottom sheet, I noticed numerous little specks on my side of the bed. "What is that?" I asked her.

Blanca replied matter-of-factly, "Blood from flea bites. You guys have fleas."

"What! We can't have fleas!" I was horrified.

"You've had them for a couple of weeks," Blanca continued. "I think Brother Joe is bringing them home from the tent."

How could that be? And what could we get to kill the fleas? Blanca knew of a dark brown powder that would kill them. I sent her to the store immediately. I covered our bottom sheet with brown powder. I covered the kids' sheets with brown powder. The instructions said to put it only on the floor, that fleas would always return to the floor. But I wasn't taking any chances.

At noon, we sat down to eat. Juan was there. I glanced over at Christy just as a flea jumped up and down on top of her head! I shrieked! She burst into tears, Joe laughed till he cried. "Jimmy" frantically ruffled *his* hair. Juan consoled Christy.

Of course, I had to tell Joe, in front of Juan, about *all* of our fleas. Joe said, "You know, I've been noticing something jumping on the floor of the platform at the tent."

"The sawdust—fleas must be in the sawdust!" the realization hit him.

The day before we opened the tent campaign, Joe had insisted on buying wood shavings. One of the helpers said, "Hermano José, we don't use sawdust here for the floors. We sweep, sprinkle with water, sweep again. After a few weeks, the ground will be packed solid. You'll see."

But Joe *knew* that a tent meeting is not a tent meeting without wood shavings. He remembered smelling that fresh wood smell whenever Oral Roberts would come to town with his big tent. But those meetings lasted only a week or two. We had been in the tent for a month now.

Joe and Bob and Juan went to investigate. The sawdust was *alive* with fleas. They hopped hungrily onto Joe's socks. They didn't bite him—he was a carrier! They apparently didn't like to hop onto my knee-high boots, but I was their prime eating target at home. Me and Chilito.

Joe and Bob and Juan shoveled the teeming, wiggling sawdust into bags to haul it off. The caretaker, Jorge Funes, began to sweep the dirt and sprinkle it with water.

We *had* to get rid of the fleas at the tent and at home before Mom and Aunt Too arrived. They had written to say they were coming on July 29. And Mother was determined to take Christy home with them.

The next day we sat laughing around the Bowden's dining room table. We laughed that not only were we spreading the gospel, we were spreading *fleas* all over town.

"And," added Bob, "I think we've discovered a new spiritual gift—like the Pentecostal Methodists. So many people are being healed around their *cintura* (waist), that we must have *el don de la cintura,* (the gift of the waistline)!"

Gasping from laughter, I realized how much I loved these people, my new "family."

I remembered the Bible verses about anyone who has left home or left his brothers or sisters or mother or father for the cause of following Christ. Jesus said that person would receive a hundred times as much in this present age—homes, brothers, sisters, mothers, and children. And on top of that, eternal life! (Mark 10:29-30)

21

Family Changes

Viña del Mar, Chile
August 1971

---

he week with Mom and Aunt Too passed too quickly. We drove north up the coastal road, watching huge Pacific waves crash on the rocks. We ate a typical meal at a restaurant in Con-cón. We rode in a horse-drawn carriage through the streets of Viña, like typical tourists. Mom and Aunt Too loved the city—the Mediterranean style buildings, the cobblestone streets, the people so nicely dressed.

Our house still sat cracked from the earthquake with workers on the roof and we still experienced slight tremors daily, but that just added to the "foreign" atmosphere.

**Margaret's Mom, Christy, Timmy, Margaret,
and Aunt Too as workers repair the house in Viña**

On Saturday, Mom accompanied me to the children's Bible Clubs. She hugged every kid, I think, and cried at the third location where the little church and parsonage had been destroyed by the earthquake.

Under the tent, Mom walked across the uneven ground toward Daniel. He beamed a huge smile as she reached over to pat his cheek. He said a few words in *Castellano* Spanish and she replied in English. Neither understood a word, yet they communicated.

Aunt Too helped me to balance the checkbook and gave out spelling words to the kids—retired schoolteacher at work.

Juan endeared himself to Mom and Aunt Too, being a gracious host and an attentive listener (though he hardly understood a word of their English). Mom invited him to the States. "Are you serious?" Juan asked, "I have always wanted to visit the U.S." Mom assured him that he was welcome anytime—in fact, she said, he should just come home with Joe and Margaret. Juan said he would apply for a visa "mañana."

Timmy was happy to follow Aunt Too around everywhere. He informed her that baby Kimberly was in the States with Aunt One (Aunt Jan).

Mom sitting on our Chilean beach (the scene of our oil painting)

I showed Mom Christy's school work. Her latest test scores had arrived from our school monitor in the States—Christy showed poor comprehension in reading and little concept of fourth grade math skills. Mom would explain all of this to the teacher in Pensacola and would also secure private tutoring for Christy from the Alexander-Smith Academy where my brother, David, recently became director.

It was really hard to say good-bye to Christy. She had just turned nine years old. But we knew that these next few months would be a time of recuperation and healing for her. In addition, she would receive undivided "Grandma-attention."

Two weeks later, Joe and I, "Jimmy," and Juan were sitting with the Bowdens at their dining room table when a telegram arrived from Puerto Montt, 'way down in southern Chile. "He is yours. Come get him," Bob read aloud. We looked at each other—what did that mean?

Bob and Joe had been down in Puerto Montt for a revival the previous March (five months earlier) and stayed in the home of a man they always referred to as "the rich Arab." Was the telegram from him? Why would he send such a cryptic note?

"Could it be that baby?" questioned Joe. "Bob, remember the teenage maid who gave birth while we were there? I drove her to the clinic. You said, 'If it's a boy, and you don't want to keep him, I want him.' You even repeated that a couple of times to 'the rich Arab.'"

Bob and Margaret were staggered. They really wanted a boy, but because of an RH negative blood factor, they had been told not to have any more children. Could this be "their boy"?

"I don't want some baby sight unseen," Margaret sighed, "but ... I sure would like to go see him."

Bob felt he couldn't go with her because of the daily radio broadcasts and nightly services in *la carpa.* I could go. But two women could not travel alone—it was a two day trip each way.

Juan offered, "I could go with the ladies." That settled it.

The farther we drove south into the cold rain, the more nervous Margaret became. "Bob said the maid looked attractive. But what about the dad? We don't even know who he is."

She bit her bottom lip, twisting her face, "What if the baby is *really ugly?*"

"Tell them you were 'just looking,'" retorted Juan, cracking a smile.

"What if it is *so ugly* that I don't even want to hold it?" she worried again, just as we pulled into Puerto Montt and stopped to get gasoline.

The ugliest man we had ever seen came to fill our tank with gas. "Ah, that is one question answered," sighed Juan, "At least now we've seen the baby's father!"

Tension broken, dying with laughter, we found a hotel. As soon as we had checked into our rooms, Juan called "the rich Arab" to schedule a time the next morning to see the baby.

As we walked into the living room, the Arab's wife approached us. She held a small, oblong bundle.

"My maid cannot keep this baby. She loves him—she wants him to have a better life than she could provide." The señora held out the bundle. "Here, take him. He is yours, Señora Bowden."

Margaret hesitated, afraid. I reached out for the baby, who was tightly wrapped in a worn blanket. Margaret crowded close to peek at him.

We looked down into bright black eyes peering from a scrunched, fat face. Suddenly, he smiled at us. He was beautiful!

Juan said, "Could we take the baby back to the hotel for a few hours? So that Señora Bowden can decide if this is 'her baby'?"

As soon as we were in the van, Juan said, "The first thing we need to do is find a doctor. Have the baby checked."

When we arrived at the hotel, Juan began to make phone calls. He discovered that an old friend from college worked at the local hospital as an obstetrician-pediatrician. He would see us immediately.

Meanwhile, Margaret and I had taken the baby to our hotel room. We unwrapped the tight bundle. Perfect little arms and legs, tiny fingers with dirty fingernails, scalp crusted with cradle cap, dirty lint between his fingers and toes, but no diaper rash.

Juan came to take us to the hospital, where his friend received us graciously and examined the baby. "I remember delivering this child!" he exclaimed. He pronounced the baby healthy.

Crunch time. Time to decide. Margaret was scared. Her daughter Connie was fifteen years old. Jeanne was twelve. Could Margaret remember how to care for a baby? But, this baby was such a wonderful surprise. Could she turn her back on this unexpected gift?

Margaret looked at me, looked at Juan, and looked at the baby cradled in her arms. "I'll keep him," she declared.

Juan called "the rich Arab" to make arrangements for the proper documents to be drawn up and sent to Bob.

Night had fallen and all the stores were closed, but the doctor's mother said she would help us. She called her friend, a shop-owner, who opened her store so that we could purchase baby supplies. We tried to remember the essentials: baby soap, baby powder, baby oil, diapers, bottles, formula, pajamas with feet, undershirts, baby blankets, and pacifier.

A few minutes later, I filled the bathroom sink with warm water and placed the baby inside. He had never before had a bath like this. I scrubbed his scalp, loosening the crust. I squeezed the toe-jam out from between his tiny toes, soaped his hands and fingernails, washed the lint from under his fat neck, and washed his chubby legs and his round buttocks.

Powdered liberally, his scalp oiled with sweet smelling Johnson's Baby Oil, the baby glowed as I took him to Margaret. She dressed him in his new diapers and pajamas and then lay down beside him on the bed. Meanwhile, Juan had tried to figure out the baby formula; he held the bottle under hot, running water to warm it.

The next day, as we traveled home, we stopped at restaurants and asked them to please warm the bottle. That night, it was 10:30 before we found a hotel and finished checking in. We went quickly to the dining room to eat. The atmosphere was peaceful, the tables set for gracious dining, two guitarists strummed softly on a small stage.

Our baby was the only child in the dining room. Chileans did not take their babies to a restaurant late at night.

227

Our baby began to cry. I tried soothing him, bouncing him on my knee, jiggling him on my shoulder. Margaret searched for the pacifier. Juan started grinning. We were a "major disturbance" in this dining room. I lay the baby on my lap and stuck the pacifier in his mouth. He didn't want it. As I raised him back up, I bumped his head against the table. Then he really *did* cry.

Maybe he was hungry. Margaret ran to the room to get another bottle and more formula. She brought them back; then she and Juan assembled the stuff there at the table and asked the waiter to warm the bottle. Finally, we stuck the nipple in the baby's mouth. Silence. For a minute. Then he cried louder than ever!

Juan turned the bottle upside down and shook it. No milk came out. There was no hole in the new nipple! Juan picked up a fork and tried to poke a tine down inside the rubber to make a hole. I jiggled the screaming baby, while Margaret wrung her hands. By the time the baby could take his milk peacefully, we had developed a case of the giggles. Here we were—three adults who could not care for one little baby! We laughed so hard we almost fell off our chairs.

The following week in la carpa, Joe began to teach the people chorus #2:

Solamente en Cristo,	It's only in Jesus,
Solamente en él.	It's only in him
La salvación	That's where you'll find,
Se encuentra en él.	His saving grace.
No hay otro nombre	No other name is
Dado a los hombres.	Given to all peoples.
Solamente en Cristo,	It's only in Jesus,
Solamente en él.	It's only in him.

It's a lively chorus, and the people enjoyed singing it.

After a few nights, Joe wanted to sing it as a solo. "It's only in the tent, it's only here ..." He paused and asked, "Is that correct?"

The people weren't sure.

"No, it's only *en Cristo*, in Jesus, where we find salvation," Joe reminded them. They smiled.

Joe sang again, "It's only in the saints, only in them ..." This time the people were ready. "No," they exclaimed.

Every night, Joe would choose another option—only in Bob, or in Joe, or in the church, or in doing penance. The people loved it, not realizing how much theology they were learning.

On August 28, Bob and Margaret, Connie and Jeanne came forward to present Robert Edward Bowden (Robby) for baby dedication. Uncle Joe performed the ceremony.

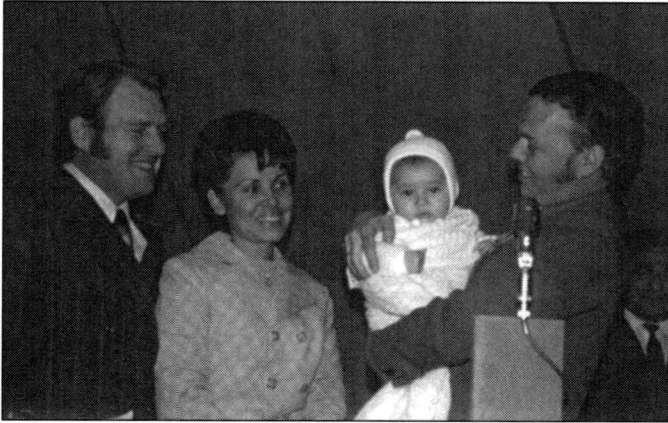

Bob and Margaret Bowden with baby Robby, Joe

22

Planting a Church—Our Philosophy

Viña del Mar, Chile
September 1971

When Joe was ten years old, he went home with the Kirbys to eat Sunday dinner. There was no butter on the table and Joe really wanted some for his bread, but he was afraid to ask for butter—for fear the Kirbys believed it was a sin.

Joe and I both grew up under legalism—a set of unwritten rules governing Christianity. If you <u>did</u> this and that or did <u>not</u> do this and that, you were a "good Christian." For example, a woman could wear a gaudy brooch on her blouse, but she could not wear even a tiny earring.

Margaret Bowden, too, had grown up with these arbitrary rules. Bob had not. He was converted after he and Margaret were married, when she dragged him to church on an Easter Sunday morning.

Juan Toro told us stories of church congregations miming legalistic traditions of "foreign" missionaries, in effect North American culture imposed on the converts.

Joe and I had lived in Latin America for three-and-a-half years now and realized how cultural so many "Christian" customs are—Sunday school at 9:45 a.m., worship service at 11:00, Sunday night service at 7:00, Wednesday night at 7:00. Where is any of that in the Bible?

In Chile, a traditional Christian belief system permeated the culture and was a tremendous advantage to our work. People believed in God-the-Trinity, in miracles, in the Bible. A Chilean would say, "Of course I am a Christian! You think I'm a dog?" Most people also said, "I am Catholic, but ... I never go to Mass, but ... I was baptized as a baby." Christianity was theory to them; most of them did not know that a person could experience a relationship with Jesus Christ.

As we sat around our dining room tables, Joe and I, Bob, Margaret and Juan hammered out our philosophy for "planting" the new church in *la carpa*.

We paraphrased St. Augustine, "In essentials, clarity; in non-essentials, liberty; above all things, charity." We determined not to preach-teach against anything that was not specifically mentioned in the Bible. We would not impose rules of dress or conduct. We would not teach against the Catholic Church beliefs or against superstitions.

However, we would definitely and clearly teach the people to read the Bible and apply what they read. We would teach the actual practice of the Ten Commandments and Jesus' teaching of love for neighbor. By doing this, we hoped the converts would "slough off" prior non-biblical beliefs and customs.

We discussed the role of the Holy Spirit in convicting of sin. The way Joe and I had been raised, some dear saint had told everyone the religious rules. The Bible says the Holy Spirit would "convict of sin." Would He? Alone?

Furthermore, our boss, Melvin Hodges, had written a book, "The Indigenous Church" in which he purported that in order for a church to be "home-grown" and to continue after the missionary left, it must be

- Self-sustaining,
- Self-governing,
- Self-propagating.

Did these principles work in fact and not just in theory?

Joe announced in the tent, "As you can see, we don't have enough benches for everyone to be seated. What if we receive an offering and you stay to help count it? Tomorrow whoever is available can go with me to buy lumber for more benches." The people loved it; someone found a hat and received an offering. A dozen people stayed afterward to count it. The next night, we had our first new benches. The practice continued.

Another night, Joe asked, "Would you like to know more about the Bible? We could meet any day you choose, at a time you choose." By consensus, they wanted to meet on Sundays. What time? They decided on 7 p.m., an hour before service, so they would have to pay only one bus fare.

Our Bible Study attendees wished the hour were even longer. So Joe announced, "Would you like to have classes a couple of nights a week to study *Curso Bíblico Elemental*? If so, meet me here on the left after the service."

We figured maybe fifteen would want the lessons—thirty-five people signed up! The course was what we had wanted to teach in Temuco, the series by Louisa J. Walker consisting of ten small books including *New Life in Christ* and *The Bible*.

And so, the people were becoming self-governing and self-sustaining. Also, by inviting relatives and friends to *la carpa*, the congregation was becoming self-propagating. Daniel had obtained a *media-agua* after the earthquake and now lived in a community of *media-aguas*. He asked Joe, "Could we get some folks together to come to my *barrio* to tell my neighbors about Jesus?"

One night a woman told me, "Yesterday two people came to my house. They said they were the only correct religion and that a true Christian did not drink coffee or watch television on Sundays. 'Fine,' I told them. 'Here is my Bible, exactly where does it say that?' They stammered around and left my house quick!" She had been a convert only two weeks. I could have shouted for joy!

María approached me, her shoulders back, and her neck rigid. "*Muy bien, Hermana Margarita*, (All right, Margaret), show me where in the Bible it says I cannot go to the casino. I like to gamble and I always win."

"María, the Bible does not specifically say you should not go to the casino; however—"

"Good, good," she interrupted, "I gamble to be able to buy gifts for my grandchildren."

I continued, "But the Bible does say we are to be good stewards of our time and our money."

"I always win, I always win," she said as she walked away.

I was thrilled. I knew the Holy Spirit was convicting her of gambling or she never would have brought it up in the first place.

Another woman walked over to me, "*Hermana*, I have always prayed to my saints, especially my birth saint. But I cannot find that in the Bible. Where is the verse about praying to the saints?"

"I don't believe it is mentioned, but there are verses about praying to the Father and to Jesus."

"I've started doing that, I'll do that more."

Jaime, a young man in his late twenties, came over to talk to me. "I have been carrying this pack of cigarettes for three days now without even wanting a smoke. I've been a heavy smoker since I was a kid. Now I don't even think about it. Do you have any idea why?"

Luís had been attending for several weeks, gradually becoming more enthusiastic and more involved. He signed up for the extra studies. As we talked about choosing our friends wisely, his hand shot up, "I am doing that now! I used to look on the bus for men, now I look here at the tent for girls!" We all burst out laughing at him. We had not known he had been homosexual. His "conversion" had been Holy Spirit orchestrated.

Another night Luís said with tears, "I have never bought anything significant for my mother. Yesterday for her birthday, I bought her a blender—she has always wanted a blender. Now with the money I save by not spending it on guys, I have extra left over to help her and to give in the offerings."

Leontina stood right in my face, beaming, "I am so glad I was deaf. If not for my deafness, I would never have come to *la carpita*, never have known this healing and this peace. Pray that my husband will come back to me. He left me months ago to move in with his *pinche*, girlfriend." (He came back.)

Isolina Cruz de López lay on her deathbed. The doctor told her adult children, "Do not tell her any bad news. Do not excite her in any way. She is dying of heart failure. It is only a matter of a few days."

A large tumor protruded from Isolina's back. Another large tumor grew in her belly. Her spine twisted sideways and also bent forward. She could not straighten up—when she stood, her head was near her knees.

Her legs were twisted, her knees crisscrossed, her feet turned inward.

Isolina had received a Bible from her niece, who had moved to the States. Lying alone, near death, Isolina dared to read the Bible. It fell open to John 11, the story of Lazarus who was dead and in a tomb. Isolina read the story with amazement. Jesus said, "¡*Lázaro, ven fuera!*" "Lazarus, come out!" And Isolina thought, "I am like Lazarus, I am as good as dead. Why couldn't Jesus heal me?"

Isolina called for her son. José thought she was dying and ran to her side. "Take me to church. Now. Call a taxi. I want to go see the priest. Now."

To honor her dying wish, José called a taxi. He carried his mom to the car. They drove to the nearest Catholic church. It was closed. No one was there. They drove to another one. Closed. No one there. They drove to a third church. No one was there. It was very unusual that no priest would be on the premises.

Discouraged, Isolina wept, "Just take me home."

As they pulled up in front of the house, a neighbor was watching. The neighbors had supposed Isolina was being rushed to the hospital to die. Now the nosy neighbor said, "Wait a minute. There is a tent down on *Calle Quillota*, Quillota Street. They say on the radio that a priest is always there, every night. Why don't you try that?"

José carried Isolina into *la carpa* and placed her on a rough bench. They were late. We had a guest speaker, a Peruvian who was short and black as night and full of the Spirit of God. The Peruvian preached a brief sermon; he prayed the sinner's prayer with everyone. Then he said, "If you need healing, come forward. Now."

People stood up from their benches and walked forward. He began to pray for those gathered at the front.

Isolina scooted off the bench. She hobbled to the end of the aisle. She shuffled her twisted feet along the rough ground. Her head was near her knees, her nightgown and robe distended over the tumors on her back and belly.

The Peruvian glanced up and saw her walking laboriously down the aisle. In a loud voice, he said, "Lady, Jesus heals you. Do right now what you could not do when you came here tonight."

Isolina paused. She tilted her head so that her eyes could see the Peruvian. He repeated, "Lady, Jesus heals you. Do right now what you could not do when you came here tonight."

She raised her head a little more. And more. Her back straightened. Her legs came uncrossed. Her feet became straight and firm. Her heart trouble vanished. Both large tumors disappeared. Her robe billowed around her as her body shrank to normal size.

There was no fanfare. Jesus healed in the Bible stories. He is the same yesterday, today and forever.

**María (casino), María Funes (caretaker),
Isolina, Margaret, Baby Robby, Margaret Bowden**

23

Spring Harvest

Viña del Mar, Chile
September 1971, continued

I took a big bite of the roast beef sandwich. Um. *Deliciosa.* The meat was thinly sliced; juice dripped from the bun onto my plate. I took another delicious bite as I perched on a barstool in the bus station in Santiago. Audrey Manning and I had just flown in from a five-day women's conference in Buenos Aires, Argentina, where some days we spent two hours riding buses, subways, and trains just to get from one side of Buenos Aires to the other. Arriving back in Chile, Audrey caught her connecting flight up to Antofagasta and I was about to catch a bus ride back to Viña.

Joe, "Jimmy," and Juan met me at the Viña bus station and we went to the Bowdens' for supper. As we sat down to eat fish, Margaret complained about the *veda*, prohibition—no selling of beef, pork, lamb, or chicken. I spoke up, "Wow, that's weird. There's no *veda* in Santiago because I had a roast beef sandwich for lunch."

Juan started grinning, "Oh, you did? And it was at the bus station? And the *beef* was really good, huh?" He laughed so hard it was difficult for him to say, "Margarita, it was horse meat!"

Veda was lifted only two weekends a month; and *veda* was merely one symptom of President Allende's socialism going awry. Allende's honeymoon year was over.

The long narrow ribbon of land that is Chile features a coastal mountain range on the western border. The eastern border is made up of nearly 3,000 miles of majestic Andes Mountains. Lying in between is a fertile valley where fruits and vegetables of all kinds are cultivated in abundance—usually ... but there had been very little planting during the past year, ever since the take-over of land by the workers.

Now there was only a small spring harvest, with practically no summer crops being planted. Hardly any sheep, cattle, or hogs had been bred. The only foods in abundance were seafood and eggs.

Since the mines had been nationalized, copper production, the primary source of export income, was down drastically. To make matters worse, copper prices had dropped on the world market. For almost every commodity, demand outpaced supply; a thriving black market sprang up, taking advantage of the shortages.

The political right had sat back, defensive and silent, during the past year. Now, seeing economic disaster looming, the political right united with the moderates to go on the offensive. They were furious that the executive branch of government had overstepped its bounds in expropriating land and businesses. The alliance tried to impeach Allende. Not enough votes. They toyed with the idea of a military coup. But the time was not right. Not yet.

The economy had begun to free-fall and the next two years would bring economic disaster. Before the actual military coup, both the government and the economy would be paralyzed with inflation at more than 500 per cent.

Well, there was still seaweed. And it was cooking in our kitchen. It smelled really, really gross. Luís insisted he was a chef and would prepare a gourmet seaweed dinner for us, the Bowdens, and the Peruvian evangelist and his wife. (The evangelists stayed with us for two weeks.)

Luís had brought the brown rope seaweed to the house the day before. "Soak it in a big pot overnight. Put a weight on the lid because the weed will swell and push the lid up."

As Joe walked by the schoolroom where "Jimmy" and I were, he paused and motioned toward the dog, "Oh, good. The way it smells in the kitchen, I thought Luís was cooking Chilito."

To accompany the slimy seaweed, Luís prepared spiny, green balls. He cut off the tops of the softball-size, bright green balls to expose the inside—orange tongue-looking strips. Luís claimed this was a seafood delicacy. I was glad for the salad and bread.

The men's ministries groups from Santiago brought four buses filled with men and their wives to the tent for a Saturday work day. With offerings (and a little extra), Joe and Bob had purchased two *media-aguas* to combine for our "educational building," our "annex."

The men also constructed and planed benches, worked to level the ground both inside and outside the tent, and gave out handbills on the street. The women cleaned up clutter on the lot.

The Valpo church women prepared lunch for everyone, and for the first time, the tent women worked together to prepare *once* (own-say) tea.

That night, after the music, the new Bible study students were dismissed to walk to the "annex." We decided to begin with two courses: I would teach one course on Tuesday nights and Juan another on Thursdays.

We began youth meetings on Friday evenings. The women wanted to meet on Saturdays, mid-morning. Then the men wanted to get together. And Joe and Juan began boys' clubs on Saturday afternoons.

Daniel did not miss one activity. He loved the studying and had learned so much since that first Bible study on Sunday afternoon, when he sat on the first row, new Bible in hand.

Joe had begun, "There are actually two parts to the Bible, an older part and a newer part." He went on teaching about "chapter" and "verse" and then had the students find John 3:16. Joe said, "Now close your Bibles and let's see who can be the first to find John 3:16." Daniel kept his finger in the spot so he would be first.

Joe, "Jimmy," and I knew absolutely nothing about snow skiing but on September 10, we drove for three hours up into the Andes Mountains to Hotel Portillo, a ski resort. Since Joe had attended the tent services for seventy-six consecutive nights, I figured he could take one night off for our wedding anniversary.

For two dollars, a ski instructor taught us the "wedge," but we fell down more than we stood up. The ski lift was the kind you grab hold of with one hand while you ski up the mountain. Since I couldn't ski well at all, when I tried to take "Jimmy" on his skis with me on my skis up the ski lift ... we went sideways so bad ... the lift bogged down and people yelled at me to "let go and get out of the way."

Joe started skiing down the beginners' slope and headed straight for a precipice. I screamed, and finally, just before the edge of the drop-off, he sat down—his legs straddling the orange pole with the little orange flag warning of danger. He scooted backward and as I tried to help him up, we both fell down. We lay in the snow and laughed until we cried.

The next day, as we started our drive down the mountain, a terrible snow storm made driving extremely hazardous. The *carabineros*, police, warned us not to attempt the drive down, but we felt we had to get back to *la carpa*. We slid and prayed all the way down those hairpin curves.

That night, the congregation gave us a surprise *once*—it was the first social event for *la carpa*. They also gave us an engraved, copper plate to commemorate our tenth wedding anniversary.

Luís, Margaret Register, the tenth anniversary copper plate, Joe, Jaime

On September 18, Chilean Independence Day, everyone was off work, so we planned a church picnic. We met at the tent, piled into our Suburbans and a rented bus, and drove to the river.

I stood on the riverbank watching Joe and Bob shiver as they walked into the river—water mixed with melting snow flowing down the mountainsides of the Andes. (September is comparable to March in North America.) Joe and Bob walked around in the river, scooting their feet, trying to find a level spot where three people could stand in waist-deep water, out of the main current. We were ready for our first baptism.

With tears in my eyes, I stood beside the seventeen people who were ready for baptism. I knew each person by name. I knew of their prior life. I knew the radical transformation that had occurred. I knew their sincerity and their passion for their new life. I remembered wondering on the way to Chile, "Will I love the Chilean people? I've never even met one." Now, each of these "tent people" was my family and my friend.

In Latin America, water baptism is not taken lightly—a person has made a rational decision as an adult and is willing to be classified as an evangelical. Many times, the newly-baptized person is disowned by his or her family.

Bob and Joe baptizing a new convert

241

As each person walked out to Joe and Bob, each one held his head high and told how he had first come to the tent and what a change it had made in his life. Then Joe said, "Upon your profession of faith in Jesus Christ as personal Savior, we baptize you in the name of the Father, the Son, and the Holy Spirit." Joe then baptized the candidate, as Bob helped. Then it was Bob's turn.

Of course, Daniel wanted to be first.

And then the picnic! I took a big bowl of potato salad and a platter of tuna salad sandwiches. All of the others opened baskets, took out meat to grill, scavenged for firewood, and built a fire! They ate at their own site, each one eating the food they brought—this was only their second shared social event.

After eating, people walked around introducing themselves to each other, talking, swimming, playing soccer. Kids played tag.

Luís' mom and dad and his sisters were there. So was a new family who had been Mormons. The man had been a church leader-in-training but a friend told him he should go check out the strange people at *la carpa*. The man was so touched, he and his family began to attend right away, and he donated paint for the *media-aguas*.

I walked up to a group of people who were having a good time laughing about the benches at the tent, how the green wood had twisted so that when people sat on one end of the bench, they pitched forward, while the other half pitched backward. One guy said, "At least I wasn't on the bench that broke!" "I was!" piped up someone else, laughing. One night a row of people had "disappeared" when their bench split in two and they all tumbled to the ground! They had stood up, laughing, and moved to different benches.

María came walking up to me. "When is the next baptism?"

"I'm not sure. Probably in a couple of weeks. Why?"

"I want to be baptized. I just cut up my casino I.D. card and threw the pieces into the river."

24

Decisions

Viña del Mar, Chile
October–November 1971

-⸲⸲⟡⸲⸲-

acked-up sewage was only one challenge at the two-day girls' retreat in Antofagasta. As national president of girls' clubs, I had organized camps for the three Chilean zones: north, south, and central.

Audrey Manning thought her house would be an ideal place for the northern retreat; she figured maybe fifteen girls would come. There were forty-five!

Our theme was *"Ser Conquistadora"*—"Be a (feminine) Conquistador." Several women helped us teach classes on hygiene, sex education, dating, drugs, etiquette, and devotion to God. We interspersed classes with swimming and handcrafts. The girls slept wall-to-wall in every corner of the house. They loved the retreat and they did not want to go home.

My favorite meal was the homemade tomato soup. The women boiled tomatoes and then mashed them through a sieve, adding milk and butter.

That night, out in the desert near the Manning's house, we made a *fogata*, bonfire. As part of our devotional, each girl held a small stick that she could throw into the fire as she dedicated herself more completely to God.

The following week, as I drove south to the next retreat, I knew that Sylvia Riquelme would be proud of me in my "modern" clothes. Thirty-five girls attended that retreat held in the Riquelme's church. Sylvia had everything so well organized that I just taught a couple of classes and enjoyed watching her work.

Then it was my turn to host a retreat in the Central Zone. Margaret Bowden and I came up with five camping tents plus a long tarpaulin to take to our favorite spot beside the river. Joe and "Jimmy" and Juan set up everything for us. Juan was lifeguard and our night-guard; Joe helped the women cook—actually, *pestered* is a better word—before he left to go back to Viña for the evening service.

There were 36 girls, plus counselors, for a total of 47. That night, around the campfire, I told the story of Esther as Margaret held a flashlight shining on the flannelgraph figures. Our *fogata* was wonderful, as each girl truly sensed God's presence. Even "Jimmy" and Juan participated, throwing sticks into the fire as a sign of surrender to God.

Joe, Dolores the cook, and "Jimmy" at camp

244

A few days later, Joe had diarrhea. He actually missed a night at the tent. He told me not to tell anyone at the service what he was "sick with," but a little old woman insisted. The next night Joe was still absent. But the little woman had brought the remedy for him: a *tapón*, stopper, she said, and handed me a narrow, longish bundle of herbs. "What is it, again?" I asked. "A *tapón* to stop the diarrhea."

Joe declares that it was to use for tea. I believed it was to be inserted. Joe decided—really fast—that he was cured.

I loved speaking to various women's groups several times a month, almost always at an *once*, tea. The Anglican Church women invited me, too. They asked me to speak specifically about the infilling of the Holy Spirit with the evidence of speaking in tongues. I read from John 14 and related Mom's story. I told the women that although we look back with assurance on our salvation experience, we can also sense the presence of the Holy Spirit "fresh and new" daily.

John Mazurek came to the tent for a week to teach from the book of Acts. His topic was "The Work of the Holy Spirit Today." Many people experienced the infilling of the Holy Spirit.

The tent was full every night now, and more and more people attended the Bible studies. The "tent people" were indeed becoming "a church," and they needed a pastor. Our furlough was coming up soon. Bob, an evangelist at heart, wanted to be free to accept the many invitations he was receiving to visit various areas of Chile and even other countries.

We taught the congregation about tithing, knowing that if ten families tithed, the offering would equal the income of the average family. This could be a pastor's salary.

Our friends Sylvia and Leonardo Riquelme came to stay with us for a week while Leo preached in the tent. The people loved them. Leo was a successful pastor down south. He was smart, sharp, and well educated. Sylvia also had her college degree as a social worker.

As we sat at our dining room table, Joe and Bob talked to the Riquelmes about becoming pastors of *la carpa*. Previously, we had hinted at this possibility, and Sylvia and Leo had been praying about it. They accepted the challenge and said they could move to Viña the first of the year.

Joe wrote to the Foreign Missions Department and requested that we be allowed to begin our furlough in January. It would be three months early, but we would come back that much sooner, therefore, better coordinating with the Bowdens' furlough. Since the new pastor would be arriving in January, it seemed logical. The FMD said "No."

Joe and I did not know what to do! Christy was in the States. We really missed her, but she was doing well in school. I'd have times of crying, but would always remember those dark circles under her eyes and how she was thriving now. We wrote to her (and she to us) in a mixture of Spanish and English.

Joe and I also talked about the possibility of my going on to the States the first of the year. I could get "Jimmy" into first grade for the second semester.

We did not know what to do.

At the end of September, our monthly statement arrived from FMD and our monthly check deposit was 0. Zero. *Nada.* Nothing. A note attached stated, "Due to the rate of exchange in Chile, we have been sending you too much money. We are adjusting for that this month. Next month you will receive half of your original salary."

We could not believe it! Joe and Bob called the other missionaries—the same thing had happened to them. Everyone called "Headquarters," and "special checks" were deposited for us.

Later, Melvin Hodges wrote, "Our office received false economical information issued as political propaganda."

For Thanksgiving, all the Chilean missionaries came to our house—there were eighteen of us. Each family brought food and we had a wonderful meal. No turkeys, of course, but chicken and dressing. And "pumpkin" pies made from *zapallo.*

One of the men motioned for me to step into another room. He reached inside his jacket and pulled out a box of candy—my favorite *Arequipe* caramels made from goat milk. "I brought this for you because I know you can't get it in Viña … I remember how much you like it."

I did not appreciate the look in his eyes or the privacy of the presentation. But I sure did want the candy. So I accepted it, telling him thanks.

The next day I waited until he was standing beside his wife. I walked over, looked pointedly at her and said, "I just want to thank you for my candy." She looked startled. "He gave me the candy you all brought me—you know, my favorite." She turned to glare at him, and if looks could kill, he would have dropped dead!

Joe and Bob received numerous phone calls as a result of the radio programs they were presenting. One was an invitation to go and "pray for a house." They weren't sure what that meant.

They took six-year-old "Jimmy" with them. As they arrived at the house, the owner said, "I used to be into demon worship and the demons followed me into this house. At night they beat on the walls, slam doors, and knock things off shelves. I need you to exorcise the house."

Joe and Bob walked through the house, anointing with oil and praying. The demonic activity ceased. But "Jimmy" was petrified! Of course, Joe and Bob didn't know the visit would be so dramatic.

Another day they went to visit a man who lived high up on a mountainside. As they entered a humble home, the wife greeted them, saying that she was the person who had called to see if they could help her husband. She led them to the bedside of a shriveled, pale man. He looked very old.

"I am dying, as you see," he rasped. "I have cancer of the stomach. It has spread now. It is eating me alive. I am only in my 50s. I am old before my time. If only 'they' hadn't done this to me!"

Joe and Bob were trying to follow what the old man was saying as his voice rose, anger and bitterness tainting the tone and crisping the syllables, "It is entirely their fault. The city. They sent me the electric bill. I paid it. They sent me a notice that the bill was overdue. I went to the office, showed them my receipt. They said they would take care of it.

"Then they sent me another overdue bill! I returned to the office. I showed them my receipt. But they made me pay! Pay! They made me pay! Again! I had to pay that *same* bill two times!

"I am *furioso*, furious. I have gone to their office every month to let them know I already paid that bill! Now, I'm too sick to go. My *rabia*, rage, overwhelms me. The doctor says it's killing me—my bitterness is eating my insides."

"How long ago was this bill?" Bob asked.

"Twenty years! They cheated me twenty years ago! And I won't let them forget it, no sir-ree. I won't let them forget it!"

He died a few weeks later—killed by his *rabia*—bitter rage.

Joe and Juan went to the American Embassy in Santiago to check on a tourist visa for Juan. He hoped that Mom was serious about her invitation, because it was his dream to visit the States.

Mom and Dad wrote to assure Juan that they were sincere in their invitation for him to visit.

I requested a schedule of classes from Pensacola Junior College. When did the winter semester begin? I really wanted to take some courses—since Joe had interrupted my college education with his marriage idea.

I asked Mom to check on openings in first grade at the church school where Christy attended. Would they take "Jimmy" for second semester?

Mom and Dad notified our renters in Pensacola that they would need to vacate the house.

We wrestled and wrestled with what to do. Furlough was not optional. After four years, we were required to return to the States to visit our supporting churches and to attend the School of Missions.

We kept wondering if I should go on home and Joe should stay for a month or two until our official furlough date. Even then, when the Riquelmes came to assume the pastorate of the tent, Joe did not want to be looking over their shoulders. They were experienced pastors; they would do a good job. Furthermore, a month or two was not long enough for Joe to get involved in a different new work.

We'd rather get the furlough year over with, and then come back to plunge into another ministry.

During these days, the *Trío Asaph* came to the tent for a week. They were an excellent musical group, four guys, actually. They sang and played guitar, harp, accordion, mandolin, and violin. Joe and Eduardo, their leader, really hit it off, and Eduardo wanted to cut a record with Joe. Joe could sing and play his sax; the *Trío Asaph* would sing backup, and Eduardo would arrange all the music. They made a demo tape to take to a producer in Santiago.

Then our landlady called, "Any way you can be out of the house by January 1? I have a renter who wants to move in."

25

Hasta Luego—See You Later

Viña del Mar, Chile
December 1971

Things were moving too swiftly—the landlady pressuring us to vacate the house, the Riquelmes coming in January to assume pastorate of *la carpa*. Also, Mom wrote that there was room for "Jimmy"/Timmy to enter first grade in January. Plus, Eduardo set the date in January with the recording company for Joe and the *Trío Asaph* to cut their record.

Then Joe received an invitation to speak at a youth camp in Argentina the first part of February. And Everett Ward contacted Joe: "Could you come to Paraguay during February and March? I am starting a church and would like to talk to you about how you and Bob went about it. Also, I have an evangelist from Texas, Doyle Jones, who needs an interpreter. But Carolyn and I need a break. Could you come and interpret for Doyle? You could preach some, too. Any chance you could come for several weeks?"

The timing seemed to be right: The Bowdens said that Joe could stay at their house during January, while he traveled back and forth to Santiago to cut the record. After that, Joe would leave for Argentina and from there to Paraguay, before returning to Florida.

251

Juan was crestfallen. He had looked forward to visiting the States, but he was scared to travel alone. How could he coordinate with Joe, since Joe didn't know when he would leave Paraguay?

We decided that Juan could travel with Timmy, me, and Chilito. Joe booked our tickets for December 30. We would leave Santiago about midnight and fly for eight hours to Miami, go through customs, and then fly on to Pensacola.

I began to sort things into three groups: sell or give away, store for our return, take to the States. We received permission to store things upstairs at the Valpo church, in an unfinished area—linens, kitchen things, major appliances, our bed, wicker rocking chair, and Joe's tools. I packed several boxes to ship to the States: our oil painting of the sea, the copper plaque given to us by the tent people, some wooden carvings and copper items as gifts for pastors and family.

Also, I had promised to compose another booklet of ideas for the girls' clubs for the coming year. Margaret and Joe helped me cut the stencils and mimeograph the pages.

I was not ready to leave Chile. Yet I *was* ready to leave—to go complete the year of itinerary, so that we could return.

Joe preached frequently at the tent now, as Bob was traveling more and more. Joe took an entire week to talk about John 3:16, taking a phrase per night: God loved the world, God gave, God gave his Son, whoever believes in Him ....

The tent continued to be full every night with people accepting Christ and being healed. Señora Marchán had a severe pain in her right shoulder. It especially bothered her when she washed clothes by hand, which she had to do every day because she had several small children. The pain disappeared and did not return.

Isolina, who had been so marvelously healed in the early days of *la carpa*, was elected president of our women's group; Juan's mother and aunt were officers, too. Isolina and her husband, along with their children (who were grown and married), came every night. After Isolina had brought her entire extended family to the tent, she began to bring neighbors, introducing them to me night after night.

Isolina's elderly mother approached me. "I know I'm an *anci-anita*, old woman, but I am deaf in this ear. Do you think God would heal an *ancianita*?" I was sure He would. And He did.

Isolina's son, José, with his right arm in a sling, came forward for prayer for healing. As Joe finished praying, he said, "Right now, do what you could not do when you came here tonight." José took his arm out of the sling and raised it straight up, high. He smiled.

The next night, Isolina motioned for us to go and talk to José. José told us that he had been at work the day before when his arm had been caught in a piece of machinery. Both bones of his forearm were broken. But the doctor could not set them because the flesh was so mutilated that it could not be put into a cast. The doctor bandaged the arm and said for José to wait until the flesh healed. Then the doctor would re-break the bones and set them properly. José had come to the tent like that—with his broken, bandaged arm in a sling.

When Joe told him, "Do what you could not do," José slipped his arm from the sling and raised it straight up. José heard the bones snapping and popping into place. The pain was gone.

When he had arrived home that night, he insisted on removing the bandage. Now he turned to us and said, "Look here. Look at my arm. The flesh is totally healed. It is as smooth as a baby's skin." And it was. The arm was totally healed, both inside and out.

Several nights later, José and his wife came forward for prayer. They asked Joe if it would be all right to ask God for a baby. They prayed. The *guaguita*, baby, was born nine months later.

Fidel Castro visited President Allende in November and gave him an AK-47 assault rifle. During that summer of 1971-72 (December, January, February), the political situation continued to sizzle. The summer weather, which made life easier for the squatters living in their *media-agua* shacks, also gave good weather for protests to intensify.

Shortages of food grew even worse.

This political and economic instability was extremely unusual for Chile. With the land isolated geographically, Chileans had learned to be independent and had a strong sense of national identity. They flew the Chilean flag at every possible occasion and sang the national anthem with pride, verse after verse of it.

Chile had been one of Latin America's most stable and politically sophisticated nations. It was a republic with a constitutional and democratic style of government. The Socialist, Allende, had been *elected*. Chile was progressive; it boasted state-run universities, a national health system, and welfare institutions. The Chilean was self-assured; his grammar was excellent, as was his pronunciation—even in all the *modismos,* catchy sayings, and their running-of-words-together, which drove me crazy! The Chilean held his head up high and looked you in the eye, certain of his heritage and his future. Until now.

At the tent, summer meant we could take off our winter coats and roll up the sides of the tent.

One night, "Jimmy" kept misbehaving with the kids sitting around him, so I grabbed his arm and ushered him outside the tent. We walked over into the shadows where I prepared to whack his bottom. Just then, he was snatched away from me. María de Funes, the caretaker's wife, held him tight. "Hermana Margarita, Jimmy is just a baby, only six years old. Don't discipline him." So ... I couldn't discipline "Jimmy" at the tent because of María, or at home because of Chilito!

One Saturday we invited church congregations from surrounding towns to come to the tent for a rally. Joe led the singing, as usual, and the people loved it—except for one particular chorus. On the third line, our tent people sang the melody one way; all the others sang it "wrong." As it turned out, Joe had only heard the melody a couple of times and remembered it ... differently. Then he had taught his "different version" to our people.

A few days later, the tent people planned a special Christmas meal of seafood paella. The men dug a hole, filled it with wood, and set the fire. When only coals remained, the men lowered a large bundle of seafood wrapped in banana leaves. They covered it all and let it "bake" all night.

This Christmas meal at the tent was bittersweet for me because it was also my *despedida*, going-away meal. Daniel brought me a large bouquet of flowers. Everyone showered me with love. At the end of January, they would have another *despedida* for Joe.

Within a few weeks, the church would be organized with one hundred charter members. I knew it was time to "cut the apron strings" and let the church "go." I knew I had to leave for furlough. But I didn't want to leave.

Where had these last four years gone? We had begun to learn the language, the culture, and the cultural nuances. We had eaten new foods, slept in tents beside Chilean rivers. Shared bread. Shared life. Shared love.

Perhaps the joy of Viña was sweeter because of the pain we experienced in Temuco. Certainly, the love of the people of Viña was stronger than one man's hatred had been.

With God's help, we had survived. We had triumphed.

How could I leave these beloved ones?

But, I was coming back. Wasn't I? Please, God!

26

Shocked!

Pensacola, Florida
January 1972

*I*had no idea that upon reentry into the United States, I would experience culture shock. There was a sense of alienation. I felt "foreign." I was shocked that I did not fit in with my family or with my church family. I was no longer *only* North American. Neither was I Chilean. I was shocked to realize that for the remainder of my life I would have a "third" culture, a blend. I was indeed a "foreign" missionary.

I was appalled at the materialism, at the super-abundance of "stuff." I saw the abundance in stores jammed with products, in homes jammed with non-essentials. The mindset of everyone seemed to be to "acquire more stuff." There seemed to be little desire to give—only to consume. Women's conversations seemed centered on hair, jewelry, designer shoes, and bags.

I grieved at the superficiality, the shallow mindset. Friendships seemed shallow. Christians' devotion to God seemed shallow. Christians' prayers seemed shallow. Christians' faith seemed self-focused.

The American church seemed almost a pseudo-church. There seemed to be little desire to reach out beyond the church walls. Where were the people whose lives were being transformed? Where was a congregation who received the Word and put the principles into action in their daily lives?

My heart broke to see the cultural decline—television content seemed more debauched, vocabulary on television more crude. People, in general, seemed more rude.

I wept at the provincialism—people seemed to think, "What world?" And their attitude seemed to be, "Who cares?" People were not interested in our experiences—the joys or the sorrows—unless we were "on stage" where people often seemed to listen out of religious obligation.

As missionaries, our lives and ministry had been integrated; our days motivated by compassion. Now I felt I had nothing meaningful to do—certainly no one wanted church services every night. I couldn't have Saturday Bible clubs because we needed to itinerate. Even if there had been women's *onces,* teas, what did we have in common to talk about? I had no women's or girls' booklets to write, no girls' retreats to plan. I missed the sense of feeling needed.

I was desperately homesick for friends in Chile. I missed our missionary colleagues. I missed our Chilean friends. I missed the lingering meals where we could sit and talk and laugh, where sharing conversation was just as vital as eating the food.

And when itinerary began, I felt I couldn't make real friends because we were in a different church every night—no one could know "me" but only my stage self. No one saw me cry or be angry; no one knew how human I really was.

I felt false because "on stage" my holy-self was demonstrated with wonderful stories from Viña. Missionaries never talked about the painful times. I dared not mention the pain of Temuco.

I felt like a plastic saint.

I was not the only one who experienced culture shock. Juan, too, observed the abundance of things in the States and was appalled.

In fact, Juan's jaw had dropped open when he stood just inside the door of the first supermarket he had ever seen. He turned his head from side to side, gazing at the items. "Why is there so much?" he asked. We walked down the cereal aisle. He drew in a sharp breath, "Why do they need so many choices of cereal? So many boxes of each one?" We arrived at the frozen food section, and I explained that inside all these boxes and bags were frozen foods. "No, there can't be. It must be just an empty box with a picture." I handed him a box, a TV dinner. He could not believe his eyes. "Who eats fake food? Why don't they want fresh vegetables? What happens when the electricity goes off?"

Mom and Dad, Jan and Barry had welcomed Juan warmly, and of course, Christy was delighted to see him. Juan's visit bridged Christy's old life and her new, as it did also for Timmy.

When Daddy took Juan to Town & Country Plaza, a strip mall of about ten stores, Juan stared at the parking lot, "Is this a car sales business?" He had never seen so many vehicles in one place. He was stunned that people did not take buses. Why did everyone need his own car?

Juan could not believe all the church buildings. So many denominations. Such big buildings. Dad took Juan to a ministers' seminar at Brownsville Assembly where Juan was profoundly touched to see hundreds of pastors in attendance.

After two weeks, Juan left by bus to visit Chilean friends in Texas and Alabama, where George Wallace was campaigning for President. Governor Wallace, who said he was Commander-in-Chief, conferred on Juan the dubious title of "Lt. Col., Field Commander, Confederate Army of the South."

Juan returned, reluctantly, to Chile the day his visa expired.

Joe arrived home in March. He had had a wonderful time, first cutting the record with the *Trío Asaph*, then preaching at the youth camp in Argentina, and finally helping with church planting in Asunción, Paraguay.

As we drove home from the airport, he bubbled enthusiastically about Paraguay—the hot climate, the Bible institute closed for lack of students, and the new congregation Everett was forming in the *barrio Republicano.*

Fear gripped my heart. I snapped at him, "Why are you talking so much about Paraguay? You don't want to go back to *Paraguay,* do you?"

"I didn't mean to tell you so soon," he mumbled. "I had no idea you would think that … this soon."

He explained that he had been praying in the Bible institute chapel in Asunción. The Bible school was closed. Not one student wanted to attend, because an Argentine evangelist had swept through the country preaching *discipulado*, shepherding, a sort of religious pyramid scheme where each person is under a shepherd who is their sole source of enlightenment.

Joe said he knelt there in the chapel at a rough wooden bench and prayed, "God, have mercy on this place. Send missionaries to this country. Help these spiritually ignorant people. They are so poor. They feel so inferior. The climate is so hot. There are so few missionaries because almost no one wants to come to Paraguay. God, send someone here."

And the thought dropped into his heart, "What about you? Are *you* willing to come here?"

Joe's tears puddled on the bench as he surrendered, "Yes, Lord, I am willing to come here."

Joe said that almost immediately he began to enjoy the hot climate, to love the people, and to have hope for students to attend the Bible school.

It was a touching story and I knew Joe meant it. But I had NOT been touched and I definitely did NOT want to go to Paraguay.

I had not seen Joe for three months. I was still in culture shock, and he wanted to change countries!

I cried. And I cried. And I cried.

I did not want to be severed from my Chilean family, both missionary and Chilean. I did not want to desert my friends who were suffering economically with Allende.

I was accepted in Chile, loved, needed. I had genuine friends. I could sit and drink *once,* tea, with any one of dozens of ladies while we talked about recipes or the *veda,* food shortage, or the Bible, or prayers answered and unanswered. Together we genuinely laughed and openly cried. There was no pretense, no façade, no hurry.

I did not want to be uprooted, again—to leave the comfort of friends in Chile and stumble into a perilous maze of unknowns in Paraguay.

"God, will I ever 'belong' anywhere?" I railed at the unfairness of having to adjust, *again*, to a different country, to another culture. Why was life so hard? I thought God's yoke was supposed to be "easy" and his burden "light." Ha! I knew by experience that fulfilling all this "religious performance" was both hard and heavy.

"Oh, God," I begged, "Help me to adjust to this itinerary stuff. And help me to endure Paraguay."

I didn't know then that I needed so much more help than that. I didn't realize my performance-based faith needed radical overhaul.

Chile Post Script
1972–2007

I did not walk again on the streets of Viña for more than twenty-five years. When Pastor Juan Mella and the church in Temuco paid our way to visit Chile in 1997, he asked if we had any special requests. Joe told him, "Yes. Could we visit Viña also?"

We flew from Temuco up to Santiago on Friday, November 7, 1997. From there we boarded a tour-style bus for the two-hour ride to Viña. We twisted around hairpin curves and zoomed through two tunnels. We dropped from the coastal mountains into the wide, fertile valley filled with grapevines and kiwi plants.

Leo and Sylvia Riquelme, still pastors of "the tent," had invited us to stay with their family for the weekend. Eight of us shared one bathroom, and I learned very quickly to take only my toothbrush, toothpaste, towel, and shampoo into the bathroom, because my time there would be very limited. Ten of us (we picked up two others) squeezed into the Riquelme's little car to go to the church.

When we approached "the tent," we noticed an elderly gentleman standing on the front steps of the church building waiting for us. A glorious smile shone on his wrinkled face. He clasped me and then Joe in a long *abrazo*, hug; we all wiped away tears ... Daniel Pozo.

People still referred to the church as *la carpa* because the tent had stood for years, until it literally fell apart. Believers filled the new building, and an outstanding worship band played lively Chilean rhythms. Joe preached Saturday and Sunday and the congregation received an offering for us!

A young couple came forward to talk to Joe—Pepe López and his Brazilian wife, Sheli. They asked for advice regarding becoming missionaries to India. We had no idea that Pepe's real name was José Antonio López, and that he was Isolina's grandson born in answer to Joe's prayer for a baby! In 2007, Pepe and Sheli left Chile to begin work with the Dalits in India.

Isolina had died before our visit. Her husband, José, continues to attend the church.

During their second term in Chile, Bob and Margaret Bowden divorced.

The divorce severed not only their nuclear family ties but also their missionary family ties. We were deeply saddened that so many missionaries and missions officials dropped Bob like a hot potato. The mantra seemed to be, "He's wounded—shoot him!"

Bob eventually returned to Chile, where he and his Chilean wife live on a twenty-five-acre ranch in the southern zone. From there, Bob has begun home Bible studies for professional people and has traveled preaching throughout South America. He wrote to us in 2007, "God has taught me a lot about grace and I thank Him for that."

Sometimes, out of the blue, Joe will say to me, "I miss Bob."

When the divorce occurred, the mission flew Margaret and six-year-old Robby to Missouri, to a small apartment where Margaret struggled to sustain herself and Robby both emotionally and economically. She had fulfilled the stereotypical role of the missionary wife—stay home, raise the kids, entertain the people that the husband (the "real" missionary) invites to dinner or for an overnight visit.

The year was 1977. I remember the date well because we came home on furlough that year. I reached out to Margaret some, but I wish with all my heart I had done more.

Then, Margaret and Robby moved back home to California where she became the director of the shipping department at World Vision for seventeen years, before her retirement in Covina.

In 2007, her emails to me were filled with the joy of her three children (Connie, Jeanne, and Robby) and four grandchildren, especially the youngest one, Robby's son, Reign Adison Bowden.

Robby became a plumber; his sister, Connie, a mid-wife. She lives in California with her husband and two children.

Jeanne, during her college years, became engaged to a young man who wanted to be a children's pastor. But, shaken by her parents' divorce, Jeanne experienced such trauma that her fiancé used that as an excuse to leave her. Deeply wounded, she turned her back on all things religious and on her family. She struggled for more than twenty years through addictions, a sense of rejection, and an abusive marriage and divorce. But through AA meetings, she found God again and also found a wonderful man, Mark, who became her husband and a good stepfather to her son.

Grateful to God for a second chance at life, Jeanne and Mark live in the Chicago area where they have dedicated their lives to reaching out to many suffering addicts. Jeanne and Mark hold recovery meetings in their home and counsel at weekend retreats. Jeanne wrote, "We spend many hours both with young addicts (who have been turned away by their own families) and with the newcomers who are so vulnerable to relapse. It really has become not only a mission for us but a way of life."

By mid-1973, both the economy and the government of Chile were paralyzed with inflation at more than 500 percent. Massive strikes by truckers, copper miners, and other workers infuriated business owners who retaliated with shutdowns and lock-outs. Street demonstrations became daily events as confrontations escalated.

The heads of the Army, Air Force, Navy and Carabineros (national police) formed a committee called *la junta*. They planned a coup under the leadership of the newly appointed Army Commander, General Augusto Pinochet.

On September 11, 1973, the military stormed the presidential palace, *la Moneda*. President Allende was prepared; he was waiting with his AK-47 assault rifle that Castro had given him. Allende turned it on himself.

Pinochet ruled until 1990 as a "military president," and even after that, he remained as Commander-in-Chief of the Army for another eight years. Some believe Pinochet's restoration of order resulted in repression. Our Chilean friends tell us of hearing gun battles waging throughout the countryside. But *la junta* felt justified in using severe measures to salvage the economy.

By 1998, Marxists, though defeated in Chile, had rallied world opinion against Pinochet. When he visited England for medical treatment, he was placed under house arrest on a provisional warrant from Spain charging abuse of power. Later, he was released and returned to Chile, where he died of heart failure in 2006, at the age of 91.

Pinochet remains a polarizing figure—condemned by some for civil rights abuse, praised by others for stabilizing Chile.

Since the late 1980s, Chile has been well integrated into the world economy, and in fact has become a model admired by the developing world. We see Chilean wine, kiwi, grapes, and all sorts of fruits and vegetables in our local supermarket in the States. I love to be able to purchase Chilean products.

27

Itinerate Again?

Pensacola, Florida
May 1972–June 1973

"*And then Joe looked down* into the cooking pot … there in the rice … was a chicken head!"

"Uuuuh," all the girls groaned.

"But it wasn't too bad," I continued, "because the cooks had gouged out the eyes … and cut off the beak … and trimmed off the red comb on top of the chicken's head …"

"Uuuuh, gross!"

"And then the cook stirred the rice … and there was a chicken foot!"

"UUUuuuuuh."

"But it wasn't dirty—the cook had scrubbed it really clean with a brush … and then she clipped the toenails…."

I loved telling stories to the girls at retreats. This chicken story came from Joe's youth camp experience in Argentina.

Gradually I assimilated the North American culture. I didn't like many of the things I observed, but I tolerated them as "the way it is here."

Joe was determined to go to Paraguay, and the Missions Board approved our transfer. During itinerary, we visited Marianna,

Florida, where Bill and Dorothy Franklin were pastors. Dot handed me a book along with the admonition, "You have to read this. It will change your life. Have you heard the new teaching about wives submitting to their husbands?" It was new to me—and not very appealing.

I read the book. I cried. The book explained that since there can be only one CEO of a company or a family, both partners, if they follow this method, can learn, grow and become more humble. I concluded that "submission" is the hardest thing we humans do— wives yielding to the husbands' decision, husbands yielding to God's prompting and to the wife's input. The husband dare not make "the wrong" decision ... it will come back to haunt him.

Joe and I formed a new pattern: we discussed, I made my opinions known, clearly. Then I shut up and left the decision in Joe's hands. At that point "submission" became *his* hardest decision— submission to God, first of all, and to the evaluation of my input.

So, I humbled myself, submitting to Joe's choice. I was sort of like the little child who was sitting down on the outside but standing up "on the inside." I was going to Paraguay on the outside, but still longing for Chile on the inside, though I never mentioned it again.

Of course, I had no idea that going to Paraguay would be pivotal in the scope of our lives.

Itinerary was hard for Christy and Timmy. Christy was nine, Timmy, seven. Every Sunday we dragged them to two different churches, which meant they had to attend a different Sunday school class every week. Timmy said later, "Since I was the missionary kid, I was supposed to know everything! It was terrible. All those people looking at you, thinking you're weird."

Both children helped during the service, dressing in scratchy costumes, holding up curios, passing out prayer cards. Years later they told me how much they ... did *not* like it.

Family Picture for Prayer Card, 1972

But in some ways, the second itinerary was easier than the first time. We had good, authentic stories to tell, such as Isolina's healing and Daniel's transformation and José's arm. We had authentic slides of Chilean mountains and the sway-back tent and photos of people we knew. We had authentic costumes—Joe dressed as a *huaso*, a Chilean cowboy complete with chaps and spurs.

And this time, as veteran missionaries, we received invitations to "round robin" conventions such as the one in Memphis, Tennessee. Several churches cooperated and invited five or six missionary couples. The organizers housed all the missionaries in a nice hotel and explained the schedule. We were to take turns in various churches on Friday night, Saturday breakfast, Saturday night, Sunday school, Sunday morning, Sunday evening. All the offerings were combined and divided equally. Usually we received monthly pledges, too, from some of the participating churches.

Also, of course, we wanted to visit the churches that had given us monthly "faith promise" pledges for the previous four years. We wanted to thank them for their prayers and offerings. Almost every church was small, the offerings and pledges small. But added together, they made our missions work possible.

Joe called churches and worked out our schedule on a big calendar. Most pastors were accessible and glad for a missionary visit. We usually were given 45-60 minutes in a service. We showed our curios and slides and told our stories. Joe played a saxophone solo and then preached. He loved to ask for the "faith promises" because he was convinced that God would repay the giver. There was no pressure or pleading, Joe just presented an opportunity to give.

Joe had shipped home hundreds of copies of the LP album he made in Chile with the *Trío Asaph*. People loved the mixture of Spanish and English in the familiar songs accompanied by the catchy Latino rhythms. I kept careful account of the sales, and as soon as we had reimbursed ourselves for the cost of production, every penny went into our missions account. Many times, album sales were greater than the offerings.

Once again, we had a set amount of cash to raise to cover our travel to Paraguay and provide a cushion for those months when the income might be low. Also, we had a monthly budget to raise for our living expenses, the children's schooling, work funds, and medical fund. The mission deducted almost all of our tithes for administrative costs ("professional dues"). They also, thank God, began to deduct retirement savings from our account.

After they retired, Dad and Mom had moved from a larger parsonage to a smaller house in Myrtle Grove, a western suburb of Pensacola. We enjoyed living across the street from them, in the little house Dad had found for us. It consisted of three small bedrooms, one bath, a living room, eat-in kitchen, and a carport.

There was a nice fenced back yard with a big shade tree. Chilito, Timmy's dachshund, just about ran his little short legs off in that big yard. But his favorite trick was to chase Dad and even bite him! Finally, Chilito became so aggressive that we gave him to Lisa Medley, Christy's best friend, who lived out in the country. Chilito lived a long life as an undocumented immigrant.

Christy was like a different person. She seemed well-adjusted and free from her school-trauma. She loved her new teacher, her new friends and her new school. We enrolled Timmy there, too, into first grade. Every thing was fine for several months. Then a rule was instituted regarding the length of girls' skirts. The girl stood quietly, while the director took a ruler and measured the height of the skirt; it could be only so many inches above the floor. Christy failed the test. I let out her hems. She always wore tights to match her dresses; she was very self-conscious since her incident in Chile. Plus, she was small for her age. She looked cute, I thought.

Second citation: Christy must have all new dresses, or she will be expelled. I could not believe it! I went straight to the local public school and enrolled both children. They finished the school year and attended the next year at Myrtle Grove Elementary School.

Once I had softened my anger toward God and Joe, I was surprised by the joy of itinerary. Most pastors' wives were friendly and invited me to speak to women's groups and retreats, girls' retreats, and children's church groups.

Driving the mountain roads through West Virginia was soothing, and conducting services in the small churches was immensely gratifying. I especially remember one little church beside a small stream in a "holler" (*hollow*, a narrow valley). The little building was filled with people who hung onto every word, every story. They prayed fervently for us, gathering around us and laying their hands on our shoulders. I was deeply humbled. I knew that the pastor did not receive as much salary as we did.

A pastor of a medium-sized church rebuked Joe. "You should not tell people that you lived in a nice house and that the missionary salary was adequate for your needs. The people think you suffer. That is why they give."

Local and district women's groups "adopted" us, giving us personal gifts of clothing or toiletries, as well as sheets, towels, bedspreads, blankets, and dishes.

Sometimes, women donated things I did not want: such as the wall hanging made from an empty margarine tub, a plastic plate and bottle caps for buttons to hold pot-holders. To make it even worse, the "thing" was covered in a weird fabric. Mother, of course, saw that I did not want it, so she said she would take care of it for me. At the last minute when we were packing for Paraguay, she sneaked it into our shipment. On an especially trying day in Paraguay, as I unpacked a box, I gazed down on that terrible wall hanging. BUT, I needed a good laugh, and the fact is, the fabric exactly matched our kitchen, so the "decoration" hung on our wall there for four years! It always brought a smile — especially when other missionaries or nationals would ask about the "unique" wall decoration.

As required, we attended School of Missions in the summer of 1972. We stayed in the air-conditioned dorm this time, in the basement, but at least it had air conditioning. We were considered veterans now. We could speak Spanish, could relate stories to the rookies. It was great.

We drove to School of Missions so that we could go through Illinois to visit Aunt Too, Aunt Ella and Uncle Harry, Uncle Mac and Aunt Jo, and Ed and Mary Bernreuter (who had given me my school shoes for first grade). This was a wonderful "perk" of being a missionary. The trip expenses were reimbursed from our offerings, but any additional expenses were personal, of course.

We were told that it was a requirement of the Paraguayan General Council that any women involved in ministry in Paraguay must be credentialed. So I asked O.L. Thomas, the West Florida District Superintendent, about my being "licensed to preach." He had the district secretary issue my license in the spring of 1973.

We were told, also, that we would be living in Asunción, the capital city of Paraguay, in an unfurnished missions house on a large lot. The previous missionaries had left a washer, dryer, and a window-unit air conditioner.

Joe went to the Naval Air Station in Pensacola where he bought three large, used, wooden crates. We began to pack our stuff. We took a couch with matching chairs, end tables, lamps, a dining room suite, refrigerator, and beds. Plus a riding lawn mower, dishes, pots and pans, linens, clothing, toys, and what continued to be the kids' favorite thing: the "treasure box" filled with surprises for special occasions or illnesses.

We also packed radio equipment. Because of the good response to the radio broadcasts in Viña, Joe wanted to begin a radio program in Paraguay.

A few weeks before we left the States, we were shocked to learn that Roland and Evelyn Blount had moved to Paraguay! I told Joe that I didn't like Evelyn and didn't want to have anything to do with her. Evelyn told Roland that she didn't like me and didn't want to have anything to do with me. Joe said to me, as Roland said to Evelyn, "No problem. You will only have to see her at meetings for official missionary business." (Ha! Little did we know ....)

All of our money was raised; our crates were shipped; our suitcases were packed. We flew to Paraguay on June 27, 1973, on Christy's eleventh birthday. Joe was 34 years old; I was 30, and Timmy was 8.

28

Arriving in Asunción, Paraguay

(ah-soon-see-OWN)
June 28–30, 1973

*W*e walked down the stairs from the airplane into a perfect winter afternoon. We had been up all night, but Braniff Airlines had served us a nice breakfast and lunch on the flight from Miami.

We had landed on a small airstrip in the middle of a cow pasture. I looked around—the land was flat as far as I could see. We walked across the tarmac to a small two-story, rectangular building, Asunción's International Airport. Hanging over the balcony on the second floor, the Jenkins and the Blounts waved and yelled to us.

Don Jenkins cupped his hands and called, "Welcome to Paraguay! We'll meet you inside, after you've gone through customs."

We walked inside the little terminal where we waited for our luggage to be unloaded from the plane. Inspectors opened our suitcases and looked very closely at everything inside, but thankfully, did not charge us any duty. We could hear a dog whining and barking in a high-pitched yelp—Tinker Belle, a little, white, toy poodle puppy that we had brought with us.

As we passed through the gate into the lobby area, Don and Betty Jenkins were waiting to greet us, as were Roland and Evelyn Blount, along with the children: Darlene (age 17) and Felicia (5) Jenkins; Howie (15) and Carla (8) Blount.

As we began to gather our luggage, Evelyn said, "Listen to that dog! Who on earth would bring a dog on a plane with them!?"

I ended up in the backseat of the Blounts' car behind the driver, Evelyn. We bumped across cobblestones onto a paved lane. We drove slowly through pastureland with tall skinny palm trees dotted intermittently throughout the high grass. Red dirt showed through patches of weeds. There were no fences, no curbs, no drainage ditches. Cows ambled across the road. When an occasional car came toward us, Evelyn would squeeze the car to the right, trying to stay on the asphalt.

Finally I blurted, "Evelyn? Since this is my first time in Paraguay, I wanted to take the main road into Asunción."

She replied dryly, "This *is* the main road; it's the *only* road to town."

As we approached the city, our road became a pot-holed street named *General Genes*. Suddenly, Evelyn braked and turned right, up a slight incline into private property. We drove up a circular drive as Roland explained the layout, "The mission owns five acres of land divided into two-and-a-half-acre lots. Your house is straight ahead behind the brick wall that cuts across the property left to right. The Jenkins live on the right half of the land.

Extending at a right angle from the front wall, I could see a six-foot-high brick wall dividing the two houses.

Both mission houses, made of brick and rock, sat diagonally on their lots; they were ranch style with a breezeway leading to a brick carport.

I walked up shallow steps, across a small porch, and into our living room. There was no foyer. I stood on a terrazzo floor as I faced a rounded fireplace on the opposite wall. I was actually in the dining area; the living area was to my right. The ceiling soared to fourteen feet at the apex, where the fireplace chimney rose. Large front windows allowed plenty of light into the room. The walls were adobe bricks covered with plaster. Every corner was rounded (you couldn't put a desk or bookcase "in the corner" because there was no sharp right angle).

To my right, beyond the living room, a doorway led into a narrow office, and then into a large room used for storage—it was piled with junk left over from several previous missionaries.

From the office, an arched doorway led to the back half of the rectangular house—three bedrooms and a bathroom with a tub. The master bedroom was at the right end of the hall and had its own tiny bathroom. The shower drain sat in the floor beside the commode. The entire bathroom became wet when the shower was turned on.

From the front door, straight back beyond the dining area, was the large kitchen. Nice cabinets ringed two walls, and a window over the sink looked out into the back yard. A door on the left led to the breezeway, laundry room, and carport.

The Jenkins and the Blounts had managed to "furnish" the house for us with odd chairs and a small table, assorted pots and pans, cots, and a double bed. We were expecting our shipment from the States within a few days, so we would "camp" until it arrived.

Evelyn invited us to their house for supper. The Blounts were living in a third mission house, just across the street and around the corner. It was actually where Everett and Carolyn Ward lived, but they were gone on furlough.

Evelyn invited us back for breakfast the next morning and said she would take me to the grocery store after breakfast.

That first night, it was hard to go to sleep even though we were dead-tired. Everything was too quiet—no traffic noise, no electrical noise, nothing except crickets and cicadas. There were no street lights. I could not see my hand in front of my face.

Our house, Paraguay

The next morning, Evelyn and I drove down the main avenue, *Mariscal López*. It was pitted with pot-holes. There were no traffic lights and no stop signs—in the entire country! Everyone drove with his foot on the gas and his thumb on the horn. The first guy at an intersection had the right-of-way, unless he was in competition with a bus or a truck. The buses and trucks billowed clouds of thick, black exhaust smoke that stung my eyes and caused me to cough.

All of the side streets were cobblestone or dirt. Strewn papers littered the sides of the streets. A few streets boasted broken curbs and rough, uneven sidewalks. There was no storm drainage system.

We walked into a small, dimly lit store, Asunción's only super-market. Evelyn grabbed a shopping cart and started happily down the aisle. I looked at the carts. They were small and rusty—every wheel wobbled unevenly. The worn handles still had some plastic attached to them, but in many places even the metal was worn through to brass.

Gingerly, I pushed a cart down the dirty aisle. Evelyn pointed out the pasta, salt, sugar, and flour, baking powder, tomato paste, puffed rice, oil, vinegar, toilet paper. That was all there was. Except for some packaged "biscuits" (cookies). Evelyn held up a package, almost hugging it to her chest. "These are delicious!"

The cookies looked dry and small and thin. I said, "I'm not cookie hungry right now."

She bought some of everything. I bought nothing. I couldn't. It was all so pitiful. So sparse and poorly packaged, so poorly arranged on rickety shelving. Finally, Evelyn began to put items into my cart, things she knew I would need.

I couldn't get out into the sunshine fast enough.

"Now we'll go to the vegetable market," Evelyn enthused.

We bumped along rough cobblestones, past men urinating in the street, past bicycles and carts both hand-drawn and horse-drawn. We saw women striding along with huge baskets on their heads.

The *San José* market was a warren of dirty streets with dirty vendors hawking everything from fruits and vegetables to cow intestines and brightly printed cloth.

Evelyn took her woven plastic shopping bags from the trunk, saying, "Come on. Oh! Look at those beautiful potatoes! And those big carrots. Ooooh, and look over there, cauliflower!"

Vendors spread out one or two vegetables on the ground or on a wobbly table. Flies swarmed. On low stools beside the vegetables, the women vendors sat with their legs apart, skirt-tails tucked up between their legs, under their thighs.

Sides of beef hung from hooks beside men with bloody aprons. Dogs sniffed the meat and wagged their tails, disturbing the flies swarming on the beef.

Evelyn bought something from almost everyone. Not I—I would *never* be able to buy this stuff. Never be able to take this dirty stuff into my house, my kitchen. We would starve first.

Meanwhile, Joe was learning from Roland why the Blounts had moved to Paraguay. After they had visited us in Temuco, they had returned to the States, where they received a letter from the Foreign Missions Department stating that they could become missionaries. Roland was amused that he had been told, "Never write to us again. You can never become a missionary because you are blind." However, because the Chilean church had written "requesting" the Blounts, permission was granted.

Roland and Evelyn had itinerated, raised their funds, and gone to language school in Guadalajara, Mexico. One afternoon, there in Mexico, Roland went up on the flat roof to gather clothes from the clothes line. He misjudged the edge of the roof and fell two stories onto a cement patio, breaking both of his arms! But he was not deterred from finishing language study. Taking care of him and the two children, in a foreign culture, as well as studying Spanish herself, was very hard for Evelyn.

From language school, the Blounts had moved to southern Chile to Osorno, a beautiful little town south of Temuco. They rented a nice house and settled in. But by now it was July, 1972, and Allende's reign was experiencing serious troubles. Demonstrations and anti-Yankee gatherings were common. The Blounts were the only Americans in a communist-controlled town. It was dangerous to be outside after dark.

Because Roland was blind, Evelyn had to accompany him to exchange dollars for *escudos*. They exchanged in stores or with businessmen (called "the black-market") because the bank exchange rate was ridiculously low. Evelyn knew it was illegal, but how else could they survive? She became increasingly nervous, paranoid that they were being watched and followed.

There was hardly any food. Evelyn would go to the market-place daily, hoping for something—anything to eat. Sometimes the vendor would say that a truck would be arriving "this afternoon" or "tomorrow" and Evelyn would make special trips back, again and again, trying to find food.

Roland was heart-sick. After all the drama of becoming mission-aries, now they were going to have to return to the States—in defeat. Evelyn had lost weight, she could not sleep, her hair turned gray, she cried day after day. She could not endure much more.

Through Bob Bowden, Everett Ward heard of the Blounts' dilemma and contacted them. "I'm due for furlough. Please come to Paraguay. I need someone to pastor the new church I've started. Live in my house. Use my furniture. Don't bring anything except your clothes. Come on now."

So they did. They moved to Paraguay in February, 1973.

When we arrived on June 28, we moved into the mission house next door to Don and Betty Jenkins. They were as nice to us as could be.

Overdue for furlough, they planned to leave in about six months. Betty was expecting a baby in just a few weeks.

Betty made home-made waffles for our breakfast our second morning. She said she would have made doughnuts but didn't have time. I was amazed! She said she frequently made cinnamon rolls, too. She promised to give me the recipes, but I told her I needed to watch her make them—just telling me would not help me much.

The following day would be Sunday, July 1. Roland said we could go to their church, but "Don't dress up." Carla told the kids that church was fun; they could ride the mule. Howie explained that he was the teacher for the children's class.

Don Jenkins invited us all to go to the country two weeks from that Sunday, to Pira Retá. (He forgot to mention the outhouse, the pigs, and the corpse.)

* * *

Betty's Cinnamon Rolls
(Though it seems complicated, once you've made them, it's a breeze! If I can do it, you can too.)
Bake at 375 for 20-25 minutes

Rolls:
4 to 5 cups flour
1 package active dry yeast
1 cup milk
1/3 cup sugar
1/3 cup butter
1/2 teaspoon salt
2 eggs

You'll need:
a mixer
a candy thermometer
a wooden spoon
a large glass bowl (in which to let the dough rise)
a 9x13 pan or two 9" round pans
a ruler
a roller or long bottle (like a wine bottle)

a pastry brush (or just use a spoon)
Filling:
1/3 cup butter, melted
1/2 cup brown sugar and 1/4 cup white sugar
2 teaspoons ground cinnamon
Icing:
1 cup powdered sugar
1/2 teaspoon vanilla
1 tablespoon milk or orange juice (plus more, as needed)
Mix a little bit of the liquid into the sugar, stirring until you could "drizzle" it.
Caramel rolls:
OR *instead of* the icing, place in the bottom of your 9x13 pan,
1/4 cup melted butter,
1/2 cup brown sugar,
2 tablespoons corn syrup
1/2 cup pecan halves.
Lay the rolls on top of the caramel mixture. Bake. Invert.

Making the rolls:
1. In the large mixing bowl (of your mixer) stir together just 2 cups of the flour and the dry yeast.
2. In a medium saucepan, heat and stir the milk, sugar, butter, and salt until the butter is melted and the temperature is between 120 and 130. (You need a candy thermometer—if the liquid is too hot, the yeast won't rise. If it's too cold, the yeast won't dissolve and, therefore, won't rise.)
3. Break the eggs into a small bowl.
4. Pour the hot liquid and the eggs into the mixing bowl with the flour.
5. Beat on low 30 seconds, scraping sides of bowl.
6. Beat on high 3 minutes, scraping sides of bowl.
7. Use a wooden spoon to add more flour (or a dough hook on the mixer). Add about two more cups of flour. It should become a solid "ball" and seem fairly "dry," not so wet that your hands will really stick to it when you knead it.

8. Lay the dough on a floured table or countertop. Mash it, double it over, mash it away from you, double, turn, mash it with the balls of your palms. (This is called kneading.)
9. Knead it only 3 to 5 minutes. It should seem pretty dry and pretty much like elastic (stretchy).
10. Oil your glass bowl.
11. Place the ball of dough in the bowl; then turn the dough over so that now oil is all over it.
12. Cover the bowl with a dishcloth and let the dough rise until double.
13. You can place the bowl in a COLD oven, on the top shelf.Put a bowl of warm water on the bottom shelf and close the door. The oven light turned on will give some heat, too.
14. In about one hour, stick two fingers into the dough. Pull your fingers out, and if you can still see the holes where your fingers were, the dough is ready. (You'll smell the yeast.)
15. Punch your fist into the center of the dough! Then pull the sides in on top of the hole.
16. Divide the dough in half. Put the dough back on the flour-covered tabletop. Cover both pieces with your dish towel and let the poor things "rest" for ten minutes.
17. Oil your pan or pans.
18. Roll each piece of dough into a rectangle 12" by 8" (use a ruler). If you don't have a rolling pin, use a bottle on its side.
19. Use a pastry brush to brush the melted butter generously on top of the rectangles.
20. Combine the sugar/brown sugar and cinnamon and sprinkle it over the tops.
21. Roll up the dough, from the wide sides – you want to end with a "hot dog" 12" long. Pinch the sides together so it won't open up.
22. Lay your ruler beside the dough, and cut into one inch circles.
23. Place the circles of dough into your pans, twelve to a pan, either in the two round pans, or place all in the 9x13 pan.
24. Bake at 375 for 20 to 25 minutes.
25. Cool slightly and invert pan onto a plate.

Drizzle with your icing. OR, invert if you chose to place the caramel/pecan delicious gooey stuff in the bottom of your pan.

PARAGUAY

The Chaco
(The Wasteland)

Concepción

Ciudad
Stroessner

Asunción--->
Pira Retá----->

Ca'acupé

Itaipú Dam

Carmen

Encarnación

29

Pira Retá

(pea-rah-reh-TAH)
July 15, 1973

araguay sits like a slanted peanut, right in the center of the South American "ice cream cone." Argentina cradles Paraguay on the west and the south. Bolivia touches the northwest and Brazil borders the east. None of the borders are important to the three neighbors, so Paraguay, about the size of California, lies isolated like "an island surrounded by land," as one man described it. On the "waist" of the peanut, at the far west, sits Asunción, the capital city.

At the time of our arrival, one paved road led from the city, to the east toward *Ciudad Stroessner*, a town on the border with Brazil. Y-ing from this road was the only other paved road. It headed south to the town of *Encarnación* on the Argentine border.

We left Asunción, heading east, about eight o'clock Sunday morning for the hour-and-a-half ride to *Pira Retá*. Don Jenkins led in his car. We rode with the Blounts, Evelyn driving, following Don. We bumped across pot-holes. We paused for cows, bicycles, and pedestrians. We stopped behind buses with people crowding out the doors and young men standing precariously on the back bumpers. Topping the roofs of the buses were rope-bound bundles and leather suitcases and chickens with their feet tied together. We slowed behind open-bed trucks piled eighteen feet high with huge bags of produce.

An hour later, we turned off the highway onto a red dirt road and navigated huge mud holes by driving on the grass pastureland. We circled around a tree in the center of the road and then turned to our right onto a lane. Bouncing along the trail in the tall grass, we could see in the distance some bamboo poles stretched across the lane to form a gate. A young boy was waiting for us. He pulled the poles back and we drove into *Pira Retá*.

Three thatch-roofed, white-washed adobe buildings sat in a field. The grass was mowed short by the cows and oxen grazing nearby. The red dirt surrounding the buildings was packed hard and swept neatly.

Rosa de Fletcha, our hostess, came to greet us. She was about 60 years old. Her head reached to my shoulders, her face was wreathed in a warm smile. She kissed me on both cheeks, "*Bienvenida a Pira Retá. Aquí tienen su casa.*" (Welcome to Pira Retá. Consider this your home.)

People would arrive shortly for the church service, she explained. Just make yourselves at home.

The first building to our right was the chapel, the second was a small store, and the third was Rosa's open-air kitchen under a thatched roof.

I needed to use the toilet; so did Evelyn. Don pointed us to a small, round, thatched-roof structure. The walls were made of sticks, placed about three inches apart. The door was a low gate of more sticks, about four inches apart. A person did not close the gate for privacy; it was just to keep out the pigs and dogs. Red dirt, packed hard, formed the floor. In the center of the floor was a hole, about three inches in diameter. We were to squat over the hole. A roll of toilet paper hung from a wire, a webbed-plastic wastebasket sat nearby to hold the used toilet paper. The roof was so low, I could not stand up. But at least, the outhouse did not have a bad odor. (Men "went" outside.)

Standing nearby, Evelyn assured me she could not see me *very well* through the sticks ... and for the first time Evelyn and I laughed together.

We walked back toward the buildings and into the little chapel. The dirt floor was swept clean. The benches had backs to them; the wood had been carefully sanded. Fresh flowers filled jars at each side of a small pulpit. Gradually the chapel filled with people who had arrived by horseback or by walking from the surrounding coun-tryside. Each woman came to Evelyn and me—kissing us on both cheeks and offering her baby to be kissed. The men shook our hands and nodded, not making eye contact.

Don led the service, Roland played his accordion and sang, and Joe preached.

Following the service, Hermana Rosa served us lunch on the veranda of the second building, a small store. It was packed with everything imaginable. The buyer would ask for what he needed, and Rosa or her granddaughter would bring out the item. Built onto the back of the store were two rooms that served as bedrooms whenever the weather was cold or rainy. Otherwise, the people slept outside in hammocks.

Extending in front of the store was a thatched roof. It formed a porch that doubled as Rosa's dining room. She had prepared a large, round table with a white tablecloth and white, cloth napkins. Each place setting boasted one shiny soup spoon. Hermana Rosa served each of us a bowl of green noodles (made from spinach) seasoned with chopped beef in a tomato sauce. It was delicious! Her grand-daughter served us fruit punch in plastic glasses.

Timmy and Carla especially loved the little pigs that rooted around our feet, snorting and sniffing our ankles. Chickens scratched in the dirt nearby, and cats groomed themselves in the sunshine while assorted dogs patrolled the perimeter.

The third building was the kitchen, where a small adobe store-room backed a very large porch, open on three sides. To the right sat a rounded, igloo-like adobe oven. Centered near a sturdy, wooden work table was a spit for roasting meat; beside it was another fire pit bordered with adobe bricks and crossed by a bar with hooks to hold cooking pots. Unlit lanterns hung from pegs on the poles supporting the thatched roof.

After we had finished eating, Rosa asked us to go about five miles farther down the road to the home of one of her church members.

As we drove away from Rosa's, Don explained that Rosa, the pastor, was a woman of great faith, as had been her mother before her. Through the years, they had endured severe persecution for being Protestants. Suddenly, Don stopped the car. "Look at that rotting log—see it? That is the tree fanatical Catholics felled across this lane. They almost killed two of our missionaries, Ray Stawinski and Paul Hutsell. The missionaries had been out here for an evening service, and when they drove their little VW back down this lane, men blockaded the road and attacked, breaking the windshield and windows of the car and causing severe lacerations to the missionaries, especially to their faces."

Sobered, we drove down the lane to the dirt road and turned right, toward the member's house. It was very similar to Rosa's—thatched roof bedrooms with the roof extending to form a large porch, an adjacent small building with a large porch-kitchen. And the dining area: a stand-alone thatched roof structure, like a picnic-pavilion, with a table under it.

We could see a group of people standing, gathered around the table. Stretched out on the table was a sheet covering a long object. Someone pulled back the sheet revealing—a corpse.

The young man had been shot the previous night in a drunken brawl. His nostrils were stuffed with cotton. His mouth was stuffed with cotton. A bandana, tied from his chin to the top of his head, kept the mouth partially closed. His eyes were half-opened.

I heard a "drip-drip." I looked under the table. A can sat collecting body fluids. A dog ambled up, drank from the can.

As the sheet was being pulled back, the young man's mother began to wail loudly—she climbed up on the table close to the body, prostrating herself across his chest. Wailing even louder, she rose up and threw herself across his chest again and again. She leaned toward his face, moaning, crying, and calling his name. She smoothed his eyebrows repeatedly with her thumbs. Loudly she moaned his name, loudly she wailed.

As the entire group of people joined in the wailing and moaning, I "escaped" if ever so briefly by glancing up to the underside of the roof. The thatch was covered with drying ears of corn, hanging by the shucks. I counted a few and then estimated—there must have been 500 ears of corn.

Dogs and cats and chickens and little pigs wandered around us as Don preached a funeral sermon. Roland played the accordion while he and Evelyn and Joe sang a trio.

Our children stood in amazement. They would never forget this scene.

In fact, Christy, Howie, Carla, and Timmy *played corpse* for years to come—one would lie on the ground *dead* while another straddled his chest, moaning and wailing and stroking his eyebrows. The other two kids honed their acting abilities by trying to be the best and most emotional moaner or wailer.

We arrived back in Asunción about four o'clock, in time to get ready for the evening service at *Barrio Republicano*.

We rode with the Blounts through the dirt streets of *Republicano*, one of the poorest, most densely populated neighborhoods of the city.

Arriving at the little, unfinished church building, we parked in a small area next to the street. A man came toward us leading a mule pulling a cart. Inside the cart sat six children and the man's wife. Hermano Juan came to greet us. His handshake was rough from hardened, calloused hands. A shock of black hair fell across his forehead. His white shirt was clean; his blue work pants were clean. His bare feet were splayed wide and had never been inside a pair of shoes.

Carla ran over to Hermano Juan, "Can we ride, can we ride now?" she asked in Spanish. He smiled, "No, after church." He unhooked the mule from the cart so the crazy North American kids could ride the mule after church.

Two vehicles were in the church parking lot: the Blounts' car and Hermano Juan's mule cart. Everyone else arrived by walking through the deep, red dirt of the poorly maintained streets. Almost everyone was barefoot—men, women, youth, boys, girls. But their clothes were clean and their bodies smelled fresh. In fact, many of the people came with their hair still damp from a recent bath.

The women kissed me on both cheeks. I kissed them back and kissed their babies. The men shyly shook my hand, looking away. When the women shook hands with Joe, they would cast their eyes down and would keep their thumbs close to their fingers, pulling their hands back from a clasp. The men would shake Joe's hand, but would not make eye contact.

Evelyn knew everyone by name; so did Roland—he recognized everyone's voice. Carla held every baby, carrying them around, one by one, on her hip.

Several dogs accompanied their families through the open doorway and lay on the dirt floor beside their masters. The benches were backless. The windows were wooden shutters, open to the evening air, mosquitoes, and bugs.

Children's and adult's Bible studies preceded the evening service (the only church service on Sundays). Roland had asked me to teach the lesson to the adults and he asked Joe to preach.

Lanterns lit the little building as Roland played the accordion and led singing. He was accompanied by one guitar, played by *Justo* (pronounced whose-toe). Justo, as dedicated a young man as could ever be found, had absolutely no sense of rhythm. Roland tapped his foot vigorously, trying to "influence" Justo. Justo paid no attention whatsoever. He sang loudly and off key, and he strummed the guitar loudly and out of rhythm.

Justo holding reins, Timmy, Christy, and Carla on the mule, Howie standing beside Hermano Juan

Following the service, the kids rode the mule; then Hermano Juan hitched the mule to the cart and began to swing his lantern as he walked with his family toward home.

We missionaries drove to a nice, quiet restaurant where a man in colorful, native costume played a harp while two guitarists, in perfect rhythm, softly strummed a romantic ballad.

In peace and quiet and calmness, we ate "bees-steak"—charcoal grilled filet mignon, boiled *mandioca* cassava, and salad made with palm hearts. We drank a delicious soft drink called *Guaraná* (guaw-rah-NAH)—all for about one dollar per person.

This closed a memorable day. We had been in Paraguay for two weeks.

30

One Week Later
July 22–August 5, 1973

⸙

*O*ne week later, Betty Jenkins waddled from the kitchen to the dining room to place snacks and drinks on the table. Though she was eight months pregnant, nothing seemed to faze her. She bubbled with chuckles as she performed whatever task was at hand.

Don was the interim pastor of *Templo Calvario*. He and Betty had invited us to their house Sunday night after church to meet some Baptist friends.

Munching snacks, we were seated around the living room when the door burst open, and in came an exuberant group, mixing English and Spanish, greeting each of us, grabbing snacks, all talking at once.

Don introduced Phil Saint, the brother of Nate Saint who had been killed seventeen years earlier by the Auca Indians in the Ecuadorian jungle. Phil, a missionary in Argentina, came up to Paraguay occasionally to hold special services. He was an accomplished chalk artist and people loved to watch him draw while he told Bible stories.

A short time later, we began to sing, *a cappella*, some choruses in English and in Spanish. Joe asked if anyone had heard the new chorus, "There's Something about That Name" by Bill and Gloria Gaither. No one had heard it. I played the piano as Joe and I sang a duet, "Jesus, Jesus, Jesus, there's just something about that name. Master, Savior, Jesus ...."

A hush fell over the group, as each of us recognized how desperately Paraguay needed to know the truth of these words. Joe had translated the song into Spanish, so he and I sang, "*Cristo, Cristo, Cristo, es el nombre sin igual. Maestro, Amigo, Cristo ....*"

A bond formed between all of us—that sense of family that exists among Christians world-wide.

The next day Phil Saint telephoned us, "I have bought time tomorrow night on television. I need you to sing that song while I draw. Could Roland sing, too, with his accordion?"

We agreed to meet him at the TV station, Tuesday night, July 24, at ten o'clock.

We were so nervous! We knew we would need to get to the television station early for make-up and to go over the script. Joe and I still did not have a car, so Evelyn drove us. We arrived at the station about 9:30. Phil had told us to drive around back to the studio entrance. The small parking lot was empty. There was a dim light burning on a wooden pole. We wondered where everyone was.

Finally, Joe went up to the big wooden doors and knocked and knocked and knocked. A man, barefoot and disheveled, came to the door. Yes, there would be a program, live, with the man who drew pictures. No, it would not begin until the soccer game ended. He closed the door.

We sat in the car. We waited. 10:00, 10:15, 10:30, 10:45, 10:50. At 10:55 a car came whirling into the parking lot. Phil jumped out, opened the trunk, took out his easel and chalk, and said, "Come on, the soccer game's almost over!"

We rushed into the studio. The cement floor was gritty with sand. Two cameras pointed toward the adobe wall facing us. The wall had not been finished. Between the adobe bricks, mortar had bulged and hardened. Three or four big lights hung from two poles. A piano on rollers sat to our left, near the center of the studio.

A man with shoes on—the director, we learned later—walked briskly into the room, conversed briefly with Phil, and left.

Phil said as he set up his easel, "When I tell you, go to the piano and sing. Roland, when I call on you, walk to the center of the room, here, and sing."

Two barefoot men came into the studio. They positioned themselves behind the cameras, a red light came on and Phil said, "*Bienvenidos, amigos*, welcome to this special program."

As Phil began to draw, a beautiful picture emerged. He nodded to us. Joe and I went to the piano and sang as Phil continued to draw. There was one microphone, a large one hanging from a pole. One of the cameramen angled it a little more toward us. We finished our song.

Phil continued to speak while motioning for Roland to sing. Joe led Roland to the center of the floor, turned Roland toward the camera, and walked away. Roland, tentatively at first, began to play his accordion and sing. When he finished, Joe went to lead him away.

Phil concluded the program. The lights were turned off. Phil thanked us for the wonderful help we had been.

We drove home. Disappointed. Disillusioned. Frustrated. How on earth could God use something so unorganized? With only one microphone? With no "set"? With the floor so dirty? With barefooted cameramen, no less!

The next day Joe went shopping for a car. The car salesman said, "I saw you on television last night! Your song was beautiful."

Joe went to buy paving bricks for a patio in our back yard. The salesman said, "You're the man who sang on television last night! I loved that program."

I went to the vegetable market with Evelyn. A little boy came to carry my shopping bags; he squinted his eyes up at me. "Hey! You're the woman who played the piano on television! Wow!"

Joe went to the paint store. "I saw you on television."

Joe went to change money, "I'm pastor of the *Filadelfia* Church. We loved your song on television!"

We needed a plumber. He walked in our door, looked at Joe, "You're the man from television!"

Every place Roland and Evelyn went, people stopped Roland, too, and talked to him.

How could this be? One song! We had each sung one short song! On an unannounced, unscheduled program at 11:00 p.m.! On a Tuesday night!

We met with Roland and Evelyn. Was this a fluke? Did people remember Roland and Joe only because they were different? The blind one and the bearded one? We prayed together. We talked for hours.

Seeds of thought began to germinate in our hearts: "What if?" "Could we possibly?" "What if we just asked?"

We talked with the resident Baptist missionaries. They encouraged us to "try" for a program.

Television had only recently come to Paraguay. There was only one channel, *Canal 9*, which covered the entire country and spilled across the border into Argentina. Old people watched *Canal 9*. So did young people. Children. Rich people. Poor people. Very, very poor people. People bought television sets on credit, and then charged their neighbors "admission."

No Protestants had ever had a "regularly scheduled" program—they were permitted only "specials" occasionally. Dare we try to buy time??

One week later, July 30, Joe and Roland walked into *Canal 9* and announced that they had an appointment with the station manager.

The manager invited them into his office. He offered them a seat, offered them something to drink. Joe and Roland drank the *mate* (mah-tay), green tea, talked about the weather, asked about the manager's family. An hour passed. At last the manager said, "Now, what can I do for you?"

Tentatively, Joe and Roland asked if possibly, maybe, would it be possible to buy time for a weekly program of, say, maybe, fifteen minutes?

The manager shuffled some papers, cleared his throat, shuffled more papers. "*Sí, es possible.*"

Now, the catch, Joe and Roland thought, he'll charge an exorbitant price!

"Ah, and that would cost how much?" they asked.

The manager scribbled some figures, scratched them out, scribbled some more, cleared his throat, "$76.00 per program—paid in advance, of course, for one year. For a thirty-minute program."

Joe said quietly in English to Roland. "I don't have that much money in my work account. Do you?"

"Yes, I could pay it up-front. You can pay me back monthly, for your half," Roland said.

Joe turned to the manager, "*¡Muy bien!* Great! We'll take it. Where do we sign?"

The manager said they would draw up the contract and schedule the program. Then he said, "If you can bring the money this week … let's see … you can begin a show …"

He reached into a drawer, pulled out the schedule, hmmed and nodded, "*This* Saturday night. At 10:00."

"Great!" said Joe and Roland.

They walked out of the office with a year's contract. They were exuberant! Stunned. In shock.

Half-way home they realized, "We don't *have* a program! We don't know how to produce a program! We're supposed to go on the air, live, THIS Saturday night! That's five days from now!"

What can we call the program?

We need a theme song.

The theme song should be meaningful, not just rhythmic.

What will we do on the program?

We can all sing.

We can play the accordion, piano, and saxophone.

We'll have a musical program. With talking in between. Dialogue.

Not preaching.

We could have interviews, too, maybe.

Joe, Roland, and Evelyn used to sing in a music group as teenagers; they could rehearse some songs.

How many songs per show? Four? With conversation in between?

Joe, you need to translate some more songs into Spanish.

We need a theme for each show. Then we'll talk around that theme.

We need a give-away. How about the first course of the International Correspondence Institute (ICI) called "Great Questions of Life"? Does Don have adequate copies on hand in the bookstore?

We should read a brief Scripture passage each week.

What Scripture translation should we use? "Good News for Modern Man" is easy to understand.

We need to pray at the close of the show.

We need a closing theme song.

What will we wear? Casual clothes. Our colors don't have to match since it's black and white TV.

Five days later, August 5, 1973, we sat in the studio in a semi-circle: the piano on the left, Joe in the center, Roland to the right, Evelyn beside him. A barefoot cameraman motioned to Joe, Joe tapped Roland's foot, Roland began to play the short introduction. I picked up the melody on the piano, and we sang our opening theme song, *Las Buenas Nuevas ...*

Las Buenas Nuevas	The Good News
Proclamaremos.	We will proclaim.
Las bendiciones	The blessings for
Al pecador.	A sinful man.
Que Cristo salva,	That Jesus saves him,
Sana y bautiza,	Heals and baptizes,
Y que muy pronto	And very soon will
Volverá.	Return again.

Joe greeted the people, "*¡Bienvenido al programa 'Las Buenas Nuevas'!*" "Welcome to the program, 'Good News.'" He read John 3:16 from the easy-to-understand New Testament. He said we would talk more about God's love in a minute, but first Roland would sing. Roland leaned forward in his chair, unsnapped the accordion, and sang. He and Joe talked. Joe and Roland and Evelyn sang a trio. Joe and Roland talked. Joe played his saxophone while Roland and I accompanied him. Joe held up the lesson, "Great Questions of Life," and said it would be free to anyone who requested it.

Joe prayed a simple prayer. We sang our closing theme song, *Hay Lugar al Pie de la Cruz*, "There's Room at the Cross for You" by Ira Stanphill.

We had been in Paraguay for thirty-seven days. We would never be the same. Neither would Paraguay.

Roland, Joe, Evelyn, and Margaret on *Las Buenas Nuevas* TV program

31

Guaraní and Home

(gwah-rah-knee)
August 1973

***

ali stood washing dishes at the kitchen sink. Her back was toward me as I asked, "*¿Alcanzaste a planchar la ropa de los niños?*" "Did you have time to iron the kids' school clothes?"

"Heh," she grunted, her back to me.

So I asked her again.

"Heh," she grunted again, slightly louder.

So I asker her again, slightly louder, "Lali, did you have time to iron-"

She stopped washing dishes, turned toward me, "Sí, Señora, ¡Sí!" she said angrily.

I was totally baffled. What had I done to deserve her anger? She was only nineteen, but she had really wanted this job.

I had absolutely no idea that Lali was answering me in *Guaraní* and that "heh" (nasal tone) means "yes."

When Spanish Conquistadors sailed down the east coast of South America, they came to a wide river basin. They hoped this river would lead them back north and westward to Peru and Bolivia, to the riches of the Inca Empire. They sailed up the Rio Paraná for several weeks until they came to a nice anchorage where they built a fort in 1537 on the day when they celebrated Mary's Ascension to heaven. They called the fort *Asunción*.

But just north of Asunción, the Rio Paraná turned back eastward, so some of the explorers set out to trek northwest across a desolate region the Indians called the *Chaco*—dry desert in summer, marshy quagmire in winter. The *Guaraní* Indians were not happy to see the foreigners trekking through their territory, so the *Guaraní*—being good cannibals—enjoyed a European dinner. But they ate only the bravest and fiercest fighters.

Meanwhile, in Asunción, the governors Salazar and Irala told their men that since they would not go back home to Spain for many years, they should take all the concubines they wanted. These Indian concubines learned to speak only a minimum of Spanish. They raised their babies to speak only *Guaraní*. (The Indian tribes are called *Guaraní*. Their language is also called *Guaraní*. Plus, the currency is called *Guaraníes*.)

The men insisted on Spanish culture and religion, so the women blended their religious practices with the Catholic traditions—for example, at the celebration of the birth of *San Juan el Bautista*, Saint John the Baptist, the custom is to walk barefoot across beds of burning coals.

To the present day, the population is 95 percent mestizo (mixed Native American and European) and the language at home is *Guaraní*. Children learn Spanish when they start to school—compulsory through sixth grade. Business is conducted in Spanish.

Though Asunción had become the center of a large Spanish province, it was isolated because of its distance from Spain and the difficulty in navigating the river. There was never a large European population in Asunción and neither silver nor gold were found in Paraguay. However the Spanish continued to rule until May 15, 1811 when Paraguay declared its independence.

Buenos Aires, down south on the Rio Paraná, was established after Asunción, so when Argentina tried to dominate Asunción in 1864, Paraguayans formed an army and fought not only Argentina but also Brazil and Uruguay! In this *War of the Triple Alliance*, Paraguay, vastly outnumbered, lost most of its male population.

Boys and women fought valiantly, too; *py nandí,* barefoot warriors, they were called.

With the population decimated, the governors said, "Have children. It doesn't matter with whom." Incest, infidelity, and promiscuity predominated the culture.

Later, in the 1930s and 40s, Bolivia tried to encroach on Paraguay's border to the northwest. Again, Paraguayans fought valiantly, this time in the Chaco, in the soaring heat and the bone-chilling frost. Since they could not build fires to heat water for their *mate* (mah-tay), green tea, they learned to drink it cold, calling it *te-re-ré* (teh-reh-reh). Again, large numbers of males were killed. Again, the mandate, "Have babies." Incest became commonplace.

Desperately poor, isolated, and attacked by large-country neighbors, the Paraguayans became increasingly paranoid of the outside world. Feeling inferior, Paraguayans retreated inside their "shells" like a turtle, for self-preservation. The mestizos became subsistence farmers clustered within 100 miles of Asunción, because only one-third of the country is habitable; the other two-thirds is the Chaco.

Months after our arrival, when we were able to reopen the Bible institute, not one student could locate Paraguay on a world map. Not one student could locate South America on the map. They honestly did not know the world was out there.

One morning, Timmy was eating a bacon sandwich. "I like this better," he said.

"What? The tomato? The bacon? The home-made mayonnaise?" I asked.

"Everything. I like living here better than anywhere else."

After two months, we were still "camping" in our house. The Rio Paraná was low and the boat with our crates could not come up the river.

But the children didn't notice the lack of "things." The kids loved our yard. They ran and climbed trees and walked on the walls. Christy carried the toy poodle, Tinker Belle, on one arm and a Barbie doll in the other. Timmy had found a stray puppy he named Bandit because it had black circles around its eyes. The kids and dogs explored every inch of the two-and-a-half acres.

There were trees of papaya, lemon, sour orange, banana, guava, avocado, pear, mango, cumquat, tangerine, pomegranate, and cherries, along with pineapple. The street was lined with royal palms. The back yard had a large "bean" tree with wide leaves forming nice shade. There was a "nut" tree that no one knew much about; no one ever ate the nuts. (The following year I used a hammer to crack the very hard shell—macadamia nuts!)

The yard was divided into the front-front yard out by the street, the front yard nearer our house behind the wall, the back yard, and the back-back yard behind a wire fence.

A rectangular brick building sat diagonally in the back yard. It held a storeroom and a maid's quarters. Attached to the back of it was a chicken coop.

The neighbors across the street had two ostriches as pets and watchdogs running free in the yard. Our next door neighbors, the Jenkins, had a macaw that could talk so plainly, it sounded like a person. It could whistle a song, too, with vibrato. (We never said "Jenkinses," though I know it is correct.)

The back-back yard had become piled with brush and trash. Joe dug a trash-burning pit and raked and cleaned up the yard. He trimmed the bushes and trees and made a bonfire. We invited the other missionaries over for a wiener roast. I had found an old percolator and I made coffee for everyone. We drank from an assortment of mismatched cups.

One day, when Joe was raking, he sent the kids in to get me. "Come right now! You won't believe this!" I hurried out to see the biggest frog I had ever seen. It was as large as a cantaloupe! The ugly, greenish-brown Paraguayan frogs spit venom that can blind a person (we were told) or can kill a small animal.

When Joe went to buy paint, he learned that it came only in two-quart cans, and the "color powder" was to be mixed in at home. The store sold paint rollers but the clerks had never heard of roller trays. Joe hired some painters to help him paint the interior of our house, and his helpers dipped a paintbrush in the can, then saturated the roller with paint from the brush, and after that, rolled the wall. So, Joe rummaged around in the junk left from previous missionaries and found an old broiler tray and an old waffle iron grid. He fashioned a paint tray for the rollers. The painters loved this new invention!

The Jenkins' back-back yard had a circular cement pond green with algae. It was actually a rough swimming pool that previous missionaries had made. We had been advised to bring a pool filter and that all the missionaries would help pay for it. It was in our shipment.

We had arrived during winter vacation from school (June–July), so the kids had two weeks to explore the yard before school started. The Asunción Christian Academy, ACA, had been formed years before by the Hutsells (from our mission) along with Mennonite, Baptist, and Methodist missionaries. At first, the Methodist missionary wife, Lucy Huston, a teacher, supervised all the children as they studied correspondence courses.

Soon, there were so many students that ACA charged tuition, rented a house for classrooms, built a ball field for soccer, and asked for volunteer teachers to come from the States to teach for a year or two. The Baptists send "Journeymen," the Assemblies of God, MAPS (Missionary Placement Service) teachers.

School began at 7:15 a.m. and finished at 12:15. A VW bus came by to pick up the children. I would have lunch ready when they returned and then we would all take a siesta. We really didn't need it so much at first, but later when the weather turned 104 degrees and stayed there for days on end, we really needed the siesta. After siesta, the children did homework and played.

Without a television or a radio, the local newspaper was our major information source. That's how we learned about Watergate.

Of course, I "had" to learn to shop and to eat the local food. But Roland and Evelyn never let me forget my first shopping trip and my saying, "I'm not cookie hungry right now." They teased me unmercifully. When Evelyn and I went to the market together, we could laugh about things that happened. But if I went alone, it wasn't so funny. I would bring the fruits and vegetables home from the market … and wash everything in bleach water. Then, anything that would not be peeled, I soaked for twenty minutes in either bleach water or white iodine water.

To buy meat, I'd ask for *un kilo* and the butcher would sharpen his big knife on a leather strap. Then he'd whack off a chunk of meat from the carcass hanging on a hook. He'd plunk the chunk down on the scales, nod, and then wrap it in a piece of newspaper. One morning, the little boy helping me carry "groceries" at the market dropped the bag. The meat tumbled out of the newspaper into the gutter … at home I washed the meat with dish detergent, rinsed it with bleach water and placed it in the dish drainer to drain. But the most difficult meat to eat was the hamburger because I could not wash it …. Are cooked flies germ-free?

Buying eggs was interesting, too. If I asked for a dozen eggs, the vendor would take a piece of newspaper, place three eggs on it, roll the paper, place three more eggs, roll it, place three more, fold it, and place the other three. Then she'd fold the paper to make a package. Evelyn and I always carried the eggs in our arms rather than in our shopping bags.

One day, on the way back to the car, Evelyn saw a storefront display of shoes. She bent over to take a closer look, cradling her eggs carefully in the crook of her arm. All of a sudden, a big dog came up behind her and put his cold nose on her bare leg, behind her knee. She screamed, jumped, and squished the eggs … yolk and egg white dribbled down her arm! I laughed until my sides ached. Of course, in the car we had a roll of toilet paper that we carried always, everywhere, so we took it and cleaned her up the best we could.

Even though the weather was not very warm yet, eggs would sit in the sunshine at the market for days. One day when I was baking a cake, I broke an egg into the flour. Green goop slid into the bowl, as the horrible, pungent odor of sulfur stung my eyes and nose. I gagged as I ran outside with the bowl. I learned to break, uneasily, all eggs into a small bowl before putting them into the other ingredients. After several rotten eggs, Joe decided we should get some chickens and make use of that chicken coop in the back yard. He bought some biddies, and soon we had our own delicious, fresh eggs!

Even though we were "camping" in our house, we had a good washer and dryer (good old Maytag) and an old kitchen stove. The stove looked terrible, but the oven worked very well. Betty taught me how to make bread, cinnamon rolls, and doughnuts, and Evelyn taught me how to make biscuits:

Evelyn's Biscuits

INGREDIENTS

    2 cups flour
2 teaspoons baking powder
1 teaspoon salt (it came in a plastic bag)
1/4 teaspoon baking soda (we had to buy it at the pharmacy)
1/3 cup vegetable oil (or light olive oil—"Crisco" was unknown)
2/3 cup buttermilk (add a teaspoon of vinegar to regular milk, if necessary)

DIRECTIONS

1. Mix the dry ingredients.
2. Add the oil and buttermilk all at once. Stir quickly until a ball forms.
3. Pinch off a small amount and roll it around in your hands, kneading it, forming a biscuit.
4. Place the biscuits in an iron skillet coated with oil.
5. Bake at 450 degrees for 12 minutes. If the biscuits aren't brown on top, don't bake longer, turn on the broiler for a few minutes.

32

A Few Good Men
July–August 1973, continued

The elderly, disheveled man walked several miles every day — from his cot at the Bible institute to the unfinished church building in Republicano. He worked hard all day and then walked back to the school.

Escoe had just appeared at the airport about six months earlier with a carry-on satchel containing a change of work clothes and a few tools. Though he spoke not one word of Spanish, somehow he had arrived at Everett Ward's door.

"Name's Escoe. God spoke ta me back in Oklahoma and said ta come help. I don't preach and I cain't speak Spanish. But I know construction. Could I build a church? If so, where at?"

Everett Ward was taken aback. He was leaving for furlough in a few days and he intended to assign the building of the little church in Republicano to Roland Blount. But Roland was blind. How could he supervise construction? In an instant, Escoe became Roland's entire construction crew!

When Roland was a young man, afraid to travel alone, his mother had held him close and whispered, "Whenever you need help, God will always have someone there to help you."

Escoe kept to himself and laid bricks. He washed his clothes once a week whether they needed it or not, and he ate one meal a day that Evelyn provided for him.

The day Escoe laid the last brick to finish the church building, he told Roland, "God wants me ta go back home now." His bag was already packed, and he left on the next flight. Roland shook his head in amazement. "God sent Escoe all the way to Paraguay just to help me build that church!"

Personally, I never exchanged more than a few words with Escoe during his time there—and I worried that if I couldn't stretch to love a disheveled North American, how would I ever truly be able to embrace the poor, ignorant Paraguayans? They were so different from the Chileans ….

Chris, on the other hand, was easy to love—he was clean-cut, cultured, well-mannered, and articulate.

Chris lived next door with the Jenkins. "But only for a few more weeks," Chris informed us over some of Betty's hot cinnamon rolls. "I'll just help Don with the accounting and then I'll go on back to Australia."

Chris Grace, in his late twenties, stood tall and thin with a mop of naturally curly blondish-brown hair and a thick beard. He had left Australia over four years earlier as a hippy, backpacking. Chris was finishing his journey around the world by traveling through the South American continent. He had already backpacked through Asia, Africa, Europe, and North America.

Chris had tried communal living, drugs, eastern religions, anything that someone told him would bring soul-peace. However, nothing lasted. Several months earlier, he had been working for a few weeks in the Bolivian jungles where he met some Assemblies of God missionaries. They talked to Chris about a relationship with Jesus, not religion. Chris listened politely but did not commit himself. Then, in the middle of the night, Chris decided to give Jesus a try. He woke up the missionaries to tell them he was "born again"!

Traveling on south, Chris had arrived in Asunción in April and paused to greet our missionaries. Within a few minutes, Don learned that Chris had studied to be a CPA. Don desperately needed an accountant. He was in charge of all the missions' funds, and he had hundreds of receipts piled in his office. The receipts needed to be sorted and recorded.

Chris volunteered to stay for a few days to help Don with the books. However, the days turned to weeks and then to months. And then, Erica arrived ....

Paint brush in hand, I stuck my head inside my kitchen cabinets. Uuuh, these had never been painted inside. I twisted my neck and saw words stenciled on the wood. I could make out "Stawinski." These cupboards were made from shipping crates!

I was humbled by the vision of the Stawinskis, Hutsells, Emorys, Sundbergs, and Baliuses in buying land for the missions' houses and the Bible school complex: classrooms, dormitories, kitchen, lunchroom, bookstore, caretaker's cottage, a small chapel, and an unfinished church sanctuary and radio studio.

But now the buildings stood empty. Deserted. I knew Paul Hutsell had given the strength of his youth to Paraguay. He had ruined his health trying to help the Paraguayan people. He and the other missionaries opened the Bible school and organized Sunday schools, women's groups, youth groups, youth camps.

I clinched my jaw in anger thinking of what we had been told regarding Juan Carlos Ortiz, the man who had been one of our Argentine pastors ... the tremendous orator Joe had gone to hear in Chile just after our arrival there .... This man, apparently obsessed with an over-inflated ego, had required his followers to become his "disciples." Ortiz set up under-shepherds to report to him. The lowly disciples could not do anything without consulting with their "shepherd." They could not call a taxi or buy a necktie or buy a pair of shoes. One man told us he even had to consult about which shirt to wear.

Ortiz declared that Bible study was unnecessary, that the shepherd would interpret the Scriptures. Pulpits were prohibited, so were pews. Believers should sit in a circle and gaze into each others' eyes and declare their Christian love.

Paraguayans fell for this error. Pastors left the country. Churches closed.

Yet the church organizational structure remained like a ghost town with a few specters dancing about aimlessly. Only four pastors remained. But the organization still had a national superintendent, a women's president, and a youth president.

Up to that time, no Protestant denomination had ever gained many converts in Paraguay. And now, to lose converts to religious heresy was heartbreaking.

"Your program was a ray of light into the shadows of my life." Our first letter from the telecast! It was from a young woman, single, 26, requesting the Bible study course. The second week, several more people wrote in.

We knew the response would be slow. We were combating current heresy as well as breaking through barriers that had stood for hundreds of years. Most Paraguayans feared Protestants. Hardly any Paraguayans had ever held a Bible in their hands. We knew our "job" was to show Christian love and to reference the Bible as the basis of belief.

Whenever Joe would make a grammatical mistake on the show, Roland would smile and say, "Aren't you supposed to say ...." Joe would laugh and say it correctly. Or, if Joe could not think of the name of something, he'd describe it and say, "What do you call that ....?"

The Paraguayans loved the transparency of Joe and Roland, their willingness to laugh at themselves. And the viewers admired their sincere love for God, their easiness in spontaneous prayer, the unassuming manner in which they read from the Bible.

A few months after we began the telecast, Joe drove through a park where the army was bivouacked. The soldiers were taking a break and had sprawled out on the grass. But when they saw Joe driving, slowly, toward them, they recognized him. A number of them stood to their feet and began singing our theme song from the television program! Soon, they all stood and joined in the singing. One guy grinned and called out, *"Cantemos, Rolando,"* "Let's sing, Roland," mimicking perfectly Joe's tone of voice and pronunciation.

Little by little by little, we were winning Paraguayan hearts.

Exactly one month after we arrived in Paraguay, Joe preached at a youth rally. His sermon was entitled, "The Lord Needs Another

Nehemiah"—someone to build up the broken-down walls. Someone who sees the need and is brave enough to accept the responsibility. Someone who doesn't give up during ridicule. Someone who perseveres until the job is done. Someone who wants to go to Bible school.

No one said "Amen" during the sermon and I wondered if anyone was really listening.

Then Joe asked, "Would *you* be willing to attend the Bible institute if it were reopened? If so, come forward."

I held my breath.

Young men and women began to walk forward! I counted twenty-seven.

33

Making an Effort
September–October 1973

---

ba'e cha pa. Íporánte. How are you? Very well. Joe and I, Roland, and Evelyn were taking Guaraní lessons. *Pa* indicates a question. There is no question mark, no voice inflection, just the *pa* added to the end of the sentence or phrase. Everything is said in a nasal tone. *Py* is "foot." *Inh* (like a grunt) is "water." *Heh*, of course, is "yes."

Sitting under a fruit tree in a dirt patio, way out in the country, a missionary friend of ours was chatting in Spanish with an old man. Our friend asked, "*¿Cómo se dice toronja en Guaraní?*" "How do you say *grapefruit* in Guaraní?" The old man replied, "*Grapefruit.*" (the English word!)

Another friend was holding a missionary service out in the country and wanted to say in Guaraní, "My wife could not come today. She has a fever." Instead, he said, "My wife could not come today. She is in heat." The people burst out laughing.

Even though we knew only a few words, the people loved for us to *try* to speak Guaraní.

We bumped down a cobblestone street and turned onto a dirt *calle* leading into *Barrio Herrera*. The little brick church, *Victoria*, sat adjacent to a vacant lot where Joe and Roland decided to hold an open-air campaign, similarly to what we'd done in Viña.

313

Evelyn led the singing, Roland played the accordion, and Joe preached. We cranked the P.A. system up really high. There was no ordinance against noise, so from blocks around, people would begin to walk to the services when they heard the music.

On Friday night, we showed the movie by Hermano Pablo, *Baal.* The movie depicts Elijah taunting the prophets of Baal, and so they cry out, "Oh, Ba-al" over and over again trying to get their god to respond. Our kids loved to mimic the amateur actors and soon added "Oh, Ba-al" to their list of games to play! But the Paraguayans loved the movie and our attendance grew to 250. Most evenings I conducted a children's service inside the church building, where I would have from 50 to 80 kids—and they were a handful.

We had intended to have services for a month, but we extended them to six weeks. The pastor at Victoria was very appreciative; his congregation tripled!

One night, Joe wanted to begin his sermon with a joke. He told about the mother who was so proud of her son. He was in the military and when the platoon marched, her son was the only one "in step"—all the others marched "wrong."

No one laughed. No one smiled. So Joe repeated parts of the joke. No one laughed. Except ... Roland. He laughed until tears rolled down his cheeks—he laughed because no one else was laughing and because Joe kept trying to explain the joke. But the joke was not funny because the Paraguayan military was not well-trained and the men did not know how to march in step!

Two important things arrived in September—baby Donnie Jenkins, and our shipment.

The baby did not actually have a name for over two months. The day the baby was born, Don added "Name baby" to his "to-do" list. We really teased Don about "baby-no-name," but he assured us that they would name the baby when it got to the top of his list.

The Jenkins and the Blounts came to our house the day our shipment arrived to watch the crates sliding down planks from the truck bed to the ground. I couldn't watch—I was sure the crates were going to topple over. We had been waiting for *three months*, camping in our house, wearing and re-wearing the clothes we had brought in our suitcases. The river was still too low for the ship to navigate, but thankfully, the crates had been transferred to a barge.

Everyone helped to carry stuff into the house! Wow, we had a couch and matching chairs in the living room now instead of lawn chairs! We had end tables and lamps! And we had real beds to sleep on! And lots of boxes bulging with goodies.

I didn't bring things for the walls (I still didn't know about the "beautiful" wall hanging Mom had packed) because I wanted to buy things in Paraguay to take back to the States with us. I had been in missionaries' homes that were "a little Americana" and I didn't want that. I wanted the children to know and appreciate their heritage but also to enjoy the flavor of the local culture. I looked forward to buying paintings and knick-knacks locally.

Unloading our crates in the front yard

The room beside our office soon became the music room. We placed chairs in a semi-circle and kept Joe's saxophone and new, electric bass guitar there. Joe would translate a song and we would meet with Roland and Evelyn every morning to rehearse and plan the following Saturday's TV show.

One morning we were practicing a song when I saw a shadow creep across the office wall. It paused when our music paused, and continued when our singing began again.

The maid! It had to be Lydia, the new maid! Why was she creeping? What was she doing? She was supposed to be in the kitchen washing the breakfast dishes!

I remembered that as Evelyn had walked to the music room, she laid her purse on top of the file cabinet in the office and mentioned that she had already been to town to change $100 into *Gs,* the local currency.

I jumped up from my chair and ran to the office door! There stood the maid holding Evelyn's open wallet! "What are you doing?" I shouted in Spanish.

Evelyn, right behind me, screamed in English, "She's in my purse! She's in my purse! She's in *my purse!*"

Joe and Roland put down their musical instruments and came to see what was going on. Joe grabbed the woman's wrist and led her to the couch. He told her not to move and he told me to call the police.

While we waited for the police to arrive, Joe told me to check Lydia's large purse, out in the laundry room. It was filled with stolen items.

The next day, when I opened the dryer door, the dryer, too, was filled with items Lydia had intended to steal. She had stashed them there to grab as she left the house.

Lali, the maid who taught me my first Guaraní word, was actually my third maid. Lydia was the second. (All the missionaries hired maids for about $20 a month.)

My first maid in Paraguay was Miriam. Miriam was a wonderful worker, she cleaned very well. She mopped the terrazzo floors every day to remove the dust seeping from the adobe walls. She cleaned the bathrooms every day. She went to buy fresh bread every day at the *panadería* to replace yesterday's rock-hard bread. She went to the market for me; she cleaned and soaked the veggies. Since everything was "from scratch," it took hours to prepare a meal. For example, beets: buy them at the market, wash with bleach water, boil until tender, peel, slice, boil vinegar and sugar and corn starch for seasoning to make "Harvard beets." Nothing came in cans. No foods were frozen. Green and angel hair pasta we could buy, but everything else was "from scratch."

One Saturday, Miriam had come to work filled with malicious gossip. She took me aside and began to talk softly but urgently. She was so excited she was trembling with joy, brimming over with her news. Had I heard about the pastor at Victoria? And what the other missionaries were saying?

Her manner unnerved me, caught me off-guard. I began to listen intently. I knew she wanted my involvement emotionally. Then something interrupted us. And during that brief interval, I realized how evil her intent was. I backed off, with an excuse, and left the room.

I was troubled all weekend. The person who had recommended Miriam told me she "talked." But, I needed Miriam's help, I depended on her. Nevertheless, when she arrived for work the next Monday morning, I handed her a week's pay and fired her. It was one of the hardest things I had ever done.

Joe drove a little orange VW station wagon up our driveway. He blew the horn and the kids and I went out to look at our "new" Speed-the-Light car, a VW Squareback. It was several years old, but it was in fairly good shape. It was standard shift, Joe explained, because we needed the "granny gear" on these rough roads. The gas mileage was good and that was important because gasoline was very expensive. And, wonder of wonders, it had an air conditioner! Policy forbade adding an air conditioner to a vehicle, but if it already had one, we were allowed to keep it.

Later that afternoon, Evelyn and I decided to drive downtown to the post office. I was not about to drive in Paraguay yet, so Evelyn drove the VW. The post office had no parking lot and street-curb parking was extremely limited. As a result, everyone double-parked. It was better if two people went, so the driver could stay in the car to move it if necessary.

We picked up all the missionaries' mail and started home. By now it was getting dark. Evelyn figured out how to turn on the lights; however, they were on "bright." The driver of every car we met honked at us, flashed his lights at us, held up his cupped hand at us (a horrible "no-no") … but we could not figure out how to dim the lights! We had no idea that the dimmer was on the blinker lever. In any car we had ever driven, the dimmer button was on the floorboard, on the left.

Several days later, I drove to the post office with Betty Jenkins. She stayed in the car, double-parked, while I ran in to get the mail, and then ran next door to have an extra car key made. When I returned to the street, a crowd had gathered and I could see broken, yellow glass on the ground. An irate man was yelling at Betty, "You should not have double-parked! Can I help it if I broke your parking light while trying to exit my parking place! We need to call the police!"

A guy in the crowd yelled, "If you call the police, you'll *both* pay big fines!"

I knew that I was at fault. (Betty, sitting in the passenger seat, didn't even have the car keys.) But it was, after all, my light that was broken. So I just gestured and yelled, "How could you break my light! Are you blind? Couldn't you see this car? If you will pay me 500*Gs* (about $3.50), I will let you go without calling the police!"

"200*Gs*," he yelled.

Betty, out of the car by now, stood at my side jiggling little "baby-no-name" on her hip. She whispered in English, "Take the money! Take it! Take it!"

"300," I yelled back.

He paid me! He was driving a big VW van, so I figured he had the money! (I do feel slightly bad about it … occasionally ….)

When Joe cleaned off the back-back yard, he decided it would be the perfect spot for a garden. Since it was spring, he hoed and fertilized and formed long rows of dirt, and planted seeds—field peas (like black-eyes) and corn. In a few days, Joe went to check on his garden. The corn was beginning to sprout. So were the peas. But the peas themselves were poking up through the dirt! Breaking the dirt apart! Well, Joe just pushed them back down and stomped some dirt over them.

Joe told Roland about it and Roland began to laugh. He had grown up in the country, and it turns out, that's what peas are *supposed* to do.

Our crop was very small. Actually, one small bowlful of peas was our entire harvest.

Christy, Timmy and farmer Joe

I needed to get my hair trimmed before our next telecast, so Evelyn took me to her beauty shop. For $2.10 she could get a shampoo, dark rinse for her gray hair, and her hair styled. Oh, yes, and a manicure. I put my glasses back on just as the girl was spraying the *laca*, hairspray, on my hair for the finishing touch. I could not believe my eyes! My hair was dark brown! She had "rinsed" my hair, too, covering up my expensive highlights from the States!

One evening as we entered the television studio, a woman stood waiting for us. She was dressed provocatively and her make-up was extreme. She was a dancer who had her own TV show. "Your program is my favorite. Sometimes I am so tired when I get home that I fall asleep on the sofa, but my husband always wakes me up to watch your show. You sing so naturally ... from the heart ... you radiate!" Her soft words and misty eyes were in stark contrast to her garish appearance.

Another evening, a nicely dressed older couple rushed up to us as we entered the studio. The man shook hands with Joe and Roland and gave them each an *abrazo*, a bear hug. "We just had to come to meet you. I'm a retired military officer. We're Catholic but ... this is the first time we are really learning about God."

His wife looked longingly at the New Testament in my hand. "Would you like to have this?" Evelyn asked, even as she tugged the Bible from my hand. The woman hugged the Bible to her chest, tears filling her eyes.

We decided to offer *Dios Llega al Hombre*, the New Testament, as a give-away on the show. We would insert the ICI Bible Course in each one.

A young wife wrote, "My husband and I really want the Bible and the study course, but we live with my parents and they would never permit us to have a Bible. Please mail it to the radio station where my husband works."

When Joe went to pick up our driver's licenses, the government employees called him by name and asked for Bibles.

I heard someone whistling our theme song in our front yard and then I heard clapping at the door. (Paraguayans clap, instead of knock, to announce their presence.) Our newspaper boy stood on the stoop grinning from ear to ear. "I need to collect for the paper. And ... uh ... I listen to your show."

"Listen?" I asked him.

"*Heh*, we don't have a TV, but I can get *Canal 9* on my radio." He walked back down the sidewalk singing our theme song, "*Las buenas nuevas proclamaremos, las bendiciones al pecador, que Cristo salva....*"

34

Good grief!
October–November 1973

———◆———

*B*y *the end of October,* spring had sprung—temperatures hovered in the 90s, barely cooling off at night, and there had already been days topping 100 degrees.

We could hardly wait to get the swimming pool cleaned out. One of the things in our shipment was the pool pump and filter. We all helped to bail the green goop out of the pool and we scrubbed the walls with a broom. The pool was about twenty feet in diameter and about four feet deep, sloping to about six feet. The cement was rough on our feet but the water felt sooo good.

On Saturdays, Christy and Timmy put on their bathing suits as soon as they hopped out of bed. They would walk through the house sighing, "Whew! It sure is hot! I sure wish we could go get in the pool! Mom, aren't you just burning up?" On Sundays, all of us would swim in the afternoon—except the Blounts. Howie and Carla were not allowed to swim on Sundays.

One day, as Christy sat on a cement bench beside the pool, she screamed, "Auw! Something just bit me!" She swiped at her chest, just above her bathing suit. I could see a welt forming so we put some baking soda on it. Within fifteen minutes, Christy, back on her bench, began scratching her arms and legs, "Mom! Where are all these ants coming from? They are biting me all over!"

I saw that she was breaking out in welts all over her body. As Joe and I rushed her to the Baptist Hospital, her face began to swell. Her nose turned red and enlarged, her ears shone red and were swollen, her eyes began to swell shut. The doctor gave her two shots, and almost immediately she began to recover. Even as he monitored her condition, he handed us a liquid medicine and said to carry it with us at all times. He was not certain what insect could have stung her but suggested that it was probably the venomous Paraguayan "flat spider." He warned that a subsequent sting could be fatal if her airways became swollen shut.

The Jardín Botánico, the zoo, consisted of assorted, stand-alone cages scattered throughout several acres. An elephant was tethered by his foot, a bear by his neck; a lion paced in a cage, monkeys climbed in their cage. Large trees provided shade where the kids climbed and scrambled over the huge roots.

Up-wind from the animals, Betty, Evelyn, and I spread our quilts and unpacked the potato salad, deviled eggs, and sliced tomatoes while the men built a fire to roast hot dogs.

The children scampered off to see the monkeys, and in just a few minutes, we heard shrieks of laughter. As Timmy had bent down to tie his shoe, a monkey reached through the bars and pulled his hair!

That day, we didn't take our two dogs to the park. Tinker Belle looked too pitiful to be out in public. The week before, we took her to the vet, who said he was also a groomer. He shaved her, unevenly, all over except for a tiny, jagged tuft of hair on top of her head and tiny, distorted tufts on the ends of her ears and feet. She was so ugly, even *she* knew it. She hid under the living room chair. After that, Joe became her groomer. Tinker Belle was so prissy, she would not urinate by common squatting; she lifted one leg. Then, she decided to lift both back legs. Then she decided to lift both back legs so high ... that sometimes she would dribble onto her tummy!

The other puppy, Bandit, was sickly, and we eventually had to have her put to sleep. But not before the maid taught us a new word. We called the dog *Bandida* because we knew *Bandita* meant "Band-Aid." Through the maid's laughter, we learned that in Paraguayan slang *Bandida* meant "prostitute." From then on, we just called the dog by her English name.

Our garden, minus the peas, was doing well. Joe's stalks of corn were head high, and began to tassel. He would go count the ears of corn almost every day. Silks extending, the little nubs were becoming bigger than his thumb! He was excited, because we had never had a garden before. Paraguayan corn had large cobs and tough, small kernels, but from these seeds that Joe had hand carried from the U.S., we would have corn full and sweet!

In early October, as Thanksgiving approached, we began to ask about turkeys. Though none were sold in the market, someone told us about a farmer who raised a few.

Joe and Roland drove out into the country and came back with two turkeys—one for Thanksgiving, one for Christmas. Joe made a pen in the back yard, so we could fatten up the turkeys. They gobbled incessantly, and they would entwine their necks trying to peck each other. Christy named them *Paul* and *Silas*.

We were still conducting the nightly, open-air services in *Herrera,* and each evening when we arrived we would see a small, old, sway-back horse hobbled nearby in a field. He was really gentle, and the children would go pet the horse. They begged Joe to buy it. Joe talked to the owner, night after night, and finally they agreed on a price.

The children were thrilled! Timmy was still a little scared of the horse, so he took charge of feeding the chickens while Christy took charge of the horse, naming him Prince Patrick the First. Every afternoon the children would ride Prince Patrick the First around our two-and-a-half acres, and then Christy would tie the horse back in its pen that Joe had made in the back-back yard.

So, our back yard was filled with turkeys gobbling, puppies barking, twenty chickens clucking, and a horse neighing. And the sounds of Joe's and Timmy's hoes getting rid of any weeds near the corn.

The children enjoyed ACA (Asunción Christian Academy). Timmy and Carla were in the third grade class. Christy was the only girl in the fifth grade, and the single, cute professor would say things like, "This paper is for the prettiest girl in the class." When Christy complained that the boys picked on her, pulling her hair, the teacher assured her that that's the way boys acted when they wanted attention.

PTA was fun! Almost all of the parents were missionaries of various denominations, plus a few businessmen and their wives. I was elected vice-president. But then, in early October, the president moved away. So, as "President," I opened the floor for discussion for our October Halloween Festival. Christy's teacher said his class wanted to do a Spook House. Timmy's teacher said that Timmy and Carla had assured her that our horse would be wonderful for pony rides.

We sold tickets and made more than $100 for the school. The horse was a big hit, providing lots of pony rides. But the Spook House made the most money. Joe had rented a cheap, wooden casket from the funeral home, and the kids screamed at the "body rising." The kids also stuck their hands down into a bowl of eyeballs (peeled grapes) and into brains (spaghetti).

We made three more trips to the hospital. First, Timmy fell out of a tree at school and had a concussion. Then, on a Saturday evening just before time to go to the TV station, Carla hopped up on the kitchen counter to get a drinking glass out of the cabinet. She wanted to take some tea to her mom. Carla caught the top of her head under the corner of the overhanging cabinet. Blood streamed down her head. Joe and Roland had to go on to the television studio, while Evelyn and I drove Carla to the hospital. Evelyn said she couldn't watch the doctor pull the skin back together and stitch it, but I said I would stay with Carla, holding her hand. I was brave ... until the doctor took tweezers and raised the skin and I saw Carla's skull through the blood ... I hurried to sit down, head between my knees.

And the third trip was because Christy had been sitting, flipping a pocket-knife. She missed catching it, and it landed on her thigh, cutting a gash that required five stitches!

The nurse at the hospital desk asked for a Bible. She knew us from TV and from our frequent visits.

When Evelyn and I went to the Post Office, six government employees asked for Bibles. As we drove away with our car windows down, a man on the sidewalk waved, "*Evelina, Margarita*, I'll see you on Saturday night, as usual."

We went into *Martels*, a department store. Five clerks surrounded us, calling us by name. They asked for Bibles and the study course.

A businessman called the television station and requested Bibles for all of his employees.

A woman stopped Evelyn and me in the supermarket. She asked for a Bible, and as she gave us her address, we realized she lived in *Barrio Herrera*. We invited her to the nightly services. She began to attend regularly.

Another woman called the station and talked to Joe, "Would you and Rolando come to my house, please? I want to pray the prayer that you say when you close the show, the one where you ask Jesus to forgive you. But I don't know how to do that by myself. Would you please come?"

The technicians at the studio wanted Bibles. So did the barefoot cameramen.

The four of us began to talk among ourselves about inviting the viewers to a musical evening. It would need to be in a social hall, or the soccer stadium, because the Paraguayans were still too scared to enter a Protestant church.

Joe and I began to fast breakfast and lunch every Wednesday. We asked for wisdom and the empowerment of the Holy Spirit, and we asked God to send a spiritual awakening to Paraguay. We continued to do this for the next four years.

Thanksgiving approached. It was time to kill Paul and Silas. Both turkeys were fat. We were going to have a real American Thanksgiving meal! And we would freeze one of the turkeys for Christmas!

Evelyn knew how to pluck chickens. She figured that a turkey would be about the same. Joe could chop off the turkeys' heads, as his grandma used to do. I could boil water and get it ready to dunk the turkeys so that the feathers would loosen to make them easier to pluck. I had seen Grandma Arnold do that.

The first turkey flopped around the yard, headless. Then the second. We dunked. Whew! Scalded feathers sure do stink!

We began to pluck feathers. The turkeys shrank. And shrank. And shrank. They were nothing but skin and bones! Ah, but the top of the breast looked pretty fat. I examined one. Wait! There was a cavity up there, by the neck. The craw. I pulled it out. Phhhuuuuttt. Air escaped. Nothing left. No breast to speak of. Skinny, skinny, tough, tough turkeys.

Betty volunteered to bake the tough thing with stuffing and to make a salad. Evelyn made pumpkin (*zapallo*) pies and eggplant casserole. She made some cornbread dressing, too, with chunks of chicken in it because we didn't know if we'd be able to eat the tough turkey. I cooked green beans, mashed potatoes, and made a fresh fruit salad. And a fallen coconut cake. When I baked the two layers for the cake, they fell. I baked two more layers. They fell, too, so I just stacked all four fallen layers. And covered them with my first "7-Minute Frosting." I made dinner rolls, too; they turned out delicious.

Everyone came to our house, because we were the only ones with an air conditioner in the living-dining room. Mission policy allowed only one window air conditioner (a necessity in the bedroom). But when Sam Balius lived in our house, he bought an additional air conditioner from personal money. We bought it from him with *our* personal money.

Our dining room table extended with four leaves and we used them all. Don, Betty, Darlene, Felicia, "baby no-name," Chris Grace, Roland, Evelyn, Howie, Carla, Joe, Christy, Timmy, and I. Our family now, in Paraguay. There were no American football games on *Canal 9* so we all went swimming that afternoon. I did make a brief trip to the bedroom, where I closed the door and cried, remembering our family in the States.

Every morning when my clock alarmed at 5:30, Tinker Belle and I would go to the kitchen and I would start breakfast—pancakes, waffles, biscuits, or bacon and eggs with hash browns. I learned to make tomato gravy (creamed tomatoes) from Evelyn and that was a treat, too, over fresh, hot biscuits.

One morning as I stood at the kitchen sink, I looked out into the back yard just as dawn broke. The horse was in the back yard, untied. I went to awaken Christy, early, to tell her she had better go and tie up the horse before Joe saw it! She staggered, sleepily, out of bed, grabbed the horse's bridle and led him back to his pen. When she returned to the kitchen, her face was ashen. Tears were streaming down her cheeks, "The corn. The horse ate Daddy's corn! *All* of it! It is *all gone!*"

Christy cried and cried and cried. Timmy and I went outside to investigate. Sure enough, every ear of corn had been eaten. Not one silk remained of one ear of corn. Big tears rolled down Timmy's cheeks and mine, too, as we stood there in the trampled stalks.

I walked to the bedroom to awaken Joe. Softly I said, "You need to get up. We have a crisis … the horse got out … and ate your corn."

Joe walked out to the garden. He stood there, pale and quiet. Tears filled his eyes.

Christy tried to imagine how terrible her punishment would be! She had failed to tie the horse properly. And she had not locked his gate securely.

All four of us sat at the breakfast table crying, the food cold on the table in front of us.

Finally, Joe said, "Christy, you know this is entirely your fault?" She nodded. "You know you deserve serious punishment?" She nodded.

Joe sighed, "There is nothing that can bring back the corn. Just as there is nothing that we humans can do to erase our sins. We all sin. We all disobey God. But somehow, God loves us so much that He sent Jesus to pay our debt—to take the punishment for our sins.

"God forgives us. And I forgive you. I will not punish you."

35

La Virgen Azul

And other stories
December 1973

Every year in Paraguay thousands of pilgrims converge on a village called *Ca'acupé*. Some people arrive on motorcycles or bicycles; others come in cars, vans, or buses. Many ride in ox-drawn carts, the wheels towering six feet in the air, dust billowing from the red dirt roads.

For eight days the village plaza becomes the gathering place where men and women in brightly embroidered clothes strum folkloric music on guitars and whisper music on hand-carved harps. Skirts whirl high as young people dance. Other "bottle dancers" balance wine bottles on their heads as the dancers dip and sway and add additional bottles, towering to six or seven bottles high.

Women erect makeshift restaurants with palm branch roofs and put pots on to boil *mandioca*, cassava. Men build fires to roast pigs and sides of beef. Vendors with wide baskets on their heads hawk *chipa*, twists of cheese-bread similar to large, soft, twisted pretzels.

Children run behind soccer balls, old men sit and drink green tea: hot *mate* or cold *tereré*. Makeshift roulette tables appear with the dealer chanting bets. To sleep, people spread ponchos under wagons and across the plaza and down side streets.

This national, religious holiday celebrating *La Virgen Azul*, The Blue Virgin, is more important to many people than Christmas or Easter or even Independence Day.

Tradition says that a carpenter walked the hills as he looked for some good trees for his trade. Suddenly, he heard *salvajes*, savages, coming toward him. Desperate, he pleaded with the Virgin to save him. He ran behind a large tree just as the *salvajes* rounded a corner of the trail. They passed within a few feet of him, never seeing him. He promised he would carve a statue from the tree to honor the Virgin who had saved him.

He carved a doll and donated it to the church.

Another legend says that some Indians were swimming in Lake *Ipacaraí* when they spotted a cylindrical case made of leather. They opened it to find a wooden statue unharmed and dry. This certainly was a miracle, so they took the statue to the church.

For as long as anyone can remember, the priest has organized an annual festival to honor the doll. "The Blue Virgin" is dressed in a blue cape adorned with golden threads and jewels.

In *Ca'acupé* after a week of partying, the celebrations culminate with a solemn parade on December 8. From the church, devotees pull a decorated "float" holding the Blue Virgin doll; then they parade through the village. All worshippers wear a light blue shirt, blouse, or blue band around their arms. And everyone carries a *limosna*, an offering of money, and an un-lit *vela*, candle.

Joining the parade, the pilgrims fall to their knees and crawl upright around the plaza and back to the church. Many tie heavy stones on their heads or pull a heavy bundle of rocks behind them. Friends scatter broken bits of glass or sharp stones along the route to increase the suffering. Other worshippers wrap themselves in large cloths and lie in the parade path so they will be stepped on.

The greater their suffering, the more pleased the Blue Virgin will be, and thus more likely to hear the *rezos*, rosary prayers. Hopefully, she will forgive the pilgrims' sins and, perhaps, even perform a miracle.

Crawling into the church, the faithful light their candles and crawl to an alcove or altar where they will leave the candle. Then they will pick up someone else's candle, which is now "consecrated by that person's suffering," and carry it to the main altar, where the Blue Virgin has been put back into her usual location. The people deposit their offering, then exit, hoping the "blessed" candle they carry with them will bring good luck, including protection from storms, lightning, sickness and other evils.

The first two weeks of December I spent standing on my head, reaching with a rag under the hood to un-stick the gears of an old, white, stick-shift, pick-up truck. It was a "field truck," which meant that every missionary could use it but no one took care of it—and the gears stuck in first-gear *repeatedly*. (Joe and Roland had driven our car to Buenos Aires to help with the *Impacto '73* crusades.)

The gas gauge of the "field truck" did not work (no replacement was available in Paraguay) so I spent considerable time walking with a gas can to the nearest service station because the old gas guzzler had run out of gas *again*.

The weather was oppressively hot both day and night. The swimming pool turned deep green because I forgot to keep chlorine in it as Joe had told me to do.

The cut on Christy's leg was not healing well.

Also, Timmy had a really bad toothache. I took him to the dentist, who deadened Timmy's jaw and began to drill out a cavity. The anesthesia was inadequate and poor Timmy squirmed and groaned in the dental chair.

For his birthday December 4, Timmy asked for a soccer ball and Match Box cars—heap guilt, heap guilt, heap guilt on my head. As we had left the States, Timmy had carried all his cars in his favorite toy, "Match Box City." But I had *insisted* he check it with the luggage. We never saw it again.

Plus, I was in the middle of an especially painful monthly period. And to top it all off, I ran out of money.

Exasperated, broke, and guilt-ridden, I sat at the kitchen table. Alone. Hot. A sense of "it is not worth it" flooded over me. I tried to "do" my best for God. Tried not to complain. Tried to be positive in front of the children. But sometimes, the heaviness of living in a foreign culture, of being separated from family, of constantly "working for God" became almost too much to endure.

Glancing up at the wall, I spotted the ugly pot-holder-marga-rine-tub-plastic-plate-horrible-wall-hanging! Slowly, I began to smile, remembering Mom's joke of including it in our shipment. She had even taped a label to it: "For when you think you'll never smile again." I smiled wider. Then I laughed until tears rolled down my cheeks.

While the men were in Argentina, Evelyn and I had to do the live telecast by ourselves. We were scared to death. Evelyn was sure she would not be able to remember a word of Spanish. She told me repeatedly that I'd have to do all the talking, but she would sing with me.

We asked our kids to be on the show to help sing the theme song, and we asked *Jorge,* a young man from Herrera, to play the bass guitar (Joe had been teaching him). Also, we asked a young man from the Church of God to play a harp solo.

The program went great! After the opening song, I greeted the people and turned to Evelyn for her to greet the tele-viewers. She began talking and did not stop! I barely got a word in edgeways.

A few weeks later, for the Christmas show, we wore our new *aho poi* embroidered shirts. And Joe asked me to tell the Christmas story. All of the MKs (missionary kids) were with us again, sitting on the floor and couch. I told the traditional Christmas story with colorful flannelgraph figures, but of course the viewers could not distinguish colors on the black and white broadcast. I gave honor to the Virgin Mary and then honor to her Son, Jesus.

Summer vacation from school is December, January, and February, and ACA planned a school camp. The kids were thrilled to attend the rustic camp. The camp organizers were two young, new teachers, and they stated that camp should be non-religious. It should be just for fun. The school director, a Southern Baptist missionary, was not happy about that. He wanted it to be like church camp. But no one else volunteered to organize the camp, so he acquiesced.

When Joe and Roland arrived home from Buenos Aires, we drove out to the camp to see the kids. One of the counselors asked us to stay for the campfire and sing for the kids. Roland had brought his accordion just in case we were asked. When the counselor presented us, he added, "And when they finish singing, Mrs. Register will tell us a story."

I wracked my brain, frantically searching for a story. I knew the counselors would totally tune me out if I told a Bible story. So I began,

When I was a little girl, my daddy told this story:

Back in the olden days, children attended school in a one-room school house. All the kids, of all ages, met together in a small building with only one teacher. When the children entered, they would hang their coats on a rack by the door and place their lunches on a bench under their coats. Everyone brought his lunch from home.

The teacher taught not only the ABCs but also the Ten Commandments, and every day he would read from the Bible. The older kids would help the younger ones with their lessons, and they would all play together outside for recess, if the weather was not too cold.

In this particular school, there was a boy who was very poor. His coat was ragged, his shoes were old and had holes in the soles. His hand-me-down shirt was frayed around the collar and was too big, so he rolled up the sleeves. And his lunch was always just a biscuit spread with grease. The kids made fun of him and no one thought to share some of their lunch of ham or boiled eggs with him.

One day at lunch time, a boy exclaimed, "Someone stole my sandwich! I know my mom packed me a sandwich and it is not here! Someone stole it!"

Immediately everyone looked at the poor kid, because everyone knew he was always hungry.

"Johnny, did you steal this boy's sandwich?" demanded the teacher.

Big tears filled Johnny's eyes.

"Johnny, we do not steal in this class and we do not lie. Tell me now—did you steal the sandwich?"

The tears spilled over and ran down Johnny's cheeks as he nodded his head.

"Teacher," he whispered, "I was awful hungry. I didn't have no supper last night and no breakfast this mornin'. There wasn't nuthin' for me to bring to eat today ... that's why ... at recess, I snuck back in the building and ... and I ate the sandwich."

"You know the rules," said the teacher. "Anyone who steals must be whipped. Six lashes with the leather strap.

"Johnny, come to the front of the classroom and take off your shirt."

Little Johnny took off his ragged coat, and slowly unbuttoned his too-big shirt. The kids could see his skinny body, his stomach shrunken, his ribs sticking out.

He bowed his head and bent his back to receive the lashes.

Tears dripped from Johnny's eyes and nose onto his scuffed shoes.

The teacher looked down at the bony ribs protruding on Johnny's back, then raised the whip ... ready to strike.

"Wait!" said a big, husky boy. "Wait, teacher. Whip me instead. I'll take his place."

The boy walked to the front of the classroom. He bared his back.

And took the whipping.

As I finished the story, the campers' eyes were filled with tears. The counselors' eyes were, too. The School Director stood and asked the children to pray with him, to receive the pardon God gives us because Jesus took our place. All the children and even the counselors repeated the prayer.

Once again, the Blounts, Jenkins, and Chris came to our house to eat. For Christmas dinner we chewed tough turkey and enjoyed more tender chicken in our "traditional" North American meal, but without cranberry sauce, a product unknown overseas.

After our pitiful Christmas trees in Chile, we knew to bring an artificial tree. It was beautiful even in the 100 degree heat. Previously, we had drawn names for gifts, so we sat around the tree with the air conditioner running full blast while the children handed out our presents.

When Carla received her gift, she unwrapped the paper to see a small box which read "*Espiral* – the best mosquito repellent available." Carla turned to little Felicia Jenkins to thank her for the mosquito repellent. Felicia said, "Carla, open the box! There's a tee shirt inside, not an *espiral!*" We laughed at this cross-cultural exchange.

We teased each other and laughed some more. "Baby no-name" finally had been named Donnie. We mimicked Evelyn screaming, "She's in *my purse!*" They teased me about my first trip to the supermarket when I said I wasn't "cookie hungry." And they teased Joe about pushing his peas back down into the dirt.

We were sharing life and building new memories. After six months in Paraguay, I was not unhappy. The house and grounds were the nicest place we had ever lived. Plenty of food was available.

But the culture was so different from Chile. The Paraguayan psyche radiated inferiority. A very small upper-class controlled the wealth. With few "industries," a middle-class could not form. So the vast majority of Paraguayans were "lower-class."

The true poverty combined with incestuous births bred a people who sensed their inferior status and dared not venture out into the "real" world, whatever that might be. Paraguayans rarely invited visitors into their homes. In fact, they did not "live inside" the small adobe rooms but outside in the cooler, dirt patios.

My heart was definitely softening toward the Paraguayan people. They were needy in so many ways. The Chilean, self-assured and patriotic, stood in sharp contrast to these barefoot peasants who barely eked out a living. Could we help? Could we educate? Could we lift even a few from the quagmire of hopelessness?

36

Anticipation
January 1974

⟶◦✥◦⟵

oe walked into the house from the back yard, his hands behind his back. "My days as a farmer have been affirmed. Here is a token of my success." He held out a large, brown marble. An egg, the very first from our chickens!

The next day Joe said to the kids, "OK, it's time to go 'gather the egg.'"

In a few days there were two or three eggs, then five or six. Would all twenty chickens lay? Every day?

We decided to use some of our delicious, fresh eggs to make homemade peach ice cream. Roland and Joe sat in the back yard, under the big leaves of the bean tree. Roland turned the handle of the ice cream churn while Joe fed ice and salt into the bucket. The kids took turns sitting on top of the freezer so it wouldn't turn over. Umm, umm, we could hardly wait!

Christy and Timmy, full of energy and giggles, were as brown as the Paraguayans and spoke Spanish without an accent. Both children were growing tall and slender; they loved summertime, the large yard, and the pool.

"Aunt Marge is coming!" I told the kids as I grabbed the mop and pail, detergent and bleach. It was almost 6:30 a.m., time to meet Evelyn and Betty to clean Marjorie Campion's house before she

arrived back from furlough. The temperature would soar to 100 degrees by mid-morning, but hopefully, we would have the cleaning almost finished by then. Marge, from Arizona, had already spent a term in Paraguay and had rented a house just a few doors up the street from the Wards'-Blounts' house.

The next day, we traveled the pitiful road to the airport where Joe and I, Christy and Timmy stood on the balcony along with the Jenkins and Blounts, waving to a short, stout, middle-aged woman as we yelled, "Welcome back to Paraguay!"

Very soon we learned that Marge was a hard worker, a bundle of fun, and that she had a "high button" and a "low button." When she was happy, she was very, very happy, and when she was sad, she was very, very sad.

All of us ate supper together and then Aunt Marge opened her suitcases to distribute gifts that Mom had mailed to her for us: for Timmy, a Big Josh (he'd lost that action figure, too, in the "Match Box City" debacle); for Christy, a Living Bible; for Joe, some seeds and some Singspiration songbooks (so he would have more songs to translate); for me, a wig and two A-line dresses. And Mom even included an outfit for baby Donnie.

Aunt Marge, Carla, Evelyn, Timmy, Christy, Margaret, Joe, Chris, and Felicia

We scheduled a missionary business meeting for the next week. With Marge arriving and the Jenkins leaving for furlough soon, we needed to talk about field responsibilities. Joe was elected field chairman; Marge, the bookstore manager; Evelyn, the ICI correspondence courses coordinator; me, the secretary; Roland, the Bible institute director; and Joe, the Bible institute administrator. Of course, there were no students yet, but as soon as school began in the fall (in March), we hoped to open the Bible school.

A woman called to invite Evelyn and me to attend a Catholic home group. She requested that we bring nine Bibles. We had no idea what to expect!

Nine women, lay leaders in several Catholic churches, met on Monday evenings at 8:30 with a priest who led a devotional study. He had a Bible, but the women did not. As Evelyn and I handed each of them a Bible, they held them reverently, in awe that they could actually have a Bible of their own.

The women asked Evelyn and me to sing "There's Something about That Name." Then the priest read from Luke 22 about Judas betraying Jesus. The priest opened the floor for discussion about whether or not Judas *had* to betray Jesus. Did he have the free will *not* to betray Him?

I mentioned that Judas' actions showed that although a person has listened to the words of Christ for many years, it doesn't necessarily mean that he has accepted Christ into his heart.

Following the discussion, the hostess served the *refrigerio,* refreshments, and the meeting broke up.

Joe and I, Roland and Evelyn wanted so urgently to teach the Paraguayans about God's love and grace for salvation. As we met daily to rehearse for the television program, we continued to discuss a "concert."

When we had gone to the airport to pick up Marge, numerous people talked to us, calling us by name, saying that our show was their favorite, the music soothing, the prayer so sincere.

One day when Joe called the VW repair shop, the person answering the phone recognized his voice and called him by name.

Joe called the long distance operator; she recognized his voice and called him by name. Everyone, it seemed, knew Joe wherever he went.

New clients who walked into the beauty shop when Evelyn and I were there called us by name.

Joe and Roland decided to go downtown to *Estadio Comuneros*, the soccer stadium, to see if we could rent it for a concert. We could! On January 25! We began to announce the date on TV, ran a newspaper ad, and told everyone we met about the coming concert.

We rehearsed 24 songs—quartets, trios, duets, solos. Jorge could play bass guitar whenever Joe played saxophone solos. Another young man could bring his drums. In our shipment we had brought a sound system with several microphones and large speakers. Joe and Roland hooked it up to test it for the big night.

We just *knew* that a large crowd would come to the stadium! We hoped to begin a church with the people who would come forward, responding to the invitation to accept salvation through Christ.

Evelyn and I had interviewed Jorge when she and I hosted the television program. His classmates saw the show, and they began to taunt Jorge at school. "Why do you want to hang out with those *Protestantes*? They're weird." The priest-teacher of the religion class at school humiliated Jorge in front of the class, saying, "They tell you to *say* you have peace. No one can find peace." Jorge's parents said, "You choose—either us and your real religion or your new friends. Don't come home if you choose them!" Jorge, only 15 years old, said, "How can I stay at home and return to a religion where I did not find God?" Thankfully, his aunt took him in.

Every day after music rehearsal, Joe went to the Bible school campus to work on the radio studio. It was just a couple of unfinished rooms on the second floor. Joe measured and framed and added a double-glass window between the control room and the recording room. He tiled the floor, made shelves and hung peg boards for all his wires. He installed a window air conditioner and ducted the cool air into the recording room. He placed acoustical tile on the ceiling and walls.

He ran cables for microphones and the reel-to-reel recorder. He learned that for about $300 per month, he could broadcast for fifteen minutes daily on three radio stations to cover the entire country. But we did not have that much money.

After our maid's attempted robbery, Joe bought a small safe and had it installed into the thick adobe wall of our office, figuring that would be better than the in-socks-in-tennis-shoes where he had been hiding money. Joe wanted to keep the combination to the safe in a "safe" place. "No one will ever find the combination," he told me, "I filed it in the filing cabinet under *Ladrón*, Thief!"

Every week, in the 100-degree heat, Evelyn and I made our grocery shopping trip—through the hectic traffic where horns blew incessantly, where there were no stop signs or traffic lights, and where the black smoke billowing from dozens of trucks choked us. We went:

1. To the meat market—early morning before too many flies descended
2. To the vegetable market—greeting each vendor
3. To *MennoTour*—the Mennonite travel agency, downtown, to exchange dollars for *Gs*
4. To the post office—while we were downtown, double-parked of course
5. To the *Total* supermarket—for those delicious cookies
6. To a *despensa* (a small corner store)—for cans of *Nido*, powdered milk. We knew of only one *despensa* that sold the Argentine product, *Nido*. We could not drink the watery milk sold in small plastic bags, so I always mixed powdered milk. We couldn't drink *it* freshly made. It had to sit in the fridge overnight to taste half-way decent.
7. To another *despensa*—the only place we knew that sold washing machine detergent.

We needed a caretaker to live on the empty Bible school grounds, especially since the radio equipment was being installed there. Joe and Roland talked to Hermano Juan (the man with the mule). He was absolutely thrilled.

Juan brought his meager belongings on the mule-pulling cart. His wife and kids walked alongside. An hour later, they had moved in.

The caretaker's house consisted of one room, adobe, with a tiled roof (no ceiling), a lean-to open-air kitchen with a wooden table and a fire-pit. In the yard was a free-standing water faucet. Out back was the outhouse with a hole in the floor.

Juan's wife stood in the packed-dirt yard, gazing at her new home. "We have our own water, our own toilet, a roof to sleep under if it rains, and a large kitchen. This is wonderful! This is just like heaven will be!"

Sam Balius flew in to visit for two weeks. He and his family had spent a term in Paraguay, in what was now our house, and had left some things stored there. Sam was a delight—funny and full of stories! Sam sorted through the barrels they had left, taking some things back to the States, but giving away most of the stuff. He stayed with us, in Timmy's room, while Timmy slept in the hallway in a sleeping bag.

Joe interviewed Sam on the television program. Sam loved the format of the show and he raved about the tremendous opportunity to reach all of Paraguay. And he helped us get ready for the concert.

Friday, January 25, the day of our much anticipated musical concert, began with rain. But our spirits were not dampened. Our songs were well-rehearsed, the words memorized. Our *aho poi* embroidered shirts were pressed and the equipment was ready to load. The men made several trips with the old, white pick-up truck to haul the sound system with the speakers and mikes and cables, a tool box, soldering iron, extension cords; chairs and decorations for the stage; saxophone, bass guitar, accordion, and drums. We had rented a piano. After it was delivered, Roland tuned it.

We took a tarp to cover things in case there was more rain. There was. But after the showers, we finished setting up and then we did a sound check.

Next, we went to a room behind the stadium to dress in our *aho poi* shirts and wait until time for the concert to begin. We were nervous, not knowing if 300 or 3000 people would come to the stadium. Oh, the wonderful church we would begin with all these new people!

At last it was time to leave the dressing-room. We rode into the stadium on a tractor-drawn flat trailer so we could wave to the crowds.

We entered the gate … the stadium was empty!

Only about 100 people sat scattered across the bleachers in the huge stadium.

But we sang our songs and smiled our smiles. We wanted to honor those who *had* come.

At the conclusion, Joe asked people to come forward to pray the sinner's prayer. Fifteen people came forward. But only four would tell us their names. They were scared.

Apparently, the spiritual ground was so hard that the seed did not penetrate. It just bounced around on top of the soil. Nevertheless, we would water the seed with our sweat and our tears.

Humbled—*humiliated* would be a better word, we knew for sure that only the Holy Spirit could soften these Paraguayan hearts.

Along with the Blounts, Jenkins, and Marge, we had planned a three-day retreat to *Tirol,* a German hotel-resort down south near Encarnación. The Jenkins said *Tirol* was a wonderful place. Sam, our visiting missionary friend, would give a daily devotional. The remainder of the time, we could just relax. We needed it. Our bodies were tired and our pride smarted.

37

Oh, no!

February 1974

Hot, tired, thirsty, and hungry, we bumped along the dirt road, with red dust flying. The sun was about to set. Where on earth was the resort? Following signs to Tirol, we had left the paved road far behind, turned onto a dirt road, and off that onto another *worse* dirt road. We rounded a curve and there it was—a collection of rustic lodges.

In the twilight, we walked over the grass and up a slight incline to our rooms. Two single beds, a night stand, and an adjoining bathroom. It was clean but spartan.

Don came by our room, "It's time for supper! Go to the dining room in the long, brick building." There was no menu to choose from, just "the meal" served to all guests. It was simple, nutritious food.

We had left home at 5:30 on that Sunday morning for the five-hour drive to Encarnación. We planned to attend church there and then drive on south to the resort hotel. We were to caravan with the Blounts and Jenkins, but the Jenkins were not ready to leave on time. They said to go ahead, they would catch up. They did. They found us broken down alongside the road.

About three hours out of Asunción, Evelyn, in the lead car, had pulled to the side of the road. Steam boiled out from under the hood; the fan belt had broken. Fortunately, we were not far from a village, so Joe went to see if there was a service station. It was closed for

Sunday. But Joe peeked through a window and could see one fan belt hanging on the wall. He talked to some neighbors and they sent a kid to get the owner of the gas station. After about a half-hour, a man walked up, opened the garage and pulled down the fan belt. But he couldn't remember how much it cost. He searched in drawers, pulled out papers, looked through a bulging filing cabinet. No price list. Joe offered him 50*Gs*. No. 100*Gs*? No, that might be too much. The price should be fair, we know you from TV. An additional half-hour later, we returned to where the Blounts were sitting beside the road.

The fan belt was too big. Joe decided he could double some of it, tape it, and wire it together. Back to the service station. Yes, they had tape, yes, they had wire.

Back to the roadside. Joe attached the belt. Now the radiator needed to be filled with water. From adobe farm houses nearby, people had gathered to watch these crazy gringos. Joe asked a kid if he could get us some water. The kid, naked except for some baggy shorts, ran to the back of his house, pulled a bucket up from a well, and filled a tin can with water. He ran his little legs off, hauling water to fill the radiator.

Two hours later, we limped into Encarnación. We would be late for the church service, but at least we could still greet the people and distribute the applications to attend the Bible institute. To our surprise, the church was empty! A neighbor said everyone had gone to the country for a wedding, even the other missionaries (the Jenkins).

By now, it was early afternoon. No restaurants were open on Sunday. We sweltered in the 100-degree heat; we were hungry and thirsty. Our purified drinking water was gone.

In the next village, we managed to find a service station with the correct fan belt. They sold Cokes. Warm. Delicious.

And then we headed on to Tirol, about forty-five minutes away.

The next morning, after our no-choice breakfast, the kids wanted to go swimming, so we walked down to the large pool. The water was as green as pea soup! The Jenkins kids jumped right in. Betty said, "It's fine. There are no chemicals in it." I could tell that! Betty explained that the pool was filled from a spring. When the water became too dirty, after several weeks, the pool would be drained and then refilled. I figured it was a couple of weeks overdue. But our kids jumped in, too, and I hoped no one would drown because we would never find the body in that thick green goop.

After lunch, the kids said we could play carpet golf. All right, at least this should be good. The hotel manager handed Joe a club and ball. Joe said there were four of us. "One ball, señor. One club. Share."

"Carpet golf" was a misnomer. The "greens" were concrete, rough and uneven. We took turns, trying to remember where our ball had been.

I was ready to go home. Three more days looked longer and longer. But the Jenkins loved Tirol. Because they had been in Paraguay for four years! We had been in Chile and the States. We had been in Paraguay only seven months. This was supposed to be a hotel resort?

I would never have guessed that three years later we would return to Tirol and I would absolutely love it!

The following Sunday, once again, we drove from Asunción to Encarnación. We had also made plans to visit a nearby Ukrainian church in *Carmen del Paraná.* Roland and Evelyn traveled with us in our car. The children stayed in Asunción with Lali, our maid.

Joe had contacted the pastor in Encarnación and he said they would provide lodging Sunday night at a small hotel owned by one of the members.

That night the little church was comfortably full, the people loved the music, and several young people wanted applications for the Bible institute. Then the pastor directed us to the hotel.

As we drove the bumpy dirt road out into the country, no lights were visible anywhere. Several kilometers later, we pulled into a small, dimly lit courtyard. A huge dog, chained, lunged at the car. He growled fiercely and gave deep, vicious barks.

A woman came to greet us and indicated to Roland and Evelyn their room, and to Joe and me, our room.

The woman restrained the dog while Joe and Roland got our suitcases out of the car. She said that as soon as we were in our rooms, she would let the dog loose to protect the courtyard.

We opened the door to our room and Joe flipped on the light switch. Roaches went flying in every direction! Hundreds of roaches! They flew across the beds, dove into the night-stand drawer, scurried under the beds, and ran up the walls and across the ceiling.

A single light bulb hung from a cord in the middle of the ceiling. The two single beds were separated by a night stand with a drawer partially opened—with a well-populated roach nest inside.

I could not sleep in this room! I would go next door and talk to Evelyn to see if she would sleep in the car with me. I would rather get eaten by mosquitoes than by roaches.

Wary of the huge dog, I scooted along the walkway to the next room. Evelyn had seen only a handful of roaches in their room. No, she would not go to the car with me because she was more scared of the dog than of the roaches.

Disheartened, I returned to the room. Joe said we had no choice and that I might as well try to get some sleep. There was no way! Joe said we could leave the light on all night; maybe that would keep the roaches out of sight.

Gingerly, I undressed and pulled back the sheets to my bed. I didn't see roach poop or live roaches on the sheets.

The next morning we walked down the walkway to the bathroom. A young boy came toward us carrying a large, hairy tarantula on his arm. "Come see him. He won't hurt you. He's my pet." Joe walked closer. I did not.

Joe and Roland promised that we would find another hotel for the following night.

Monday morning, we located the village of *Carmen del Paraná* and met the gracious Ukrainian people. They hosted us for lunch, where we stood behind our chairs and prayed for the food both before and after we ate.

The pastor directed us to the Hotel Munich in Encarnación. We checked in, rested for a few minutes, and then dressed for church. This one-story hotel was built around a courtyard. Our room was on one side, the Blounts' on the other side of the courtyard.

That night after church, Joe and I returned to our room, eager for a good night's rest. Taking off my wig, I stood near the door while Joe went straight to the bathroom.

I glanced up toward the window on the other side of the room just as a brownish black, furry creature crawled out from under the wooden shutters. It inched down the wall and onto the headboard. It slid down the headboard, slithered across my pillow, across my sheet and onto Joe's bed that we had pushed next to mine. The creature was about five inches wide. Its tail dragged behind it as it crawled sideways and forwards. Its webbed feet and legs clung to Joe's pillow as it glided across. And then the creature crept under the pillow.

"Joe? Joe! JOE!"

He couldn't come immediately. By the time he came out of the bathroom, the creature had disappeared into Joe's bed.

Joe flipped his pillow off the bed. No creature. He flipped back the sheet, no creature. He pulled the two beds apart. Nothing. He folded back his mattress. Flipped back my sheets. Folded back my mattress. Pulled the bedding off his bed. Off my bed. Nothing.

He stretched, pulled, heaved, and moved things so much that he ripped his underwear!

No creature. But there was no way I was sleeping in that room! Joe shook out his pillow once again, folded his arm around it and said, "Let's go to Roland and Evelyn's room. There are three beds in their room."

I changed into my gown. I had forgotten to bring a robe, but it was dark outside. We would come back to the room early in the morning.

We knocked on Roland and Evelyn's door. "Yoo hoo," Joe sang. "We've come to spend the night with you!"

As we told them the story, I said that I didn't have to worry about Roland, being blind, seeing me in my nightie. We laughed and talked for a long time.

The single bed was hard; it sank in the middle and was very narrow. Finally, I put my head at the other end, hugging Joe's feet. We slept fitfully.

Early the next morning, we opened the door to walk back to our room. The patio was full of people! It was an open-air restaurant! Waiters with white towels folded across their arms filled coffee cups, silverware clinked on dishes.

I hugged Joe's pillow, trying to cover myself as best I could. Joe's hair was tousled, we were barefoot. My hair was plastered to my head from wearing a wig the day before. We weaved our way around the tables, through the patio to our room.

I had never been so embarrassed in my life! I prayed that we looked so horrible that no one would recognize us from TV.

What on earth must these people think? What were these gringos doing in someone else's room? They had obviously spent the night there!

Back in Asunción, we found a notice in our mail box. We had received two packages from the States. We must go to the customs office to retrieve the packages.

We were able to get one package with only a few days' delay and 1000*Gs*. The small package was addressed to Christy from a girls' group. Winter pajamas. Well, this was February. But the temperature was consistently 100 degrees.

For the other package we would have to hire a customs agent. Why? "Because the package is larger, more expensive," the customs official told us. So Joe hired a customs agent. We did a mountain of paperwork. We paid the agent and the customs tax.

Several times Joe asked, "What does the box contain?" Each time the agent replied evasively, "Ah, bonbons."

Finally, a notice appeared in our mail box. We could retrieve the package at the customs office, in another building, at our earliest convenience.

We were so excited!

Joe came home with a large, cardboard box. It was from another girls' group. It was addressed to our family.

Slowly, the kids opened the cardboard flaps and peered in. They saw orange construction paper figures filling about one-fourth of the box. They reached in, pulled out small, orange construction paper pumpkins. On the back had been taped a stick of chewing gum and a small sucker. Several dozen orange construction paper pumpkins lay in the bottom of the large box.

Most of the suckers and gum had come off in the Paraguayan heat. They were clumped in the bottom of the box, a melted mess.

Halloween treats, in February, after days of paperwork, and expensive customs fees. We laughed and laughed and laughed.

*   *   *

No Bake Oatmeal Cookies
Timmy's favorite cookie to make by himself

INGREDIENTS
One stick butter
1/2 cup evaporated milk
1 cup sugar
4 tablespoons cocoa
1/2 teaspoon salt
1 teaspoon vanilla
3 cups quick oats

DIRECTIONS

1. Combine butter, milk, sugar, cocoa and salt in medium sauce pan. Bring to a boil and continue boiling for 5 minutes.
2. Remove from heat. Stir in the vanilla and oats.
3. Drop by teaspoonfuls onto a greased cookie sheet. Let cool. Wolf down.

(You can add 1/2 cup peanut butter, but we did not have peanut butter in Paraguay.)

38

Students
March 1974

I *did not want to teach* Spanish Grammar. I could teach *New Life in Christ*, or *Survey of the Old Testament,* fine. But Spanish grammar to Latinos?

Reluctantly, I walked to the front of the classroom and greeted the students. Fifteen sets of dark brown eyes looked back at me. The students looked almost as scared as I felt!

Twenty-six students had enrolled in the Bible institute: fifteen live-in students and eleven more for the night classes. The school had the auspicious title *Instituto Teológico Asambleas de Dios,* ITAD (Theological Institute of the Assemblies of God).

I had no idea of the students' level of vocabulary, punctuation, spelling, or verb and subject agreement. So I decided to begin with essays.

Since not one student could afford to buy school supplies, I handed out paper and pencils as I explained that I was interested to know why they chose to attend ITAD. "Please write on your paper, 'Why I Came to the Bible Institute.'"

Very studiously, the students picked up their pencils, leaned over their papers, and began to write. Wow! I was pleased and surprised. They were not at all shy about beginning the essay.

After a few minutes, I walked around the room to peek over some shoulders.

I looked down at the first paper: "*Porqué vine al Instituto Bíblico. Porqué vine al Instituto Bíblico. Porqué vine al Instituto Bíblico.*" The student was just copying the title on every line! "Why I Came to the Bible Institute."

I looked over some more shoulders. All the students were writing repeatedly, "Why I Came to the Bible Institute."

I held up a student's paper, turned it over and explained to the class, "I'm sorry, I didn't explain myself well. On this side of the paper, tell me why you wanted to come to the Bible Institute."

"*Sí, Hermana, sí, sí,*" they nodded and began to write.

Relieved, I walked slowly around the room.

They were doing it again—writing "Why you wanted to come to the Bible Institute" over and over and over!

All except one guy, Fernando, the most unlikely student of all. Fernando was as skinny as a rail, his back was twisted, his eyes were crossed. Now in his late twenties, he lived on the street. He slept in doorways and abandoned buildings or in someone's home if he was invited. He was an orphan who, as a child, had bounced from one foster home to another. He owned only the clothes on his back and a shoeshine kit consisting of one dirty rag and a half-empty tin of brown polish.

When he turned in his application to attend ITAD, we debated whether to include him. We were afraid he was looking only for a bed and food. However, Fernando said, "I realize I have no money for my tuition, but I can shine shoes. I will go out on the streets every afternoon. And every day I will bring back the money I earn and give it to Hermano Rolando. I think God will give me enough customers to pay my tuition."

Faithfully, every afternoon, Fernando would walk the streets to look for shoes to shine and then turn in small amounts of money, sometimes as little as 10*Gs* (about 7 cents).

Now I was amazed to look over his shoulder and read, "I came to the Bible Institute because I want to know God better day by day until I arrive at having the mind of Christ."

"Fernando," I asked, "would you please explain to the class in *Guaraní* what I want them to do?"

354

The essays in the grammar class were replete with errors of spelling and grammar. Sentence construction was poor.

We knew the students were not "college material." Most of them had barely finished sixth grade, the mandatory schooling. They had not owned Bibles and did not know Bible doctrine.

Our organization has a wonderful resource for standardizing all the Bible institutes in Latin America, the loose-leaf notebook, *El Plan Básico (The Basic Plan)*. It was compiled by missionaries Verne Warner and Monroe Grams, along with the members of the Christian Education Committee for Latin America. As Joe and I studied the procedures, the course titles, and the textbooks available, we realized that our first task was to bring our students up to par. They were not ready for these college courses. We would have to start with the basics—Luisa J. Walker's *Curso Bíblico Elemental*, the Elementary Bible Courses that we had used in the tent in Chile.

Because the Paraguayan style of learning was by rote, the students had not been taught to think for themselves, to reason. Our students were diffident and tentative, with poor self-confidence. They did not think they were capable or worthy of learning. Yes, they were ignorant. But we believed they could learn. We just had to convince *them* of that!

Joe was thrilled as, little by little by little, the students began to open up and began to discuss issues in the *Bible Doctrine* class he taught.

Marge and I each taught two classes four days a week. Evelyn taught one class. Joe and Roland taught the night classes, conducted chapel every morning at 7:30, and led chapel on Friday nights.

After the first week of classes, we figured the students would hurry home for the weekend, but they didn't! Only one boy went home and only for a couple of hours. He told us, "We're all happier here at school. Our families ridicule us."

We had set tuition at 500*Gs*, only $3.75 a month. It was a pitiful amount, but the students did not have even that much.

We worried about how we missionaries could afford to provide meals. Food for fifteen students would cost us about $500 per month!

Several years earlier, I had written the story of José, the Chilean carpenter in jail for murder. Our mission's magazine published the story with the title "Tears in Temuco." In New Smyrna Beach, Florida, a woman read the story just before Roland and Evelyn, en route to the mission field, had visited her church. She began to donate to them monthly. Now, she wrote a letter, "I want to donate $500 to a worthy project." Roland wrote back, explaining our need at ITAD.

As we calculated the time-frame, we realized that she wrote her letter the very day we had decided, definitively, to open the Bible institute, even though we did not have funds to support it. In response to Roland's reply, the lady sent $1000!

The other class I taught was entitled *Holy Spirit.* As we read through Jesus' promise and then Acts chapter 2, the students hung onto every word. I told them the story of Mom and Dad receiving the baptism in the Holy Spirit. The students' eyes filled with tears. When the bell rang for a break between classes, two students remained at their desks, their heads bowed to the desktop.

Justo, the musician from Republicano, motioned to me from just outside the door. "The Lord is breaking my heart," he said. "I want to help people in my church and also here at school."

"Why don't you start with those two?" I indicated the two boys still in the classroom.

As Justo put his hand on Isidro's shoulder and began to pray, Isidro sobbed, feeling God's presence for the first time. Isidro was a mischievous kid. We almost didn't allow him to attend. Joe and Roland had given him a stern warning that if he misbehaved, he would be expelled.

The other boy, Gustavo, was just as broken before God. Of course, we did not know, then, that one day shy Gustavo, tall and lanky, would become a faithful, steady pastor. One by one, the other students drifted quietly back into the classroom and began praying.

The following day, we concentrated on the last part of Acts chapter 2, where it is recorded that 3000 people came to faith in Christ. I asked, "Could 3000 people come to Christ in Paraguay?"

The students shook their heads, no. They had never considered the possibility. They had never seen a Protestant church with more than fifty people.

I pressed the point, "Could 2000 come to Christ? 1000? 500?"

Fernando raised his hand, "Maybe fifty could come to Christ here, and fifty there and fifty more in another village."

The Bible school campus contained the shell of a large church building where Joe was having workmen install a terrazzo floor, even while our class was in session.

I waved my hand toward the empty building and asked, "Could fifty people come to our chapel — right here?" They nodded, yes.

"Could 100?" They looked at each other doubtfully.

"300?"

They looked at me in amazement.

March was busy. April would be worse because we were planning a month-long nightly campaign in *la Plaza Italia*. Hopefully, there would be more new converts who would become students the following semester.

Our ITAD students

39

Gladys, Pablo and Tani

La Plaza Italia, Asunción, Paraguay
April–May 1974

Three extraordinary people in their twenties were at la Plaza Italia: Gladys, Pablo, and Tani.

Gladys electrified the air around her. She radiated personality, charming everyone she encountered. Her sister, Edith, sat beside her on the front row of chairs that first evening of our crusade in la Plaza Italia. Gladys was elegantly dressed, her jewelry shimmered, her shoes and her hair were the latest styles.

The Plaza, located in an upper-class neighborhood, was surrounded by cobblestone streets, not dirt streets. The open square, a city block in size, sported sidewalks, streetlights, trees, and grass.

We rented 200 folding chairs and arranged them in rows with a wide center aisle. Joe built a rectangular platform with storage underneath. Every night we stored the chairs under the platform and secured them with padlocks. From home we brought, every night, the P.A. system, light bulbs, and musical instruments. We printed song sheets to distribute to the attendees.

Though we announced the meetings on the television program, we wondered if any upper-class people would dare to attend a Protestant gathering.

Within a few nights, there were 300 people! The seats were full and people stood around the perimeter.

Demetrio Montero (who had come to Temuco while we were there and who became Joe's mentor on evangelistic crusades) was our speaker. Demetrio's deep voice resonated through the park. People were mesmerized by his eloquence and authority. Gladys was one of them.

When we greeted her, Gladys looked us in the eye and called us by name. She held her head high, chin up. She was totally different from any other Paraguayan we had met.

We invited Gladys and Edith to lunch at our house, where we learned that Gladys worked as a musician, arranging orchestrations for radio and TV commercials. She said she was also a professional singer.

When we took Gladys to tour our little radio studio, Joe asked her to sing something for us. She nodded, closed her eyes and began to sing softly, swaying gently from side to side. Enchanting music filled the air. Husky blues with a touch of folk. My mouth dropped open! Gladys was *good!*

She did not know any hymns, but we had just translated the song "Something Beautiful" by Bill and Gloria Gaither. I sat playing the piano as Gladys read the music over my shoulder and began to sing the Spanish words,

Vida hermosa,	Something beautiful
Vida mejor,	Something good
Todas mis dudas,	All my confusion
Él entendió.	He understood.
Entregué a Él el mal,	All I had to offer Him
Y Él me perdonó,	Was brokenness and strife.
Y ahora,	But He made
Vida hermosa,	Something beautiful
Él me da.	Of my life.

I had never heard anyone sing more beautifully. Tears filled my eyes. Gladys was *why* we had come to Paraguay!

Gladys sang on the television program that Saturday night. She oozed confidence, she was a professional. She did *great*.

Gladys' mother saw the show and stormed into Gladys' apartment early the next morning. "How dare you appear on a Protestant show!"

"Edith and I accepted Christ," Gladys tried to explain.

"No, you most certainly did not!" screamed her mother. "I would rather you were a prostitute than a Protestant!"

For about three months, Gladys sang at church and on TV. Then, one day, she came to our house, crying. She really needed some money. She owned a car, a Fiat, practically new. She could sell it. Did we know of a missionary who needed a car at a really good price? We did. Mr. Joule, a teacher at the children's school.

Gladys sold him the car. When he went to transfer the paperwork, he discovered that the car was contraband, smuggled across the border from Argentina ... the papers were false.

We called Gladys. She didn't answer. We went to her house. She wouldn't come to the door. We continued to try to contact her, and eventually, she paid back the money to Mr. Joule.

We never saw her again.

Pablo sat on his motorcycle in the shadows at the back of the Plaza Italia. Coming home from playing soccer, he heard the music and paused to listen for a few minutes. When Demetrio began to speak, Pablo was mesmerized. Such a command of words! Such beautiful Spanish! Such a rich vocabulary! "Oh, man," he thought, "I would give anything to be like that one day!"

For three weeks Pablo came every night, sitting on his motorcycle, staying in the shadows. He perused the crowd—one, two, three ex-girlfriends sat there. He had paid for abortions for all three girls. He would remain in the shadows.

But on the twenty-first night, Pablo pulled the motorcycle up near the last row of chairs. He climbed off and sat down in the last chair in the last row. When Demetrio finished his sermon and asked people to come forward to accept Christ, Pablo could not stop himself. He stood quickly and walked forward.

During the following week, Pablo sat in the chairs, inching forward row-by-row each night.

For the fifth week, Joe announced that we would be moving inside a building and would continue with Bible teaching. Everyone who attended would receive a Bible and study book.

We met at the plaza and "paraded," singing all the way to the church on *Catorce de Julio* Street, a block away. Of our 300 attendees, we wondered how many would dare to follow us. Pablo and thirty-nine others ventured inside the church building.

They were forty of the happiest people I had ever met! Though they were surprised that the walls were bare with no paintings or statues, the new converts devoured the nightly classes. When Joe talked about being baptized by going down into the water, they burst out laughing! They teased Joe by asking him if they could swim some, too, while they were in the water. The only baptisms they had ever seen were "infant sprinklings" with holy water.

When Joe handed out applications for the Bible institute, Pablo took an application. He knew he could only attend the night classes because he needed to work. His widowed mother, an invalid, depended on his income as a refrigeration technician.

Evening by evening as Pablo studied the booklets *And Now what?* and *The Great Questions of Life*, his desire intensified to attend ITAD full-time. So, he decided to pray for his mother to be healed. If she could get a job, he would be free to attend the Bible institute full-time.

He prayed. She was healed! She found a job and Pablo turned in his application.

It was only when he handed us his application that we learned his name. He was so shy and unobtrusive that he had blended into the crowd.

It would be three more years before we would see Pablo Villalba stand on a platform in this same plaza and preach with the authority and eloquence that Demetrio portrayed. Pablo would become the first full-time Paraguayan evangelist. Also, he would marry one of our best and sweetest students, Betty!

Tani (Estanislau Cándia), the new pastor of the church on *Catorce de Julio* Street, was practically on his honeymoon, having recently married a girl from the Russian-Ukrainian colonies down south. Because Nadia was blonde, Christy and Timmy were certain she was a North American. Speaking English, they ran up to her. She smiled. She did not understand one word.

Tani was one of the earlier eight graduates from ITAD, back before it had closed. The church averaged only about twenty people because the "shepherding movement" had decimated the congregation, and even the former pastor had fled the country.

Every night in the plaza, Tani helped set up the chairs, helped with announcements, and greeted the people. Then, when the campaign ended, Tani and Joe taught the night classes at the church.

Now, with forty new converts from la Plaza Italia, Tani's congregation tripled! He was so young that we really worried whether he would be an adequate pastor. Though overwhelmed at times, Tani grew, little by little, into his responsibilities.

How could we know, then, that in several years Tani would become the National Superintendent of the Paraguayan Assemblies of God. A position he still holds as I write these words, thirty-three years later!

During the month at Plaza Italia, Joe and Roland alternated teaching the week-night classes at the Bible institute and providing the music at the crusade. On Saturday evenings, we would hurry from the Plaza to the television studio.

Night after night Joe unloaded the equipment, set up the chairs, then, when the meeting ended, stored everything away again. One night, while pulling stuff out of the back of our car, Joe hesitated, looked up into the night sky and prayed, "God, *why* do we have to go to all this trouble?"

He sensed that God said to him, in reply, "Joe, your job is to get people's attention. Then I can speak to them. You help them pause ... I will speak to their hearts ... each person will choose his response."

40

Changes and Visitors
April–July 1974

*J*uly 4 *dawned crisp and cold.* Christy and Timmy shivered in their heavy jackets as the Asunción Christian Academy (ACA) school choir prepared to sing from the steps of the American Embassy.

Marines stood at attention around the flagpole and slowly began to raise the American flag. Tears filled my eyes. We felt we were "in America" on this sparse grass on the embassy grounds.

I adjusted the accordion straps, and when a designated Marine nodded to me, I began to play the first song.

After the ceremony, the ACA students followed a Marine for a guided tour of the embassy. Timmy could hardly contain his joy. Christy, who had just turned twelve, could hardly keep her eyes off the handsome Marine.

About 100 of us North Americans gathered at the refreshment table to *ooh* and *aah* over the doughnuts flown in from the States especially for the Fourth of July. So what if the doughnuts were so stale I could scarcely bite into one? It was authentic American food. And the hot, strong espresso coffee helped to wash down the stale doughnut.

Never before had I cried at the raising of the flag or felt such patriotism. I was happy to be able to participate in this most solemn

U.S. holiday. But even among the other expatriates, I felt alone ... vulnerable ... sad.

Joe and I had not seen any other family members in over a year, and our friends Roland and Evelyn had left Paraguay on July 1 for a year of furlough.

But, I shook myself, enough of this sadness. I needed to hurry home and get ready to welcome two college interns. Rachel Placeres and Erica Frigoli were coming for eight weeks.

Rachel, Cuban-born, lived in Texas where her dad, a pastor, had fled from Castro. Rachel, fluent in Spanish, enjoyed grading and answering the International Correspondence Institute (ICI) courses that we mailed to each person who wrote in to the television program. One letter especially intrigued her—Lucía's.

At the bottom of Lesson 4, Lucía wrote, "Is it possible to meet one of you in person? I have many questions since I prayed asking Jesus into my life."

Rachel rode the bus for over an hour to the barrio where Lucía lived. After waiting another hour for Lucía to "show," Rachel rode the bus back home. A couple of days later a letter arrived, "You came! My friend saw you! I didn't go to the bus stop to meet you because I didn't believe anyone would actually come to see *me*. Please return next Saturday."

When Rachel returned, Lucía, seventeen years old, cried with joy to see her. They sat in Lucía's aunt's patio while Lucía asked one question right after another.

Then, quietly, Lucía asked, *"Raquel, ¿puedo tocar tu Biblia?"* "Rachel, could I touch your Bible?"

Reverently, Lucía touched the Bible with her fingertips, then she ran her hand across the surface and finally she cradled the book in her arms as tears rolled down her cheeks.

"I have never touched a Bible before. I've seen one—the big one on the table at the Catholic Church. But the priest says we must never touch it and that we shouldn't want to read it because it is too difficult to understand." She continued softly, "Is there any way I could keep your Bible overnight?"

The next evening, Rachel met Lucía at our church in Republicano. In addition to Sundays, there were services on Tuesdays, Wednesdays, and Thursdays, and youth meetings on Saturdays. Lucía could not believe her good luck. She could attend church almost every night!

A few weeks later, the youth leader announced, "There is a young woman present who has accepted Christ as Savior. Would she stand and give her testimony?"

Lucía looked around to see who would stand, never dreaming she was the person. Finally, she stood and, with knees trembling, told her story. She added, "My dream is to become the person who grades the ICI courses and answers the letters from the television audience."

And, of course, the following year, she did!

Howard and Jerry Nutt came from Bolivia to speak at our annual, national church convention. (We had met Howard and Jerry on the road to language school in Mexico.) Tall and skinny, Howard had a Texas drawl even in Spanish. He spoke slowly and thoughtfully and loved to teach on the Holy Spirit. Joe figured he would be great for Council, and sure enough, many people received the baptism in the Holy Spirit through his ministry.

An average of two hundred people a night attended the Council meetings as a result of being converted in the campaigns in *Victoria* and *Plaza Italia*. The year before, according to Roland, attendance had averaged about twenty-five people.

A few weeks later, at Howard and Jerry's invitation, Marge Campion and I visited Bolivia as speakers for the joint women's and girls' retreats. When we stepped onto the cobblestone streets of Santa Cruz, Bolivia, we felt right at home. We even heard people speaking *Guaraní*. Marge and I climbed up into the Nutt's Land Rover and held on for dear life as Howard zoomed through traffic. We bounced over potholes so deep that our heads hit the roof of the Land Rover (no seatbelts in those days).

At the retreat center, hundreds of girls and women walked quietly across the grass to the auditorium. They looked like little dolls floating along the ground on billowing multi-colored skirts. A prim, black bowler hat perched on each head, and from beneath it, a single black braid flowed down each woman's back and swished gently from side to side. The faces were stoic, but black eyes danced with sparkles of excitement.

As the service began, the girls and women stood and sang and clapped in happy rhythm. When they all sat down, their clothing fluffed around them and a terrible odor wafted through the auditorium. I thought I would throw up!

Jerry whispered, "These Bolivians live in an extremely cold climate at a high altitude where to bathe would crack the skin."

Thankfully, I always carried a little Avon "pot of perfume" in my purse. I cupped the "pot" in a handkerchief in my hand and tried to hold it nonchalantly under my nose. It was the only way I could keep from gagging.

After the air settled, it was my turn to speak. I loved speaking to the girls. They listened attentively and followed my every movement with their big, black eyes.

Later that week, Howard and Jerry took Marge and me out into the country where only a Land Rover could travel. There was no road, no lane, not even ruts from carts. We bumped across fields for about an hour until we came upon a village nestled in a valley. An adobe church sat surrounded by adobe houses with thatched roofs. It was an Assemblies of God village!

We walked up to the little house of the pastor, whose wife had given birth to twins there the day before. Without hesitation, Jerry picked up the babies and cuddled them, one in each arm. Jerry's Spanish was not good. She had cried many tears over her ineptitude with the language. But she spoke a more meaningful language of love, and the people loved her in return.

As soon as I returned from Bolivia, Joe left for Chile to speak at the third anniversary of the church in Viña. The congregation still met in the tent, and Joe said all the "old ladies" cried for joy to see him, especially Isolina, who had been so miraculously healed.

How I wished I could have gone, too! I missed the friendships I had enjoyed in Chile. I certainly was busy in Paraguay. I "gave of myself" every day. But after a year of living in Paraguay, I did not have one Paraguayan friend.

41

Erica's Amazing Grace
July 1974

We received a letter from Erica Frigoli just before she arrived to intern for eight weeks. As an MK (missionary kid), Erica had contracted liver disease from amoebas, probably from eating "off the street" in Bolivia. Erica's liver was so badly damaged that her body could not tolerate even a drop of grease or oil. She could eat only fruits and vegetables. Anything cooked must be boiled with no seasoning.

I was angry. Joe listened to me rant and rave about having to cook separate foods. I'd had visitors for weeks and weeks. I would have to cook for the other college intern, Rachel, and I certainly didn't want to have to worry about catering to special-food-needs at every meal! Unseasoned, boiled food, no less, that no one else would eat!

Joe gave me one of his famous lectures, "Margaret, what if she were your daughter? She can't help her illness. She says she will prepare her own food. Lighten up. Give her a chance."

I was ashamed. I was still apprehensive, but I would give her a chance.

A slender, pretty girl about 5'2" tall with long, black, naturally curly hair stepped off the airplane stairs onto the tarmac. She carried a guitar case and wore a tentative smile.

Her frailty, combined with her inner strength, melted my heart. I opened my arms and so did Joe and Christy and Timmy.

Erica had been born in Bolivia to missionary parents who were Italian. She grew up bilingual in a warm, open Italian family. One night as her parents came home from church, a truck was stopped in the middle of the road, with no lights on. In the terrible wreck, Erica's mother was killed. Devastated, Erica helped to care for her brothers.

Erica's dad, Bruno, had been a bodyguard to Mussolini in the old country, but Bruno was at a loss as to how to care for three small children. Even after Bruno married an American missionary woman, life was still tough for Erica. She began to learn English, and when her dad became an American citizen, so did Erica. But then she possessed three passports: Italian, Bolivian, and North American. When she turned twenty-one, she would have to "choose a nationality."

"OK, Erica and Rachel, I've just been elected Missionette President for Paraguay. Let's plan a girls' retreat," I said.

They planned the list of activities, printed the programs, made posters, and contacted all the churches. They wrote skits and starred in them, *"Paco and Paquita."* Since school was dismissed for winter break, we held the girls' retreat at the Bible institute.

"OK, Erica and Rachel, I've just been elected Youth President for Paraguay. Let's plan a youth retreat," Joe said. We held the youth retreat at a rustic campground out in the country.

Never once did Erica complain about her food or physical condition. She wore loose sweaters and blouses with big skirts or long pants to disguise how thin she actually was. She wore platform shoes and a long, stylish jacket. She walked briskly, her head held high, as she looked straight ahead.

Erica played her guitar and sang on the television program. She taught preliminary classes to the new Bible school students who had registered for the following semester. Soon, Christy was walking and talking just like Erica and was begging for guitar lessons.

Erica was soft-spoken, eloquent in Spanish (not quite as fluent in English, since it was her third language).

One day Erica came back from the Bible institute by walking rather than riding the bus. When we asked her why, she said, "I like to walk. I guess I'm just a streetwalker." We burst out laughing.

To my surprise, food was never an issue. Erica took her place in the kitchen, alongside me, and prepared her own foods. She taught me not to overcook pasta and she showed us how to twirl spaghetti on our plates with a fork and spoon.

She loved apples and told us about a college student who wanted to date her—he sent her apples every day.

Another day, Erica confided, "I'm engaged to a guy at Southwestern Bible College. But being here this summer renews my doubts about marrying him. I just can't see him fitting into missionary work. And I love doing all this! I think I want to be a missionary."

By the time summer was over, Erica had promised us she would return the next year. She did. And the year after that, too.

When Erica returned for a longer stay, she taught regular classes at the Bible institute, taught at ACA, helped with more girls' and youth retreats and camps, and sang on the television program. She never complained or turned down a "job."

Someone else noticed Erica, too, and admired her quiet beauty and inner strength: Chris Grace. Chris was the Australian, former hippy, world traveler, accountant who had been passing through Paraguay and had intended to stay for "a few weeks." The weeks had turned into months and then into years.

When we opened the Bible institute, Chris enrolled. Even though the classes were simple and far beneath his level of intelligence, Chris enjoyed learning the Spanish as well as relishing in the theology of his new faith in Christ.

"Caballeros, hoy el tema es escupir," Chris began. (Gentlemen, today our topic is spitting.) "More precisely," Chris continued, "spitting on the floor of the dorm."

The fifteen guys looked at Chris with amazement. Why was he fussing about spitting? Every man needed to spit. Even in the middle of the night.

Fernando shook his head, muttering, "First he handed me those two big cloths, 'sheets' he called them, and showed me how to put them on the bed. Then, he gave us each a toothbrush. And a towel and a bar of *jabón de coco,* coconut soap. We're clean, we make our beds, surely we can spit wherever we want!"

Chris sat with his guys in the one room adobe dorm. Sixteen beds lined the walls where Chris had chosen to live with the men.

"*Hermanos,* Brothers, please know that gentlemen do not spit beside their beds. If they need to spit, they go outside, *even* in the middle of the night. And outside, they do not spit near the door. They walk around the building. Neither, as I've told you before, do gentlemen urinate near the door, *even* in the middle of the night. They go to the toilet to urinate, *even* in the middle of the night."

The men groaned and fussed, but to a man, they promised to obey. They loved Chris. They had never seen anyone like him, this counselor, prayer-partner who was patient and kind, respectful to them, helpful in every way.

When Chris had accepted the responsibility of Dean of Men, he envisioned helping the young men with their homework, making sure they obeyed curfew, clapping a hand on their shoulders to encourage them in their studies. He had no idea that he would become a father-figure to these students, most of whom had no other male role model.

Sometimes as Joe and I looked at Chris with his curly hair, scraggly beard, and sandaled feet, and as we observed his humble concern for these young men ... sometimes ... Joe and I wondered if we were "entertaining an angel unaware."

By the time Erica arrived, Chris had become the Dean of Men. Joe and I could see the "sparks" between Chris and Erica and we could not think of two more wonderful people to form a new family.

Chris and Erica

"Hey, Chris, want to come over for supper tonight?" Joe would ask.

"Sure, mate," was Chris' ready answer in his Australian accent.

He helped Christy with her math homework and when he would say the name of the school, ACA, it sounded like "ICI." This was confusing because that was what we called the correspondence courses we mailed to TV viewers.

Chris transformed a cookie sheet into a wobble board and taught Timmy to sing, "Tie me kangaroo down, mate."

One evening when I asked Chris to help by placing the napkins on the table, he replied, "Actually, I won't place nappies—'diapers'— on the table, but I'll be happy to put on the 'serviettes.'"

That first year, Chris and Erica never touched each other. They just talked. Joe and I, Christy, Timmy, and Rachel would think of excuses to leave the dining room so that the two of them could be together. Erica made no commitment to Chris and he did not press her for anything. She needed to finish her years of college—and break up with her boyfriend.

Of course, Joe teased Chris unmercifully and Christy wrote some new verses to "Amazing Grace" which she sang, loudly, around the house. Timmy wrote a love letter, signed Erica's name, and slipped it in Chris' backpack.

The following year, July, 1975, when Erica returned, our house was the place where Chris and Erica "courted." He did not want to be improper in any way, and Paraguayan standards rarely included "dating." Besides, Chris wanted to graduate from the Bible institute and apply to the Australian Assemblies of God Missions Board for missionary appointment.

Soon after Erica returned to Paraguay in 1976, Chris stated that they were officially engaged to be married and would be married shortly! When Erica told me they would be going home to her parents in Bolivia for the wedding, I wanted to cry. But I understood Erica's need to do that.

When Mr. and Mrs. Grace, Chris' parents, decided to fly to Paraguay from Australia for the graduation ceremony and to meet Chris' new bride, they called the travel agency to book their flight. The agent said, "Where? Paraguay? No, you don't want to go there. How about Brazil? Or Argentina? Or Chile? Nobody goes to *Paraguay*."

Postscript:

As Aussie missionaries for fifteen years, Chris and Erica Grace taught in Bible schools in Bolivia and Chile and worked in tent evangelism.

Chris and Erica's prayer card

In 1995, Chris and Erica moved to Australia, where Chris continued to be part of the Foreign Missions Leadership Team. They have five children, three born in Latin America, and two born in Australia.

From 2005 to the present, Chris and Erica pastor a church in Melbourne, Australia.

42

New Friends—and Old
August–December 1974

───◆───

he *tree branch rustled* as Timmy shook it over our heads while Christy said, in Spanish, "Look at that man up in the tree!"

The organ music, dramatic and sustained, rippled beneath my fingers.

"I am just trying to see Jesus better," Don Gould said in Spanish, standing in the corner and projecting his voice.

Joe nodded from the control room, flipped open his microphone and announced, "Good evening, friends. Welcome to another radio broadcast of *Las Buenas Nuevas* (The Good News)."

Lorene Gould looked over the script once more. I was amazed that she had such talent to write these dramas. She and Don, with their two boys, Scott, eleven, and Randy, nine, were a new addition to our missionary team.

We invented our own sound effects and laughed as we rehearsed in Joe's little radio studio.

Since our television contract had expired and Roland and Evelyn were in the States on furlough, Joe produced a daily radio broadcast. He taped the shows and once a week added the "dramas." The response was good. We received a number of write-in letters, but nothing to compare to the telecast.

The children ran through the house as I sat at my desk trying to plan my stories for the Missionary Retreat. Lorene and I were in charge of the children's activities for the five-nation retreat.

"What would be great would be a song," I thought, "just for the MKs (Missionary Kids)."

Christy and Timmy ran through the room again, singing to the top of their lungs a song they were learning at school, "You're a grand old flag, You're a high flying flag...."

The melody stuck in my head, la la la-la-la ... La la la-la la-la ... I began to write:

> As you look at me,
> You may wonder what you see.
> I could be tall, thin or short, dark or fair.
> I could have long hair
> Or freckles there,
> But I'm something extra special,
> Don't you see?
> For my heart beats true to the Red, White and Blue,
> And I love the Lord Jesus, too.
> Now, you old-timers, don't forget –
> I'm an MK, a Missionary Kid – Yeahhh!

We could add motions to it. The kids could point to their noses for the freckles, put their thumbs under their arms for "extra special," place their hands over their hearts at the patriotic phrase, bend over for the old-timers and sing in a croaky voice.

The MKs loved it! They all went back to their countries singing it, and Loren Triplett, our new boss, asked for the words to pass along to other countries.

The Retreat that December was held in Bahía Blanca, 'way down in southern Argentina. Actually, it was about the same latitude as Temuco, but east, on the Atlantic Ocean. We flew to Buenos Aires and rode by bus with other missionaries for eleven hours to reach the campsite.

Also attending was a missionary from Uruguay, Reginald Stone, who had previously been a pastor in West Virginia. Reg said,

"Margaret, please tell your dad that I am using his notes on the Holy Spirit. Rev. Arnold taught at our camp meeting back home, and I've translated his teaching into Spanish."

The retreat speaker was Robert Spence, who had just been elected president of Evangel College.

Along with several other MKs, Christy was baptized in the cold ocean waters. At twelve-and-a-half, Christy was enchanted with the teens. And Warren VanDolsen seemed to notice Christy especially … giving her her first kiss … and writing to her later….

Timmy, too, (he had just turned ten) was smitten in love, by Cathy Campbell. Back in Paraguay when he received a letter from her, he said, "Mom, Cathy really is mature to be eight years old."

"Don't tell me what to do, I'm not your mother!" barked little Natalie Ward, three years old, her hands on her hips, her blond curls shaking as she defied all the other MKs. She was the youngest of the bunch in Paraguay now. We died laughing at her wording, and it soon became a catch phrase, "Don't tell me what to do, I'm not your mother!"

Everett and Carolyn Ward, with Brad, age nine, and Natalie, age three, had returned to Paraguay after their furlough. While Carolyn settled into their house, Everett and Joe worked out the Bible institute teaching schedule and planned campaigns in *Calvario* and in *Barrio Jara.* Everett would be "in charge" of the campaigns, Joe would help.

We had acquired a tent, and the Paraguayans loved to attend the services. One man in a wheel chair would arrive by 5:00 waiting for service to begin at 8:00.

"Hello, welcome," Joe greeted a new man who was clean-shaven and dressed in old but clean clothes. The man grinned at Joe, "Don't recognize me, do you? I'm the *borracho*, drunk, you've prayed for night after night. You're lookin' at a changed man!"

An old woman walked up to me. Her Spanish was halting because she usually spoke only *Guaraní*, the Indian language. Her wrinkled face shone with a toothless smile. "It's true! What you are saying about faith in Jesus is true! I didn't understand this Protestant teaching … so I asked God to show me *la verdad*, the truth. And last night … "

Tears formed in her eyes and began to roll down the grooves in her cheeks, "Last night Jesus came to my bedroom. He stood at the foot of my bed and explained everything to me *in Guaraní.*"

Weeks later, a tallow candle sputtered and sparkled, sending the fragrance of frying bacon across the room. I held the Rook cards close to my chest and grinned at Lynn Trout. We were gonna beat the men. Joe didn't have a good hand, or he'd have raised the bid. Bob Trout must not have a good hand either; he had dropped out of the bidding, too. When the generator suddenly shut off at 10 p.m., the silence seemed deafening, and Lynn and I had scrambled to find the candles and matches so that we could finish our game.

For three days, we were on vacation in the middle of nowhere, down a dirt road, in a large field, beside a small river. We were the only guests at the *Villa Florida* Resort, an adobe building with six rooms, a thatched roof, and an outhouse-bathroom down at the end of the building. The kitchen-dining room, open on three sides, smelled of wood smoke from the cook-stove. Thankfully, the room was screened to keep out some of the flies, mosquitoes, sheep, goats, dogs, cats, and little pigs.

Bob took Christy and Timmy with Beth Ann, age nine, Holly, seven, and Jeffery, four, fishing and on a boat ride in the slow-moving river. The kids rode a horse, too. Lynn and I just rested and waited for the next meal when the cook would fill our plates with the delicious food of the day, much larger portions than we could ever eat.

Several months before, when Bob came up to our door in Asunción and clapped his hands in the Paraguayan manner of greeting, I had almost fainted! Bob and Lynn were fellow students in language school! They had served a term in Peru while we were in Chile and now had transferred to Paraguay. They were with ABWE (Association of Baptists for World Evangelism).

We cried on each others' shoulders, laughed together, and learned together. Lynn taught us to eat chocolate chip pancakes and how to make tuna melts. Lynn seemed to whistle all the time and she wore red high-top tennis shoes.

When Lynn rescued a kitten in the rain, she gave the kitten to Christy. The cat became T.H.E. Cat, Thomas Hughart Edward Cat. When Thomas had kittens, she would kill iguanas two-feet long and drag them up into the breezeway to feed the kittens.

To our menagerie of chickens, ducks, kittens and toy poodle, we added a soon-to-be-very-big, lovable boxer that Timmy promptly named Leader.

Joe received a letter from Roland: "We've raised funds for a girls' dorm, go ahead and start construction. And, we were invited to appear on the PTL Club, a new show in the States. Another guest, Willard Cantelon, gave us $1000 to pay for *Las Buenas Nuevas* television programs. Then Jim Bakker gave another $1000 and asked people to call in to give offerings. We'll have the money to go back on television as soon as we return to Paraguay in July!"

43

Rook and Rockin'
1975

We stretched a large banner across the balcony at the airport: "Hey Y'all! Welcome back, Blounts." The Varig plane landed and people began to deplane and walk across the tarmac. The line dwindled. And then stopped. Joe and Everett went downstairs to check the passenger list. Yes, the Blounts were listed, but they had missed the connecting flight in Sao Paolo.

We congregated in the parking lot: Aunt Marge, Chris Grace, the four Wards, the four Goulds and the four of us. Everett began, "I plugged in the coffee urn before we left so I have forty cups of hot coffee."

"I've already taken the *sopa paraguaya* cornbread out of the oven," I added. "And baked the cake."

"The potato salad is ready," Marge chimed in. "And the veggies," added Lorene.

"We've cancelled the classes at the Bible institute."

"We've taken the children out of school."

"So, let's have a party anyway!"

For the first time together with no ministry agenda, we just relaxed. We even had a Rook tournament. It was wonderful simply to slow down for the day. All of us were exhausted from the preparations, not just the food, but from painting and cleaning the Blounts' house (formerly the Jenkins' house, but the Jenkins had transferred to Central America). The following day, we welcomed the Blounts … with leftovers and laughs. Joe had rescheduled the harp and guitar *conjunto*, musical group, to come to serenade the Blounts, so that afternoon was special, too.

Tim and Brad, both ten years old, crouched in the bushes beside the street. "Brad, when the next car comes along, toss your water balloon at it." "OK, I will if you will. Let's both toss our balloons at the same time!"

They did not have long to wait. As a car slowed for the pot-holes in front of the Wards' house, Timmy stretched his arm back, Brad stretched his arm back.

Whheeewww. Splattttt.

"Oh, man, one of the balloons went inside the open window!"

"That girl sure screamed when it landed on her lap!"

Terrified, the boys ran away as fast as they could. They ran to the back of the house where Mari, the maid, told them to hide in her room. She would protect them. It was no big deal, this was *carnaval* week and everyone did mischievous things.

The boys hovered, sweating, waiting. Five minutes passed. Ten. Fifteen.

With big sighs of relief, Tim and Brad emerged from hiding to fill more balloons with water. Laughing, they rounded the house and headed for the bushes once again.

They crouched, waiting for the next car.

Suddenly someone grabbed them by their collars. The man, the driver, had been waiting for the boys to reappear!

The man dragged Brad and Tim to the Wards' front door.

"You will not believe what these boys have done!" the man shouted angrily, the minute Everett opened the door.

"Come with me!" the man growled. "Right now!"

Everett accompanied the man to his car, which was parked around the corner.

A young woman sat in the passenger seat. She was crying.

"My daughter and I were on our way to the University. She is an architectural student and has in her lap her semester project, a meticulous design she has spent weeks drawing."

Everett looked down at the large drawing in the girl's lap. Water-stained and smeared, the drawing was ruined.

Everett offered the man some money. But money could not fix the problem. Neither could the boys' regret or the spankings they received.

One day after I had made some purchases downtown, a merchant handed me a letter opener about three inches long. It was made of bone and honed to a very sharp point. "Take this, señora, carry it with you always for your personal protection." I didn't understand. He continued, "When you ride the bus, you'll see. You will need this."

A few days later, I boarded a very crowded bus to go to the Bible institute. Every seat was taken and the aisle was crammed tight with people. To my surprise, a man got up to give me his seat on the aisle. Then he stood beside me, at the end of the seat. Whenever the bus would rock side to side over the pot-holes, the man would rub himself against my shoulder. I could not believe he was doing it deliberately. I angled my body, pulling my shoulder away.

But the next time the bus rocked, so did he! I drew away from him as far as I could, scooting closer to the person seated beside me, making that person very uncomfortable. But the man followed me, arching his body to press against my shoulder.

Then I remembered my "personal-protection-very-sharp-letter-opener." I unfastened my purse and made an obvious show of taking out the letter opener. The man moved back. I would have jabbed him where it would have hurt the most. And he knew it.

Joe and Everett could hardly wait to tell Roland about an occurrence at the Bible institute. A young man had gone to the office to talk with them. Of course, the conversation was in Spanish.

"Brother Everett, I've asked for this meeting so you can tell the other students to quit throwing rocks," the young man began.

Everett and Joe were very concerned! This was the first they had heard of this!

"Who is throwing rocks?" Joe asked.

"Well, I hate to name names," the young man replied. "But a number of students are involved."

"Where?" Everett wanted to know.

"At the dorm."

"Are they throwing rocks onto the roof?'

"No," replied the student, smiling.

"Against the outside of the building?" Joe asked

"No, señor," the student explained patiently. "Inside. Inside the dorm. And it is very painful. All of us suffer from the throwing of rocks."

"Is this during the daytime? Or at night?" Everett asked.

"Almost always at night. Sometimes when I'm asleep, in the middle of the night, I'm awakened by students throwing rocks."

Joe and Everett shook their heads in disbelief. "Have you talked to Chris (Dean of Men) about this?"

"Yes, I have," the student informed them very seriously. "He talked to the guys, but they just keep throwing rocks."

Joe thanked the student for his concern and Everett stated that the matter would be resolved without delay.

Joe went to get Chris to come to an important meeting.

When the men were gathered, Joe and Everett explained, in English, the problem.

Chris was mystified. He didn't remember any such conversation with any of the students.

The more they talked about it, reverting back and forth in English and Spanish, it finally dawned on them—that was the Paraguayan expression for 'passing gas'!

As Joe and Everett told Roland the story, they all three laughed until tears rolled down their cheeks.

44

Busyness
December 1975

"*I wish you could come home* in December. I'm pregnant!
Is there any way you can 'break the rules' and fly home
when the baby is born?"

I started crying as I read the letter from my sister, Jan. I had
missed the adoption of little Kimberly. Would I have to miss the
birth of this baby?

When we left the States, we knew we were not allowed to return
until we had completed our four-year term. Could Joe somehow get
permission for me to fly home?

I was tired after two and one-half years of constant activity day and
night.

The heat was oppressive for most of the year. The temperature
would hover at 104 degrees day after day. One day we felt chilly, and
as I looked for sweaters, I noticed the thermometer: 90 degrees!

This semester, I taught Algebra II at ACA and became home-
room teacher for the ninth grade. I would get up every morning at
5:30 and cook breakfast. Joe would drop me off at ACA and I would
ride the bus later to the Bible institute.

I would rush home (on the bus) to cook *almuerzo*, our big meal
of the day (with no prepared foods), and then clean up the kitchen

before falling into bed for a siesta. For supper we warmed leftovers before we headed out to church.

Afternoons, I gave accordion lessons to students at the Bible institute, and piano lessons to Christy, Timmy, Howie, and Carla. I helped the children with their homework, worked on my lesson plans, and scheduled committee meetings for those morning hours when I would be free.

Some of the committee meetings were for the PTA. I was still president. We planned school activities, programs, suppers. There were end-of-school banquets and luncheons to welcome new teachers and teas to welcome new students and their families.

Joe was director of the ACA, so we hosted teachers' teas at our house and school board meetings. We planned summer camps for December, January, and February.

Fifteen missionary wives of various denominations met every month for a "coffee." We conducted a Wednesday morning Bible study in English.

As national Missionettes' president, I held monthly committee meetings, and once a month a girls' meeting, many times in our patio. We hosted camps for the girls, too, and retreats. Lorene was a wonderful help, and the next election, I nominated her as national president.

As vice-president of Women's Ministries, I met with Ercilia Bogarín to plan the monthly women's meetings.

Joe was national president of the youth, and we had monthly rallies plus retreats on every holiday weekend and camps over longer holidays.

We held monthly meetings at a penitentiary. I taught children's church and Sunday school. Some Sunday mornings, Joe preached at the English-speaking Union Church.

Once a month was the Missionary Field Fellowship, which lasted for hours as we hammered out where to have another campaign, how best to request release of our "work funds" from the mission. I was secretary. Joe was chairman for several years.

Plus, one day a month I spent in bed, doubled over with terrible cramps. I would cry out if anyone so much as touched the bed, shaking it even slightly. I was anemic from loss of blood and continued to suffer with fallopian tube and ovarian infections.

Then, our maid, Lali, (who taught me *heh* meant *yes*), quit. I really "couldn't be angry," because she enrolled full time in the Bible institute. But I prayed and prayed for some relief in the kitchen and with the cleaning. I needed help in going to the market and in washing the vegetables and meat.

God in his wonderful grace sent us Oscarina, a young woman in her late twenties. She cooked and cleaned and picked up after us all. She made green *tallarines*, noodles, with meat sauce and cooked the food for the dogs (no dog food available). Oscarina made *flan* and *albóndigas,* meatballs. She made her way into our hearts, where she remains to this day.

Every evening we attended either special classes at the Bible institute or another campaign. After the evening services, while Joe taught the new converts' courses, I taught the new Sunday school teachers the following Sunday's lesson.

Joe and I did not make Christy and Timmy attend every night. One night as Joe and I left the house, he said to the children, "Remember, do not open this door for anyone!"

"Not even for Grandma?" Christy asked.

"Not even for her."

Christy grinned, "Well, if she comes, I'll just go outside and sit on the porch with her until you return."

Another day, after I had made cupcakes to take to one of my many meetings, the children and Joe began to chant,

Char-i-ty be-gins at home.

Char-i-ty be-gins at home.

So, I learned always to make two batches of brownies or cookies or cakes.

One night at the tent, some children were running around outside playing during the service. Just at the close, when the speaker was giving the invitation for people to come forward for prayer, the children ran into the tent and down the aisles, laughing and chasing each other. As they made a pass in front of where I was sitting on the front row, I reached out and grabbed a missionary kid. I set the child down and whispered sternly, "We do not run in the tent while service is going on."

I thought nothing more about it, until a few weeks later when the child's mother accosted me.

"Margaret! How dare you discipline my child! I know what you did though I couldn't see you. I was in the back of the tent, but someone told me how cruel you were to my child! How you jerked my child by the arm and talked harshly to my child."

I was dumbfounded. I opened my mouth but no sound came out.

The missionary glared, "You think your children behave the best. And are the most talented. Just because Christy plays the guitar and Timmy is learning the harp. Well, for your information, your children are not perfect!

"You think you are *so holy*. You do all these *wonderful* things. You think because I stay at home and take care of my family that I am not as good a missionary as you. Well, miss-know-it-all, I like to stay home!

"I don't *want* to attend the services, but I like to go out to eat. When my husband comes home from church, I have the children in bed asleep. The maid watches them while we go out.

"I don't neglect my family as you do.

"Furthermore, I don't *want* to teach at your so-called Bible institute. I haven't set foot on that campus in months. And I don't intend to do so now.

"You think you are *so righteous* because of all your religious activities. Well, you don't fool me!

"You don't really care about me or my children. You are just interested in doing all your precious good works!"

I was shaking. No one had ever before talked to me in that tone of voice. She walked away and I searched for Joe.

I felt as if I were sitting in a garbage dump and the woman had been heaping basketful after basketful of garbage over my head.

I knew I needed to sort through this stuff. I needed to pick up each piece and evaluate it, to see how much truth was in each accusation she made.

All my life, my mother and dad were dedicated to "church work." And I followed their example.

I loved teaching. I loved inspiring girls and women. I loved stretching students' minds and watching them grow in knowledge and practical experience.

Was this wrong? Was I wrong? Was I neglecting my family—to "do God's work"? Was I attempting to attain God's approval by my good performance?

Where was the balance?

Was I only a hollow plastic shell without warmth? Did I care only about "the work" and not care about individuals?

Was this woman envious of the gifts God had given me?

It would take me years to sort through all of this. Years of growing and changing. Years of being humbled and humiliated. Years until I realized that I was redeemed not by my good works, but only by God's grace. Years until all my "works" were swept away and I felt that I was lying prostrate in the mud at the foot of the cross.

I wanted so very much to get away from Paraguay for a few weeks—to go home to Pensacola for the birth of Jan's baby. And Joe obtained permission for me to go. We pinched pennies and Mom and Dad pitched in to help with my airfare.

At the last minute, National Airlines went on strike and I had to fly three different airlines to make the connections from Asunción to Pensacola.

In Pensacola, as Jan's due date neared, she and I would time her pains and call the doctor if any two or three contractions were close together. Once, we drove all the way to Sacred Heart Hospital, but as soon as we arrived, Jan's pains stopped. We went into the women's restroom and laughed until we cried.

On December 12, 1975, William Shawn Hammac was born. I held him and rocked him. And I held his big sister, Kimmy, and loved on her, too.

And I rested. Mom cooked wonderful meals. Dad was recuperating at home from a second heart attack, and I could be with him! In the rest and good care and joy of being with family, I gained six pounds.

One day Mom told me about a pastor's wife who was gossiping maliciously about her. Shocked, I asked Mom, "Do you ever pray for her?"

"Every day," Mom replied. "I pray, 'God, work your will in her life.' That alleviates my anger and lets God do whatever He wants."

After being gone for three weeks, I was ready to return to Paraguay. I had been worried about leaving Joe and the kids for so long.

When I arrived back in Asunción and walked into the living room, I could not believe my eyes! The room was a terrible mess. Dirty socks strewn, crumpled newspapers lying around, toys everywhere, shirts, slacks, shorts, shoes piled in every available space. I was appalled!

Then Joe and the kids began to laugh. They had deliberately "staged" the messy living room just to see my reaction! The rest of the house was clean. Of course, Oscarina had taken really good care of the family, plus, the other missionaries had frequently invited Joe and the children over for meals.

New Year's Day approached. What lay ahead in 1976?

* * *

Oscarina's recipe for delicious, baked custard pudding:

Paraguayan *Flan*
325 degrees for 55–75 minutes

INGREDIENTS
6 eggs
2 cans sweetened condensed milk
2 empty cans (above) filled with milk
1 teaspoon vanilla
1/2 cup sugar
a baking pan (I use a bundt pan)
a larger pan (a 9x13 cake pan) with about one inch of water in it

DIRECTIONS

1. Preheat Oven.
2. Melt the sugar in a skillet over medium heat until the sugar becomes a golden liquid. (This takes a while, so begin it first.)You can add a tiny bit of water if the liquid is too thick.
3. Beat eggs well. Add the condensed milk and vanilla.
4. Fill the "empty cans" with milk and then pour the milk into a microwaveable dish and heat until the edges of the milk just begin to bubble. Cool and add to egg mixture. Beat well (by hand is OK, with a whisk).
5. Oil your baking container well (the bundt pan). Pour the melted sugar into the baking container. Pour the flan mixture on top of the melted sugar.
6. Set the pan in the larger pan of water (you can use warm water from the faucet). Carefully transfer both pans to the preheated oven.
7. Bake for 55 minutes at 325 degrees. Test with a knife inserted in the center. Continue baking until knife comes out clean (as much as 20 or 30 minutes more).
8. Carefully remove bundt pan from the water, and let the flan cool for about 10 minutes. Run a dull knife around the edge of the flan to loosen it. (It shrinks some as it cools.)
9. Continue cooling until the pan is cool enough to refrigerate. Refrigerate at least a couple of hours, overnight is best.
10. Invert the pan onto a serving dish. Leave the pan on top for several minutes so the melted sugar can drip down over the flan. Keep refrigerated.

45

Surprise, Surprise
1976

"*J want to sing a duet* in chapel next Friday night," Fernando told me.

"Great!" I assured him. We were so proud of Fernando, now in his third year at the Bible institute. He continued to shine shoes every day. And already, his tuition was paid for the month.

"Nery will play the harp, I'll play the guitar, and you play the accordion."

"*Muy bien*, OK," I said, looking at his sparkling eye (the other eye traced its own path).

"So, what song do you want to sing?" he continued. "The duet is with you!"

Margaret, Nery, and Fernando

Actually, I did not want to sing with him. His voice was not great and neither was his guitar strumming. But overriding those things was the certainty that I did not want to disappoint him.

We practiced, we sang, and the students loved it!

One day Fernando became really angry. I don't remember why, exactly, but he stormed off the campus, stomped down the sidewalk, and yelled back, "You can keep your old Bible institute. I am never coming back, never! Never!"

Two days later, a very repentant Fernando appeared at the Bible institute office. His eyes were bloodshot, his clothes were wrinkled, his breath was rancid, and his head hung low.

"Will you take me back?" Fernando muttered. "I have greatly sinned."

"What have you done, Fernando?" Everett inquired.

"I have really sinned ... I was so mad ... I walked and walked and ended up near the riverfront ... and for fifty cents ... I bought a prostitute."

"You didn't!" exclaimed Everett.

"Yes, and that is not all," continued Fernando. "Then ... I bought three cigarettes ... and I smoked them all."

"Oh, my," Everett said.

"And one more thing, I bought a bottle of wine. And I drank all of it."

Fernando's head ached but his conscience hurt even worse. Everett and Joe suspended Fernando from school.

Fernando also confessed to his pastor and then willingly obeyed the church board's "discipline," which was to confess his sin to the congregation and be prohibited from exercising any leadership positions for three months. The pastor admonished the congregation to show love to Fernando and not to mention his sins again. (The interim pastor was Joe.)

"A man prayed the sinner's prayer with us," reported a team of our Bible institute students.

"A teenage girl really listened to what we had to say," stated another group.

With students on three levels of study in the Bible institute, we wanted to include practical ministry experience. We had organized the students into groups of three. The teams were thrilled to report on their first outing.

"Well, we have you beat! Two people prayed the sinner's prayer with us," piped up Nery.

He continued, "But it was at the *manicomio,* insane asylum. So we're not sure if that counts." The students laughed uproariously!

After chapel on Friday nights, the students gathered in the grass patio to enjoy refreshments and play games. They often played a tag-game similar to "two deep" that I had played as a child. There were no cliques, everyone participated. Christy and Timmy loved the sense of camaraderie and family.

Easter Sunday dawned cool and crisp. We were scheduled to attend *Victoria.* This was the church where we'd had our first crusade and where many of our Bible institute students had been converted. The pastor, as did most Paraguayans, spoke primarily *Guaraní.* Because there is no "s" in *Guaraní,* this dear old pastor wanted to be sure to speak Spanish properly. However, he over-corrected with too many "s-es" and introduced us as "Brothers Joes and hiss wives."

The sunrise service began at 6:30 a.m., followed by a break for hot, strong, sweet coffee. Then, after the regular morning service, the ladies served *almuerzo,* lunch, prepared by our own Águila de Santa Cruz, the cook at the Bible institute.

As I sat in the early morning service, wrapped in my poncho, I became sad. Christy and Timmy were to my right, sitting on the floor on the adobe pavers, with their backs against the wall. The children were not "dressed up." No one was. There were no Easter hats, no Easter lilies. No anthems, no choir. I felt sad that Christy and Timmy would not know "a real Easter" such as I had known as a child in the States.

I had settled into my gloom when the pastor announced, "Brother Santa Cruz, please come forward."

I hunched lower as Águila's husband, an elderly gentleman, walked slowly down the aisle. My eyes were focused on my lap when I heard the first strains of music.

I looked up to see gnarled, carpenter hands cradling an old violin. Sweet sounds floated across the adobe chapel. Classical music! Played beautifully!

The notes flowed into my heart, straight to my soul. Tears rolled down my cheeks.

I repented for thinking this was not a "real" Easter.

A few months later, the phone rang. Mrs. Moses whispered, "The baby has arrived! Go pick up Doris Ann and come to get the baby!"

"All right," I said, nervously. I jumped into our little car and hurried to pick up Doris Gaona.

Doris had moved to Paraguay from Washington state to teach first grade at ACA. She had fallen in love with Eladio Gaona, one of our pastors, and though they'd been married for five years, they had not been able to have a child. Mrs. Moses told them of a teenager who needed to give up a baby for adoption.

The teenage girl, an orphan, lived with her aunt and uncle. But when she became pregnant, they kicked her out. In desperation, she walked to the Red Cross hospital, where an obstetrician took pity on her. "You can live with me until the baby is born. But you must give up the baby for adoption."

On August 3, the baby girl was born. The doctor-friend attended the birth and then quickly excused herself. Wrapping the baby carefully, she placed the tiny bundle into a shopping bag and nonchalantly walked out of the Red Cross hospital. She went straight to Mrs. Moses' house.

Cradling the newborn infant in her arms, Doris crooned, "Ooh, I love you already. Your name is Marci, my sweetheart. And I'm your new mommy."

That afternoon, I drove Doris and Marci to the Baptist Hospital, where Dr. Skinner examined the baby and pronounced her healthy. Later that afternoon, Evelyn and I helped Doris bathe Marci and prepare baby bottles.

A few weeks later, Doris went to apply for a birth certificate and passport for Marci. All she had to do was declare the child's name, write down the child's birth date, and say the child was born at home.

Doris stood at the counter and stared at the forms. So easy. Just a few little white lies. Then it would all be over with. No one would ever know. Besides, Marci *was* her child. "No one" in Paraguay would condemn Doris for what she "had to do" to have a child of her own....

But when the time came, Doris could not do it. She could not write lies on the birth certificate and passport application.

Years of paperwork followed, along with enormous expenses. Doris and Eladio had to run ads in the newspapers to try to locate the father. The birth mother needed to sign endless papers, but she had moved from the city, and no one could find her. Thankfully, little Marci stayed with her new mommy and daddy during this time and eventually became an official member of the Gaona family.

Joe and Roland negotiated and negotiated and negotiated, but the station manager would not budge. We were not able to buy the Saturday night time-slot for our television program. The only time available, the manager told the men repeatedly, was at the noon hour on Tuesdays. We were really disappointed at first, but then realized that since everything closed for siesta from 11:30 to 3:00, maybe people would watch, after all. And they did!

➤ A priest invited us to visit a home group. He introduced us by saying, "*Son más conocidos en Paraguay ¡que la mandioca!*" (These people are better known in Paraguay than cassava!) This was a real compliment to us because *mandioca* was a staple, served at every meal, like bread.

➤ Luís Palau came to Paraguay for a two-week crusade. We invited him to be on the television program, and he invited us to sing at the crusade. Also, I played the piano for the mass choir and congregational singing. The stadium was packed with hundreds of people.

➤ The Christian and Missionary Alliance invited us for a three-day campaign, with emphasis on the Holy Spirit.

➤ The head of the Salvation Army, from England, was one of our guests.

➤ A Methodist musical group, led by a teacher at ACA, sang regularly on the show.

One day, at the conclusion of the television program, Roland held up the little book, *"La Cruz y el Puñal"* ("The Cross and the Switchblade"). Antonio Vitar, lying on the couch enjoying his siesta, heard the words "hope" and "drug addict." His head snapped up— his son was a drug addict!

The family had lost all hope of breaking the addiction to drugs. They had tried every program available in Paraguay and Argentina. Antonio's sister, just back from the States, said no hope was available there, either, for an effective cure. Nothing really worked. Every counselor told them there was no hope. Antonio's son would die an addict, a broken young man, a university student, his life thwarted, ruined by drugs.

Antonio wrote, *"Estamos desesperados.* (We are desperate.) Please send the book."

Antonio read *"La Cruz y el Puñal."* His wife read it. The son read it. Together they prayed, "God, if you could deliver Nicky Cruz, you can deliver us."

The son was transformed!

The father was, too. Why couldn't he be like Dave Wilkerson and offer hope to other young people in Paraguay?

Antonio Vitar approached the President of Paraguay and asked if he could begin a Teen Challenge-type center for faith-based drug rehabilitation. The President's wife gave Antonio an entire city block for the project. And the President gave Antonio a new car and told him to go to every high school in Paraguay and give a copy of *La Cruz y el Puñal* to every student.

(We had no idea any of this was happening.)

Several years later, Roland's phone rang. Antonio said, "Rolando, my new grandson is born! Would you dedicate him to God at your church tonight?"

That night, Roland stood in front of the congregation. He held the baby son of the former hopeless drug addict. Three generations were now transformed by the hope of *las Buenas Nuevas*, the Good News!

46

Sleepless Nights
1976

"*Pull the sheet up over your head,* I'm ready to spray," Joe told Christy and Timmy. They held their breath as the mosquito spray filled the hallway. Then Joe swiveled, turning the tank and tube toward our bedroom. He pumped the handle.

Every night we repeated this ritual. The mission allowed us to have a window air conditioning unit in the bedroom but the cool air did not reach into the children's rooms, so the kids spread sleeping bags in the hallway.

Within a few minutes we would drift off to sleep. But many times I would awaken in the middle of the night with the sense of a heavy weight pressed over all my body. It would be hard to breathe. I had a sense of being smothered, my limbs felt paralyzed, my mind felt squeezed inside my skull. I would pray, feebly at first, asking God for help. We called it "pleading the blood of Jesus," asking God to remember Jesus' death that freed us from the effects of sin. As I pleaded with God to apply that grace to me, gradually I would sense the heaviness lift and I would begin to breathe freely. I would feel a sense of release, like "clarity" being restored. The oppression would retreat.

For many months, I did not realize that Joe, too, experienced the same thing.

Paraguay was so different from Chile. There had been a freedom, a spiritual freedom, in Chile. Sometimes I wondered if all the demons that fled from surrounding countries came to hover over Paraguay. A spiritual oppression seemed to fill the air. A constraint, a struggle, restrained a free move of God's Spirit.

Yes, we had converts to Christ, but in small numbers. No evangelical church in Paraguay averaged very many people. Even in the Luís Palau crusade, when Christians of all denominations united to fill the soccer stadium, only several dozen people accepted Christ as Savior. The fellowship was great—the converts were few.

When a missionary (I'll call him Bill) came up from Argentina to visit, he scoffed when we tried to explain all this to him. He said, "If I were here, I could plant a church, a large one. Paraguay is not different from any other place in Latin America. You're just not going about it right." Several years later, "Bill" transferred to Paraguay. The next time we saw him, he said humbly, "I want to apologize to you. I was wrong. Paraguay *is* different. Only God's sovereignty can break the demonic hold and bring a spiritual awakening to Paraguay."

The very act of living drained us emotionally, physically, and psychologically. We lived in a pressure-cooker environment with the other missionary families. Small tensions that should not amount to anything became enlarged. It was like living in a fishbowl, and this increased anxiety and drained our strength.

Joe and Roland wanted to begin a church on the Bible institute campus. A building stood there, empty.

We stretched a banner across the road announcing services every night beginning March 16. A strip of grass fringed the campus, just inside the wrought iron fence. We set up chairs there, in the open air, so everyone could see what happened and, hopefully, no one would be afraid to participate in these Protestant services.

María Paniagua and her mother were riding in a bus when they saw the banner. "That's tonight," exclaimed María. "Those are the people from *Las Buenas Nuevas*, the television show. Could we go, please?"

That night only a handful of people came, but when Joe gave the invitation to pray to receive Christ, María and her mother prayed.

Then Joe asked anyone who wanted prayer for healing to come forward.

I think I loved María from the moment she came forward. She was frail, timid, sincere, and suffering. As Joe and Roland prayed for her, faith grew in her heart. She glowed with her new faith and the assurance that God was with her.

María Paniagua

Sixteen-year-old Maria did not live in Asunción. She had come to the capital from Concepción to see a cancer specialist. She was scheduled to be admitted to the hospital the next day for a biopsy on an egg-sized lump in her left breast.

The biopsy came back positive for cancer. But María asked for a few more days before surgery, because she wanted to attend the crusade every night. After almost a month, the doctor said María could wait no longer.

We promised to visit her in the hospital. We assured her that God had touched her.

Joe and I entered the government hospital lobby. No air conditioning. Gritty sand crunched beneath our shoes on the terrazzo floors. We climbed the concrete staircase to María's room, a ward containing a dozen beds lined up against opposite walls. The stench of urine and sweaty bodies mingled with the smell of food cooking.

The hospital did not provide meals, so relatives of each patient brought bundles of food, or cooked on hibachis on the balcony.

Awaiting surgery, María was pale but tranquil, as she lay on the rough cotton sheets. Her mother held a paperback Bible she had purchased at the campaign.

"My mother has been reading to me," María said. "The woman in the next bed told her to read a little louder so she could hear, too."

Joe took María's hand and prayed for her, for God to be with her during surgery the next morning.

The surgeon removed María's left breast, and he removed four ribs from over her heart. I could clearly see her heart beating underneath the sheet. She showed me her scar. The surgeon had opened her skin, like a book, and removed everything beneath it. My heart broke for her. To be sixteen years old and suffer so.

The other patients and their families noticed María's tranquility, the peace her mother possessed. As they saw María's mother reading aloud to her, they, too, wanted to hear the Bible.

When Joe visited the next afternoon, María's mother was standing farther down the ward reading aloud to the people in that area. And every day she extended her reading to people in other beds and in other wards.

Because María was in the hospital, dozens of people were hearing the Bible for the first time. Her mother literally wore out a Bible; the cover came off and pages fell out from so much use.

And every day María had new requests for prayer. "*Hermano José*, Brother Joe, would you go to the room next door to pray for a boy injured in a car wreck?"

"Three doors down, a man who fell from a horse."

"Go down the hall, on the left, there's a boy who was hit by a falling tree."

"An Air Force captain who's been in a plane crash." The captain told Joe he was "finished with life" since he'd been so badly injured. But he accepted Christ and soon recovered his health.

"A woman on the third floor is scheduled to have her leg amputated." Joe followed María's mother's directions to the third floor. The teenage son of a woman who had been in a car wreck greeted

Joe. Joe prayed. The next day as soon as Joe arrived, María said, "Go up there right now! They want to see you!"

In tears, the teenager reported, "The doctor opened the bandages on mother's leg, one last time, before amputating the leg. He was shocked! The leg was healing! He did not amputate!"

Dozens of patients were praying with Joe and with María's mother, who was growing stronger in her new faith. Patients were being healed up and down the hallways ... because María was in the hospital.

María's sister, Dilma, came in from the country. In her twenties, Dilma was bitter, her face hard, her attitude brittle. But, everyday she, too, listened to her mother read the Bible. And Dilma's heart softened. She and her aunt began to attend the crusade every night. As Christ's love flowed into her, Dilma's entire countenance changed. She became soft, gentle, and approachable.

The aunt had problems of her own. She took prescription drugs: to sleep, to awaken, to cope, to be calm, to be alert. With her eyes dilated, the aunt talked too loudly, her body twitched. But then as God worked in her heart, she too was transformed.

Was this what God would use to bring "an awakening" to Paraguay? All these people and their relatives who knew personally, now, of God's grace? They could spread the word and revival would break out all over the country! Our new church would bulge with people. Where would we put all the new converts?

As soon as God would raise up María, healing her from any further cancer, the news would spread. "Paraguay's Spiritual Awakening" was coming soon!!

María looked forward to Joe's daily visits. Every afternoon following the siesta, he would spend two or three hours visiting all the patients María's mother had contacted. María began to tease him that he was just dropping by to see her on his way to pray for everyone else. She loved him dearly.

But María's health did not improve. She did not get better. Every day she grew weaker. The radiation was not working. The skin over her left chest was black, like a shiny plastic garbage bag, from over-radiation.

Joe and I fasted. We prayed for hours. We pleaded with God in the night hours. I knew God could perform this miracle—and I knew He would. After all, Paraguay was pending, waiting for this healing.

When I walked to María's bedside, I would kiss her on both cheeks, smooth the hair off her forehead, hold her hand. I took her some cucumbers, which she loved. And I took talcum powder for the rough sheets.

María grew weaker day by day. Her legs became paralyzed. As the cancer spread up her spine, her headaches became excruciating.

When the pain became severe, María would plead, *"Ora, Mamá, ora."* "Pray, Mama, pray." And the pain would ease.

The doctor told the family to take María home to die. But she did not want to go back home to the country. She did not want to leave Joe.

One day, María said, *"Mamá,* when I die, don't cry. Sing. Sing Psalms. Sing for me. Don't cry."

On July 15, four months less one day since we had met María, I kissed her forehead and whispered to her listless body, "María, we love you so much. Brother Joe could not come today. Do you want me to tell him hello for you?"

She roused, and with a mischievous smile, said weakly, "No. Tell everyone else hello. But you tell him to come up here. I'll tell him hello myself."

I walked out of the hospital and sat in our car in the parking lot. I was angry at God.

I beat my hands on the steering wheel and cried out, "Why? Why? Why? Why don't You heal María? I know You can. Why don't You? This healing could change the nation!"

As I paused for a breath, into my heart dropped the certainty that God is sovereign. He could do what He wanted. He did not need my counsel or my permission.

That realization broke my will. I leaned my head on the steering wheel and bawled.

"All right, God. I give up. I release María, I won't beg for her healing any more."

The next morning the phone rang, and Dilma said, "María died in the night."

That afternoon, July 16, Joe and I walked down the steps into the morgue in the hospital basement. María's mother had asked us to hold a brief service there before she took the body home to Concepción for burial.

María's body lay in an open wooden casket, curved to fit her body. She was clothed in a white cotton robe, like a choir robe. Her arms were crossed on her chest; her dark hair flowed over her shoulders. Her little bare feet stuck up at the end of the coffin.

Joe stood, his Bible in hand, and read to María's mother, sister, and the small group of aunts and cousins assembled there. Joe read about the new body promised to us in heaven.

Roland played his accordion and we sang Psalm 117.

Alabad a Jehová
Naciones todas, pueblos todos
Alabadle.
Porque ha
Engrandecido
Sobre nosotros
Su misericordia.
Y la bondad de Jehová es para siempre, Aleluya, Amén.
Y la bondad de Jehová es para siempre, Aleluya, Amén.

Praise God
All nations and all tribes.
Praise him
Because he has increased to us his mercy.
And the goodness of God endures forever.
Alleluia. Amen.
(my translation from the Spanish)

The hospital staff gazed in amazement at the people gathered there. No one had ever seen a family like this. They were not screaming, keening, and throwing themselves on the coffin. They were actually peaceful. Tranquil.

I thought of the words of Jesus in John 12:24 that unless a grain of wheat falls to the ground and dies, it remains alone. But if it dies, it produces much fruit.

When would the harvest come to Paraguay?

47

Trips

1976

❦

The four kids trouped down the sidewalk on their way down-town to a little restaurant called *El Lido Bar*. Christy was thirteen, Timmy and Carla, eleven, Howie, seventeen. I thought nothing of letting the kids go alone on the bus. Crime was almost non-existent due to President Stroessner's zero tolerance policy: "Jail first, trial in the distant future maybe."

As soon as the kids were out of sight, they began their drama: Timmy, the crippled one, dragged his right leg and bent his crippled arm. Carla, the blind one, groped to find her way. Christy, the deaf one, signed furiously. Howie, the caregiver, ushered the little group along. They continued the charade all the way to town, the entire time in the restaurant, and all the way home!

One afternoon they all went bowling. I use the term broadly because Asunción boasted one bowling alley where two boys set-up the pins on two warped lanes. Fortunately, the kids didn't mind "gutter balls." Our phone rang. It was Timmy, saying, "I'm calling from the hospital."

I panicked, "Hospital? What's wrong? Who's hurt? What did they break? How bad is it?"

"Mo-*ther*, calm down. Nothing's wrong. There's no telephone at the bowling alley. We came across the street to the hospital to use the phone, that's all. Can we go to the little restaurant down the street for a snack?"

The nurse at the emergency room knew us by name, from scratches, bruises, eye infections, and worm eggs under toenails.

When the Blounts had returned from furlough and moved next door to us, Timmy and Carla became practically inseparable. They walked on top of the walls, they climbed trees. They both gathered eggs, walking through the chicken yard and squishing you-know-what between their toes. They talked to biddies and held momma chickens.

At the new church, when we divided the girls and boys into two separate Sunday school classes, Carla was angry. She did not want to be separated from Timmy.

To pass the time while we adults met for business meetings, the kids wrote, produced, and presented dramas. They would wrap Tinker Belle around their necks for a fur stole; they would turn on the vacuum cleaner for the sound of an airplane. They arranged kitchen chairs in a row, very close together, and played "getting on and off a Paraguayan bus." They would lip sync to LP records. They produced "radio broadcasts," adding an assortment of sound effects.

**Timmy with the boxer, Leader, Carla with a chicken,
Christy with the poodle, Tinker Belle**

They played Barbie and Big Jim for hours, making houses out of boxes. Timmy wrote Mom a letter informing her that Big Jim was a tough outdoorsman but Ken was a puny wimp, so *don't* send Ken clothes for Big Jim.

When Randy and Scott Gould both came down with the "hard, red measles," Timmy developed all the symptoms. He stayed in bed all day ... almost. At least until he finished reading a new *Charlie Brown* book Mom had sent him.

Tim and Randy dug an underground hideout, fortified it with boards, and furnished it with candles and rugs. Tim said it was "perfectly hidden until Mom ratted us out because she felt sorry for Carla's being excluded."

Christy made numerous trips to ACA to practice for the school play, *Cheaper by the Dozen*, to practice duets with her best friend, Beth, and to practice for the ACA choir.

"Take one valium before you leave the house. Take another as soon as you reach the waiting room. Take a third when we call you to come back to the dental chair."

The dentist held a chisel in one hand, a hammer in the other. "Open wide." Wham. "Keep your mouth open." Wham. He walked around to my other side. Tap, tap, wham. He moved behind my head, tilted me back even farther. Tap, tap, wham.

I didn't know which was worse—the throbbing pain of an impacted wisdom tooth, or the hammer and chisel treatment to remove the tooth, whose roots wrapped around the bone.

I wasn't the only one in pain. Don Gould suffered from a bleeding ulcer. It had begun during itinerary, continued throughout language study, and now caused Don tremendous pain. The doctor advised him to return to the States for treatment. Don received permission to take early furlough. I really missed them, especially Lorene, who had taken over the girls' clubs.

Everett Ward, too, suffered. But in a different way. He worked really hard—in evangelism, church planting, and teaching at the Bible institute. But his philosophy differed from Joe's and Roland's. Everett wanted the students to be on a true college level. Joe and Roland wanted students, period. Just like with Barnabas and Paul, the division became so painful that Everett asked for a transfer. The mission assigned him to Chile, of all places!

Years later, we talked with Everett and Carolyn. They said moving to Chile resulted in a wonderful move for them. They had lived in Paraguay their entire missionary career, and had no idea the Chileans would be so warm and welcoming and of such a different intellectual level. They said their lives and ministry had been enriched, changed, for the better.

Joe, Roland, and Timmy climbed up into the old, white pick-up truck to travel to the interior for a week. They would sleep in the back under a camper-topper.

At the annual national church's General Council, Joe had been elected Superintendent of Paraguay. This meant that he should travel throughout the country to bring unity to the handful of existing churches and inspire workers to begin new churches.

Pablo (from la Plaza Italia) began a church! As Joe assisted Pablo in baptizing his new converts, Joe said, "I'm baptizing my grandchildren!"

Roland became pastor of our new *Buenas Nuevas* church, while Joe traveled even more, visiting the Russian colonies in the south.

In the early 1900s, attempting to populate the country, the Paraguayan government had offered free land to immigrants. From the Ukraine, young men came to work the land. They married Paraguayan girls and carved thriving farms out of the wilderness. Some of them had been members of the Russian Assemblies of God. And now, with Joe's urging, they sent three of their sons to the Bible institute.

One of the sons, Pedro Polonski, loved the Lord with all his heart. At seventeen, he played soccer very well, studied hard, and worked on his dad's farm during summers and holidays. Pedro also noticed our Christy ... but since the Paraguayans didn't date, Pedro would come to our house, where he and Christy could "talk." Ahem. I was glad furlough came the following year. Christy was too young to be interested in boys!

On December 20 we were entertaining twenty-five Christian workers plus their children at our house when a telegram arrived. "Funds deposited to your account. Go to retreat."

We could not believe it! Another five-nation missionary retreat began the following week in *La Leonera*, Chile. But Joe and I had not planned to go because we did not have the money. Now, the mission had deposited the money for us to go!

I scurried to get our clothes ready. Joe hurried to get the car serviced. When we checked our passports, both kids' passports had expired! Joe rushed to the Embassy for new passports.

Chris Grace would travel with the Blounts in their car. Aunt Marge Campion, the older, single woman, would ride with us in our VW.

We left Asunción on Friday morning, December 24, in searing summer heat. At the border crossing into Argentina, we sat in the steaming car for hours, it seemed, waiting on the customs officials to approve our exit papers. I began to sing a little ditty to keep the kids occupied, "Hottie, hottie, hot, hot, hot. Hottie, hottie, hot, hot, hot. We are all so ver-y hot." I sang numerous verses, all with the same lyrics. (To this day the kids remind me of their torment, and they sing the endless song as loudly as they can, just to drive me crazy.)

Finally, our papers were cleared and we drove onto the ferry to cross the river into Argentina, to sit and wait *there* while customs officials cleared our entrance visas. By late morning we were headed south toward the *pampas*, wide plains. After about an hour, Joe said the car was acting funny and would accelerate to only 50 mph. We stopped at the next little town. "A burnt valve," said the only mechanic. "I'll work on it this afternoon and tonight. $160.00." We checked into the only motel. The Blounts decided to keep on driving.

Saturday, Christmas Day, the car ran fine, but after lunch, Joe felt something weird with the steering. He pulled over: a balloon had developed on the left rear tire. As Joe put on the spare, rain began to fall. We limped into the next village in pouring rain. A man at the hotel sold us a tire, at double the price (because it was Christmas, he said).

On Sunday morning, December 26, Christy was listless and Timmy had developed an angry-looking sore on his chin. We traveled on. Just after lunch, Joe said the steering was veering to the side. He pulled over. There was a balloon on the right rear tire—both tires had been new, from Brazil. Joe put on the spare. We limped to the next village. Almost every business was closed for the holidays, but the mechanic at the only open garage said he could put a tube in the tire. He did and we traveled on for about two more hours. Then the tube blew!

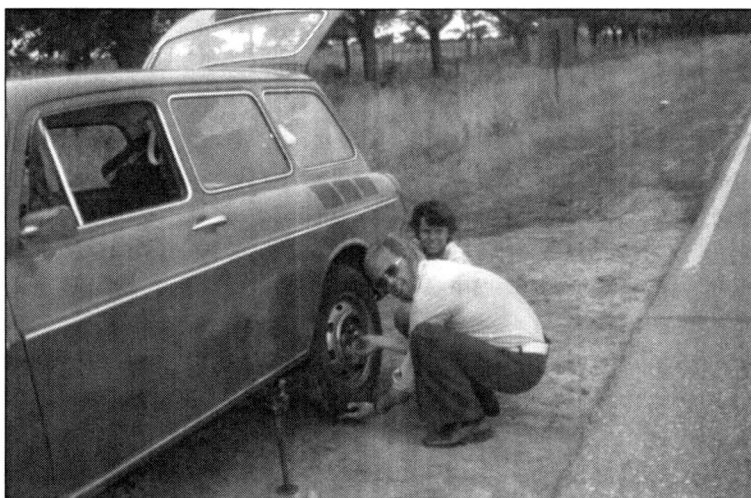

Joe (and Timmy) changing *one* of the tires

When we stopped for Joe to change *that* tire, we finally laughed. The elastic in Joe's underwear was loose, he had a wedgie, his pants were drooping, and as he crouched in the dirt, trying to place the jack *again*, he said, "The first thing I'm going to do, if we ever get to a hotel, is throw away this underwear!"

We drove on. We came to an Auto Club that opened just long enough to sell us a tire. We drove on. Then Joe said, "Oh, no. The car is losing power—just like it did two days ago. Surely we don't have another burnt valve!?"

We limped into the next village to the only service station, where the lone attendant said, "There is no mechanic in this town, but *mañana* we'll send for a tow truck, to pull you to Mendoza, three hours away. There is no hotel here but there is a rooming house where you can stay tonight."

Thoroughly discouraged, we unloaded our suitcases. I took Christy's temperature, 102. I looked closely at Timmy's chin, the infection had spread. We had hardly any money left. Aunt Marge pooled her money with ours.

Joe and Aunt Marge and Timmy walked to a "greasy spoon" to eat. I did not want even to think about food, my stomach was churning. I stayed with Christy at the little house. I put her to bed, grabbed my Bible out of the suitcase, and went into a small sitting room. I cried and cried and cried.

I opened the Living Bible to my marker, II Chronicles 20, and read verse 12, "We have no way to protect ourselves against this mighty army. We don't know what to do, but we are looking to you." Verse 15, "Don't be afraid … For the battle is not yours but God's." Verse 17, "Take your places … see the incredible rescue operation God will perform for you." Verse 22, "At the moment they began to sing and praise, the Lord caused the (enemy) … to destroy each other." Verse 26, "On the fourth day they gathered in the Valley of Blessing."

When Joe, Timmy, and Aunt Marge returned, I read the verses to them, and we cried together. Hope blossomed in our hearts as Joe led us in a beautiful prayer, thanking God for our problems and thanking Him for the solution.

Just as he finished, the landlady arrived. She said there was *one* mechanic who *did* live there. She would take Joe to see him. And a doctor was a friend of hers. She would call her to come over immediately.

The *doctora* shined a flashlight in Christy's mouth. "Come look," she motioned to me. Christy's tonsils were coated with white infection. The doctor gave Christy an injection and handed me a prescription for six vials of antibiotics. "Every morning and evening, find a nurse to administer the injections," she said.

The doctor looked at Timmy's chin and wrote a prescription for an antibiotic cream.

The next morning, December 27, my 34th birthday, the mechanic fixed the car in ten minutes' time. A loose connection. Exactly the same thing that had been wrong before, but this time the mechanic was honest.

We drove out of town and up into the foothills of the Andes mountains. About noon, we arrived at the Argentine border checkpoint near the tunnel. A rough tunnel connecting Argentina to Chile ran through the belly of the tallest mountains. It was actually a railroad tunnel, with no lighting, but when no train was scheduled, cars bumped across the ties. Going through the tunnel saved hours of dangerous travel.

However, the tunnel was closed for repairs. We had to take the high, narrow mountain road, past the Christ of the Andes statue. The border guard gave us instructions: vehicles climbing have the right-of-way. Any vehicle descending must yield space to the ascending ones. Do not stop. The air is so thin and the grade so steep, you probably will not be able to get started again. Buses will not stop. They will push you out of their way.

We began our ascent. The narrow road was loose gravel, slanted toward the outside, no guardrail. Most of the road was one lane only. At the widest areas, there was barely enough room for two cars to pass.

Slowly our car crept forward, put-putting in the oxygen-deprived air. We rounded hairpin after hairpin until a big car came down the mountain, the driver laughing, and forced us to a stop. We could not start again. Joe slipped the clutch, stepped on the gas. We crawled to a large bump at a hairpin curve. The car would not move forward over the hump. "Hop out," Joe told us. "I'll back up to the precipice, slip the clutch and maybe, without the extra weight, just maybe, the car will make it. When I get across the hump, I can't stop. You'll have to climb back in while we're rolling."

Aunt Marge, Christy, Timmy, and I stood in the narrow road just beyond the hump. Joe backed up. The brakes did not work well; neither did the emergency brake. We held our breath. Just before Joe released the emergency brake and applied the gas, we heard the bus.

Several hairpins down the mountain, a bus was ascending, blowing his horn to say, "Get out of my way, I will not stop, I will push you off the road."

Joe gunned the motor, slowly came toward us, inched over the hump. I opened the door, the kids and I and Aunt Marge scrambled over each other trying to get inside. The bus horn sounded, one hairpin below.

We continued to inch forward, mostly on prayers, I think.

Around the next hairpin we could see the Christ of the Andes statue. A broad area extended from the road toward the statue. We pulled onto it. The bus zoomed by. We resumed breathing.

We got out of the car on unsteady feet. Timmy went scampering up the mountain toward the foot of the statue, but he could not get his breath in the high altitude and sat down abruptly, almost fainting.

Gratefully, we climbed back in the car and began our descent, down the mountain to Chile. The next day, we had no more problems reaching *La Leonera* hotel, about an hour south of Santiago.

As we drove through Chile, Aunt Marge was surprised to see a sign for Bresler's Ice Cream. Joe said, "Yes, Aunt Marge, you know Bresler's Ice Cream was invented here? Yeah, George Bresler was marooned here during World War I. His ship sank off the Chilean coast. But somehow, in the wreckage, an ice cream freezer made it to shore. George took that freezer and churned ice cream. People liked it so much, ole George formed a company...." On and on, Joe wove his tale. Aunt Marge fell for it hook, line, and sinker. Finally, as he made the story more and more ridiculous, she realized he was making up the whole thing. We laughed and laughed.

At the Retreat, we renewed acquaintances, the MKs bonded, and Timmy was baptized in the swimming pool. Monroe Grams asked Joe if he would conduct a service in Spanish for the hotel employees. Joe read John 3:16 and talked to them about God's love. Almost all of the employees prayed the sinner's prayer.

As we drove for four days back to Paraguay, now in the new year of 1977, we had no car problems at all. Joe said the car just scooted over those mountains.

48

Camps and a Country Wedding
January–April 1977

We pulled into our driveway after four long days of travel, driving back in our little VW Squareback from the Missionary Retreat in Chile. We hit the ground running, with only two days to get ready to host CADSA, the South American Retreat for Latino Leaders. I hurried to begin laundry. Joe hurried to the retreat center to double-check that everything was in order.

Joe rushed to the post office to collect the mail to see peoples' arrival schedules. Then, he began making runs to the airport. Philip Hogan, Executive Director of World Missions, was our honored guest. Joe was Rev. Hogan's chauffeur and translator in conversations (another missionary from Bolivia translated the preaching).

As soon as CADSA ended, we began camps for church youth, women, girls, school kids, and then for our Paraguayan ministers and workers. Because Joe was superintendent and I was national Women's Ministries president, we were busier than we had ever been.

From December through February, on most mornings the temperature reached 86 degrees by 5:30 a.m. and during the day hovered from 100 to 104.

At the end of February (end of summer), school started again. Christy was in the eighth grade, Timmy in sixth. Also, at the Bible institute we once again conducted day and night classes.

The weather began to cool down a little in April, in time for another month-long crusade in la Plaza Italia. But this time we were helpers only. The evangelist, eloquent and personable, who spoke with authority and authenticity, was our own Pablo Villalba who had first attended there on his motorcycle three years earlier! Tears filled my eyes as I watched Pablo standing on that platform surrounded by a crowd of people.

April also marked ten years for Joe and me as missionaries.

And in April, Hermana Rosa's granddaughter was married in Pira Retá, the little village where we had gone two weeks after arriving in Paraguay. This time we did not attend a funeral but a wedding.

Once again, we drove out of Asunción on the Pan American highway. We dodged cows and pedestrians and buses with people hanging out the doors. We turned onto the red dirt road, around the tree in the middle of the road, turned onto the lane, and then drove into the field through the gate at the wooden fence. We drove across the pasture to the little white-washed, thatched roof chapel, next to the little store with a wide porch and the open-air kitchen under a thatched roof.

Large barrels of water gathered from the creek sat to one side. Joe explained that Rosa's husband traveled by ox cart to the creek to collect the water. The wheels of the cart were around six feet in diameter, and the cart sat high up off the ground. (Joe had visited here several times during the last three years and had helped with the water gathering.)

Cases and cases of Pepsi were stacked on one side of Rosa's patio. I figured she must be stocking those for her little store. Sweet-smelling smoke rose from the outside cooking pit. A young boy turned the spit, which held a large pig. Chickens roasted on a wide grill made from adobe bricks with rods across them. *Mandioca*, cassava, boiled gently in big pots. Heat waves radiated from the igloo-like oven where *sopa Paraguaya*, Paraguayan cornbread, baked.

A strip of red carpeting lay in front of the little chapel door. Two white, wooden folding chairs leaned against the wall nearby. Toward the center of the patio sat an oblong table displaying the one-layer wedding cake. (The bride and groom did not cut the cake while we were there. The cake was for immediate family only.)

Rosa had asked Joe to perform the marriage ceremony, which was set for 6 p.m. Of course, being good *gringos*, American foreigners, we arrived early, around 5:00.

By 6:00 no one else had appeared. About 6:30 I saw some people walking slowly down the lane toward us. A few minutes later, I heard a motorcycle. It carried four people. Three people came on a bicycle, one person peddling, one on the handlebars, one sitting on the back. A bus arrived jammed with nicely-dressed people. A dump truck came barreling down the lane, the back of the truck filled with men, women, and children. Cars came driving across the fields. Trucks. Vans. Donkeys. Horses. Horse-drawn carts. Ox-drawn carts.

By now it was dusk. I saw a man walking across the field toward us swinging a kerosene lantern, his family trailing behind. A woman and her two small children came walking from the other direction. She was swinging a lantern and leading a horse. On the horse sat her husband. Flashlights danced across the field from every direction. Lanterns bobbled, coming closer.

As the people arrived, they set their lanterns on fence posts to light the scene with twinkling flickers. There was no electricity.

About 8:00, Hermana Rosa asked me if I could play the wedding march. "*Sí*," I told her. She motioned to her husband and he came bringing me an old accordion. As I put it on and opened the bellows, a stuck key sounded a note, long and sustained, both as I opened and closed the bellows. Rosa nodded to me. Trying to ignore the stuck note, I began to play the traditional wedding march "la la-la-la." A young couple appeared at the back of the crowd. The young man was dressed in a nice blue suit. The young woman wore a shining, long white dress and carried a *ramo de flores*, bouquet. The couple walked slowly across the grass to the red carpet. Someone placed the white folding chairs there, outside, by the chapel door. The couple sat down.

Hermana Rosa stepped forward; she served as pastor of the little chapel. She welcomed everyone and then asked José Bogarín, who had been superintendent of our churches in Paraguay for many years, to come forward. He stood near the bride and groom, faced the people and began to preach a sermon in *Guaraní*. He preached for an hour.

Later Rosa told us there was no way she was going to pass up this opportunity to let the entire community hear the gospel. In fact, she told us, everyone's attitude toward her had changed dramatically since we had begun the television program.

"Before," she said, "they ridiculed me. They thought I was a crazy Protestant evangelical. But because of the television show, they know what we believe and they respect me. They see you here and they know for sure, now, that we are one team. We'll have new people in the church because of tonight!"

Joe performed the ceremony, in Spanish, and then Hermana Rosa fed everyone a meal and gave everyone a Pepsi.

More than 500 people came to that country wedding!

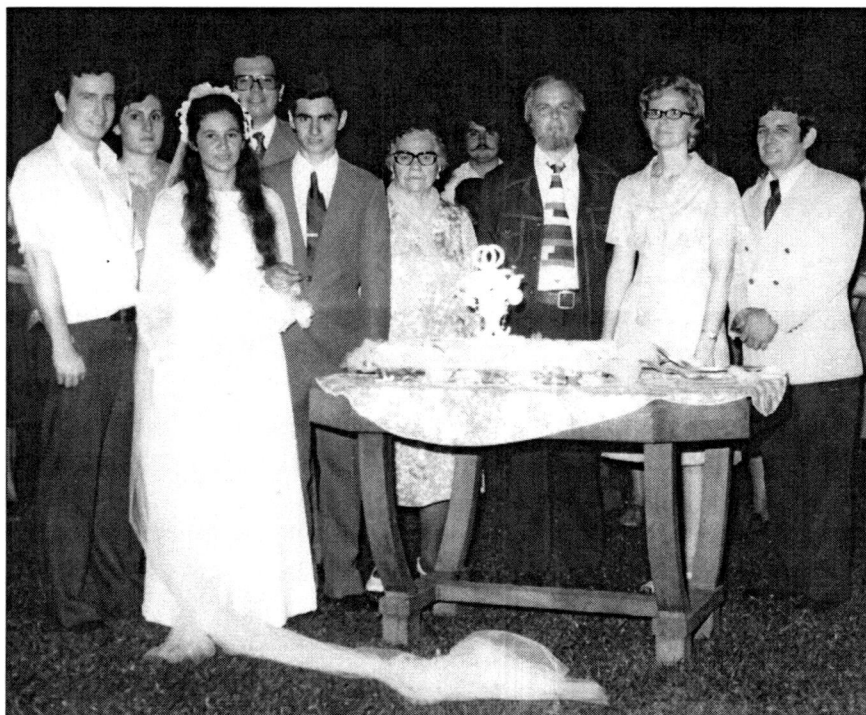

The country wedding
Far right, Eladio Gaona (baby Marci's dad). Next to him,
behind the table, Margaret and Joe

Roland loved being pastor of the new *Buenas Nuevas* congregation on the Bible school campus. Every person there was a brand-new convert, bubbling over with joy. One day Roland said, "These people are about to enthuse me to death!" Case in point: Mariana and Izzy (easy).

Mariana, a middle-aged woman, could walk only in a slow shuffle. She had spent the last eighteen years in bed, sometimes too weak even to sit up. Mariana had had five major surgeries. She suffered from "nerve trouble," from heart trouble. She took sleeping pills every night. She rarely left her house, except to go to the beauty shop.

Mari, her beauty operator, had accepted Christ during the Luís Palau crusade. She watched our television program, and when we invited viewers to the new church, she dared to attend. Mari told Mariana that she should go visit the *Buenas Nuevas* church. It couldn't hurt, could it?

That very night, Mariana came and Roland prayed for her. She was healed! Her husband could not believe it! Izzy said if God could do that for Mariana, then he, too, would serve Jesus and not be ashamed to be a Protestant. Mariana's aunt came, also, and was healed, and her life was transformed with happiness.

Izzy was an old man, white-headed, and very talkative. A veteran of the war with Bolivia, he loved to tell stories of his hardships. He had never attended a Protestant church, and as he learned to participate, he would talk with every visitor informing them of how different and great everything was. One night we heard him tell a visitor: "Here you have to be baptized with your head actually under the water!" Laughing, Joe suggested Izzy should run an information booth at the back of the church.

I enjoyed teaching Sunday school to these new converts. They would hang onto every word. One day they asked me about the differences between Protestant denominations. I explained that just as the Catholic Church has many different branches, such as the Jesuits, Dominicans, Carmelites, and Franciscans whose beliefs are essentially the same, the Protestant churches do, too. However, some Protestants did not believe that God would still heal people today. Spontaneously, my class burst out laughing! Because every one of them had been healed during this crusade or had a family member who had been healed.

As I described the baptism in the Holy Spirit, these new converts wanted to pray right then and there to be filled. Later, at the conclusion of the church service, fifteen people quietly and reverently raised their arms slightly, and each one received the baptism in the Holy Spirit.

Joe and I were due for furlough in June, just eight weeks away. It was bittersweet, because by now I loved the Paraguayan people and did not want to leave. As I had let go of my anger at God and at Joe for "making me" move to Paraguay, I had begun to accept the new reality: I would always miss my Chilean friends, but I could also make room in my heart for others. In fact, I felt much more "needed" in Paraguay. The women and girls, though not eloquent with words, shyly accepted me and allowed me into their circle of love.

Living in Paraguay, Joe and I had not experienced terrible heartaches or tremendous miracles as we had in Chile. But we had walked through everyday life, side-by-side with common people. And we had learned to love them deeply.

Christy said, "If we just had McDonald's and Grandma down here, we'd stay forever!" Then she added, "Oh, yes, and the babies, Kim and Shawn."

But Joe and I were tired. Especially Joe. I'd had the break of going back to the States for Shawn's birth. But Joe had not stopped for four years. The intense heat took its toll physically. The pressure of the television program, day and night classes at the Bible institute, camps, crusades, retreats, interaction with nationals and missionaries, the responsibilities of national leadership—all worked to drain us spiritually.

Joe was exhausted. And frustrated. Because he could not figure out what to do next term—where to go. What exactly to "do." He saw the tremendous impact television was having all over Paraguay. And even when Joe and Roland had traveled several times to Argentina to help with evangelistic crusades there, people would call the men by name. In Argentina, people stopped them in the airport, in the aisle of the airplane, at the customs office, in restaurants and service stations.

Inside Paraguay, everyone, it seemed, knew Joe and Roland by name. The blind one and the bearded one, *Rolando y José*. During these four years, hundreds of people had stopped to say, "Your show is my favorite!"

If television could have this much impact in one country, why couldn't someone produce a program for international airing? Was this why Joe didn't feel compelled to return to Paraguay? The work was progressing. We had three new churches in the capital city, new workers, and graduates from the Bible institute who were eager to preach and begin new works. But Joe's burden had shifted. He kept wanting to produce television programs for other countries as well. But no one had ever done that before. Would our mission give him permission to try?

As we agonized over our future, Joe retreated to Villa Florida, the little thatched-roof hotel in an isolated area, where we had gone once before. He went alone for three days to fast and to pray. While there, he dreamed of a palm tree with its fronds dried and hanging down from the top. People had gathered around the tree with machetes and were preparing to chop down the tree. Joe ran to the crowd and said, "No, don't chop it down! Just cut off the dead leaves. Leave the tree, it will grow new leaves." The people listened to him, did what he had suggested, and new leaves began to sprout.

Joe did not try to interpret the dream, but he could not forget it. Some time later, Victor Hedman, a friend and missionary in Argentina, sat at our kitchen table and said, "Joe, the dream shows your leadership. And it shows that growth will come to Paraguay." We had no idea that Vic would ask to transfer to Paraguay and would be a key person in conserving that new growth.

So, even as the burden began to lift from Joe, God was calling others to come, to reap the harvest from the seeds sown on *Las Buenas Nuevas* television program.

* * *

425

Here is Evelyn's recipe for that delicious cornbread Hermana Rosa served at the wedding.

Sopa Paraguaya
(Paraguayan cornbread)

Oven 450 degrees   Bake for about 25 minutes

INGREDIENTS
3 cups of Martha White cornbread mix (check the label to be sure it is white cornmeal)
6 eggs, beaten
1 3/4 cup milk (non-fat works fine)
1 lb Monterrey Jack cheese, cubed (about 1/2 inch cubes)
3/4 cup oil (I use Extra Virgin Olive Oil)
4 cups chopped onions (about 2 very large onions)

DIRECTIONS
1. Grease a 9x13 glass baking dish. (olive oil)
2. Chop onions.
3. Preheat the oven.
4. Sauté onions in the 3/4 cup of oil and leave on stove.
5. Cube cheese into 1/2 inch cubes. (Do not use shredded cheese. It will disappear and the secret of this good cornbread is the melted cheese-chunks inside.)
6. Measure cornmeal into a large bowl.
7. In a separate bowl, beat eggs. Add milk.
8. Pour milk mixture into cornmeal, all at once, beating with whisk to eliminate lumps.
9. Add cubes of cheese.
10. Pour hot oil/onion mixture into the cornmeal batter. Quickly, mix well. Pour into greased pan.
11. Bake at 450 about 20 - 25 minutes, until golden brown and knife inserted in middle comes out clean. Scrumptious!

49

The End and the Beginning
May–June 1977

I sat on the airplane with tears rolling down my cheeks. I had cried on the flight to Paraguay, not wanting to come. And now I cried, not wanting to leave. Christy sat beside me with tears dripping off her chin.

Christy was five years old when she became an MK (missionary kid). Now she was fifteen. Timmy had been only two; now he was twelve.

How had the Paraguayans penetrated so permanently into our hearts? We had not shared a meal in one Paraguayan home. There was no "middle class" and poverty shamed the vast majority of the population.

Somehow, walking through the last four years, I had accepted the slow pace of life. To the best of my ability, I had integrated into the culture and become involved in the simple ministry there. Though the Paraguayans could not help us with our Spanish grammar, we had learned fun words from them, like *pirapiré* for "money" and *macanudo* for "great!"

Our first graduating class, ITAD
Aunt Marge Campion, Gustavo, Betty, Pablo, Elizabet,
Justo, Chris, Roland, Evelyn

I would miss the shy manner of the Bible institute students as they approached the first class of their first semester. I would miss seeing them grow in knowledge and in confidence, gradually learning to hold their heads up high, to face the world boldly yet God-dependent.

I would miss the smell everyone radiated of *jabón de coco*, soap from coconut. It smelled like suntan lotion. And I would miss smelling and seeing the *talco*, scented talcum powder. It stuck to the folds in peoples' necks and gave a clean-smelling fragrance as I greeted the women, kissing them on both cheeks.

In spite of the intense heat, rarely did one smell the "body odor" of Paraguayans because they bathed several times a day. Construction workers carried clothes in little black satchels on the bus. Arriving at the construction site, the workers would undress (for the entire world to see) and put on their work clothes. Of an evening, the workers would bathe from a faucet at the construction site, dress again in their nice shirt and trousers, and then board the bus for the ride home.

I would miss the torrential rains when all dirt roads were closed to traffic, when lightning played a constant movie for hours as it danced from roiling cloud to roiling cloud. Because of inadequate storm drainage in the city, enterprising youth would wade into the flooded streets, place adobe blocks as pillars and run planks across the "stream." Pedestrians gladly paid a "tip" to cross the improvised bridges.

I would especially miss Oscarina, our faithful friend and maid. Oscarina, from her poverty, gave us abundant love and care. She cooked and cleaned and spoiled Christy and Timmy … and Joe and me.

I would miss the beautiful wood carvings. And the intricate and delicate Paraguayan lace called *ñandutí*, meaning "spider web" in *Guaraní*. The fragile threads formed concentric circles creating colorful patterns, each unique — because the ladies randomly selected colors of threads.

And the harp lessons! Every restaurant featured a *conjunto* consisting of a harp and two guitars. Soon after we arrived in Paraguay, Joe talked to Felipe Aponte and arranged for him to give me (!) harp lessons. Joe located a harp manufacturing company: a shade tree beside an open-air thatched roof in a back yard where a couple of true artists created hand-crafted harps. The men selected wood and sanded it smooth again and again. They scored the wood and inset tiny strips of white plastic PVC for decorations. They carved small pegs for tuning keys.

When Felipe came for my first harp lesson, I sat rigidly in a dining room chair, the harp before me. Joe sat nearby to watch. Felipe demonstrated how to hold my fingers. Stiffly, I complied. The idea was to teach me the first chords of a folkloric song. I strummed the strings *phlat phlat phlat*. "Good, good," Felipe said, "you practice more and I'll be back in two days."

Awkwardly, I tried to pluck the strings. At the second lesson, I couldn't figure out how to bend my thumb into position. Joe piped up, "Here, let me try." I did. I never touched the harp again. Joe had a natural agility to play. And Felipe came twice a week for three years to teach Joe — and Timmy! He, too, was a natural.

We would miss the twice weekly visits of Christy's guitar professor, with his coke bottle eyeglasses and his garlic breath.

And Christy would always remember being *quinceañera*, celebrating her fifteenth birthday with her best friend, Beth, who also turned fifteen. We rented tables and chairs, ordered a wedding-like birthday cake, and served a meal to about thirty teens as Felipe's *conjunto* serenaded with Paraguayan folkloric music on the harp and guitars.

We would even miss the chickens with dozens of fresh eggs for home-made ice cream. The children would miss the *yerba mate,* the green tea sipped through the metal spoon-like straw. Oh, and the *Guaraná!* That delicious, unique soft drink similar to cream soda.

We would miss being able to visit the *Foz do Iguazu,* waterfalls larger by far than Niagara Falls.

Though we had seen definite signs of growth in the church work, progress was painstakingly slow. When we moved from holding crusade services outside, near the street, to inside the building at the new *Buenas Nuevas* church on *Choferes del Chaco* Avenue, our attendance totaled 62 people: 18 adults, 17 teens, and 27 children.

The largest student body at the Bible institute numbered 28 students.

Our annual General Council in May consisted of 12 pastors from the entire country. Hopefully, new workers, recent graduates, would become licensed and ordained in the years ahead.

The television contract ended with our return home. (But Roland vowed to begin again just as soon as new missionaries arrived—and he did.) For our final program, we featured our families. Roland and Evelyn sang with Howard and Carla. Timmy played the harp, Christy the guitar, Joe the sax. I sang a new song that Mom had sent to us and that Joe had just finished translating: "It's All in the Name of Jesus" by Stephen Adams.

Timmy, Joe, Margaret, Christy on the last TV show

The next morning, our phone rang. "Please forgive me for calling you at home. I persuaded the television station to give me your home number," said a woman's cultured voice. "May I please come to your house to accept Christ as my Savior?"

Half-an-hour later, a shiny, black Mercedes pulled into our driveway. A uniformed chauffeur stepped out and opened the back door for a tiny, elegant, elderly lady.

Doña Rebeca walked briskly to our front door. We invited her in to sit on a lawn chair, as we had already sold all our furniture. *Doña Rebeca* sat poised and composed in the old lawn chair. She folded her hands in her lap, and began, "During four years I have watched your program while faith has grown in my heart. I have always loved God, but I have yearned to know him personally. Yesterday I wanted to pray what you call 'the sinner's prayer' along with you as you prayed on television. However, to be sure, certain, of the prayer, I decided to impose upon you at your home."

Joe explained to her that Jesus loved her and was waiting, knocking on her heart's door, awaiting an invitation to enter. As *Doña Rebeca* prayed with Joe, tears rolled down her aristocratic

431

cheeks. Rarely did Paraguayans cry at salvation; they usually just accepted the facts as presented to them. But a chord deep inside *Doña Rebeca's* heart moved her to tears.

After the prayer, she drew a deep, satisfying breath and asked, "Oh, José, could I please bring my son tomorrow? And my daughter? I so want them to know Jesus, too."

The next day she returned, chauffeur and all, with her adult children. They both reverently and gratefully prayed with Joe. *Doña Rebeca* handed me a small package of colorful coasters she herself had crocheted. They are a treasured gift I still possess.

As *Doña Rebeca* prepared to leave our house, she walked to the door and then paused. With her hand on the door handle, she turned to Joe, "Hermano José, we Paraguayans love the music on the television show. We love the way you read from the Bible. We enjoy the humor you display and the testimonies people give. But what speaks to our Paraguayan hearts, more than anything else, is the peace that we see on your faces."

Joe was stunned. He had prayed and prayed for confirmation as to whether to continue his vision for producing television programs. How would he justify to our mission board his rationale for "television"? Radio was cheaper. The printed page was even less expensive. Crusades touched hundreds of people. But not tens of thousands. Not a nation. Not nations. Now, *Doña Rebeca*, sent by God, gave him precisely the assurance he needed: "What speaks to our Paraguayan hearts more than anything else, is *the peace that we see on your faces.*" Joe never again wavered in his determination to produce television programming.

Epilogue
1977 and forward

PARAGUAY

No one realized that a new hydroelectric dam, just now beginning construction on the *Itaipú* River, would transform the country. Eventually 40,000 workers would be employed there, and the money they earned would give Paraguay a middle-class! The subsistence farmers could have electricity. Major change lay ahead.

The following year, 1978, Loren Triplett, Missions Director for Latin America, began to organize crusades for fifteen sites in Paraguay. He ordered yellow and white tents and implored evangelists and missionaries from all over Latin America to converge on Paraguay during the next ten years. He established the "Paraguayan Task Force" to blanket the country with workers and prayer. Slowly but surely, congregations began to form in town after town.

Don and Lorene Gould returned from furlough to remain in Paraguay for thirty years. They established Bible institutes on the eastern border and began churches there. Cindy Lucas and Eve Shellenberger came as teachers to Asunción Christian Academy, where many Chinese and Korean students had begun attending to improve their English. Dozens of students accepted Christ. And later, Roland and Evelyn pastored a congregation of Korean believers.

Roland said, "At least twelve youth from our *Buenas Nuevas* church became pastors and helped in the great Paraguay Awakening. Evelyn and I left the country in 1983, but we returned for visits in 1987 and 2001. On both occasions at the airport in Asunción, we were recognized and called by name."

In 1985, Victor and Jan Hedman became acquainted with a new convert, Emilio Abreu, a famous athlete. Emilio met for Bible study with a small group of friends in his home on Saturday afternoons, but Vic talked to Emilio about expanding that group to form a church for middle and upper-class people. By 1993 *El Centro Familiar de Adoración* (Family Worship Center) had grown from 12 friends to 2,500 members! Vic even loved to see the traffic jams in front of the church on Friday and Sunday evenings—these people owned cars!

Vic wrote to us, "I believed Joe's prophetic dream about the dead tree that came to life and flourished. We were part of the fulfillment." Jan told me that her job was to interview new converts before they could be baptized. As she questioned them concerning when they had first heard the gospel, many replied, "On *Las Buenas Nuevas* television program."

By 1990 there were 14,950 people worshipping in 172 Assemblies of God churches! By 2005, Emilio began construction on a church auditorium to seat 10,000!

REGISTER FAMILY

For Joe and me, and for Christy and Timmy, our furlough year was tough. Each of us coped with culture shock as we tried to adjust to North American life.

We moved to Springfield, Missouri so that Joe could attend AGTS, the Assemblies of God Theological Seminary, to obtain his Master's Degree in Cross-Cultural Communication. I attended Central Bible College, taking classes toward a B.A. (which I eventually finished, but not until 1989, with our grandchildren present and hollering, "Yeah, Grandma!" as I walked across the stage).

Christy suffered through a terrible year of adjustment, her first year in a *gringo* high school.

Timmy also suffered through a terrible year of adjustment, as he became a teenager and entered junior high school in a "foreign" culture.

Joe's tele-*vision* was put on hold for a year because the Foreign Missions Committee (later they told us) thought he was crazy. No one had ever produced television programs for all of Latin America. However, Joe did not lose his deep desire, and every month for twelve months, he pestered Loren Triplett, our boss, with the dream that would not die.

In June, 1977, we visited Joe's brother, Kenny, near Tampa, Florida. While there, we just "happened" to meet a television producer named Paul Garber and we just "happened" to encounter our old pastor, Tom Waldron, who had retired to Florida. Tentatively, Joe shared his tele-*vision* with these men. Their encouragement and involvement would change the course of our lives for the next thirty years!

With God's help, we would build a television studio where we would produce award-winning programs for adults and for children. We would laugh at puppets who forgot to open their mouths when they talked! And we would meet Dottie, the make-up artist who had worked at a funeral home and wanted everyone to lie down and hold their breath while she applied their make-up.

As we began to produce television programs for an international audience, we knew the shows should be "professional" so that the Chileans would watch them. We also knew the shows should be simple so that the poorest Paraguayan could comprehend the truths presented. Finally, we would understand "why" we had needed to live in both Chile and Paraguay.

Producing the shows would be costly, not just in money, but in long hours, and in the intense physical and emotional investment we would be required to make. I would continue to stretch and grow, to try to "do" God's work. I would need to adapt to living in another new place, with new co-workers. I still had so much to learn! I needed to learn what it means to "be," not "do." I still needed to grow beyond being a plastic saint to one filled to overflowing with God's grace.

Over the next thirty years, the telecasts would reach every country in Latin America, would be dubbed into various languages, would reach Europe and India, and would be scattered all over the world via fourteen satellites.

But that is another fabulous story I can hardly wait to write!

Breinigsville, PA USA
26 October 2009
226490BV00002B/2/P